A TASTE FROM

Grandma's Kitchen

A touch of the old,
a bit of the new—
The Schlabach family
shares favorites with you

ISBN-1-890050-66-0

First Printing October 1997
Second Printing June 1999
Third Printing June 2000
Fourth Printing November 2000
Fifth Printing July 2001
Sixth Printing June 2002
Seventh Printing April 2003
Eighth Printing January 2004
Ninth Printing June 2005
Tenth Printing December 2005
Eleventh Printing September 2006
Twelfth Printing June 2007

Carlisle Printing
OF WALNUT CREEK Ltd.

2673 TR 421
Sugarcreek, Ohio 44681

Dedication

eing grateful for my heritage of faith and the art of cooking, this book is dedicated to:

  … Grandmothers and mothers everywhere who have passed on the art of good cooking.

  … The cooks of today who are busy in their kitchens now.

  … Our children, the cooks of tomorrow.

  … Daughters Julia, Hannah, Larisa, Marnita, and Kari, helpers in my own kitchen.

Mrs. Mary Esta Yoder

As you partake of the delicacies of this book, we trust you will find much delight in them. We believe God has made possible our enjoyment of these good things. "And Jesus said unto them, I am the bread of life; he that cometh to me shall never hunger; and he that believeth on me shall never thirst." We enjoy the temporal things of life, but we must also give thought to the eternal things.

Expression of Appreciation

We wish to thank all of you who generously contributed their favorite recipes. Some are treasured family keepsakes and some are new, but all reflect the love of good cooking.

A special "thank-you" to our family for their encouragement and their willingness to help in this project. Without their help my dream of compiling a family cookbook would not have been realized!

Also, a special thanks and recognition go to Melissa Mast for the artwork on the category pages and to Sarah Schlabach for the art on pages 164 and 216.

We hope you will enjoy the many outstanding recipes on the following pages.

David Ray and Mary Esta Yoder

Table of Contents

Memories
of Grandma

Honey Delights cookies

1 cups Butter
2 cup Honey
2 Eggs
4½ teas cinnamon
½ „ cloves
½ „ alspice
4 „ soda
2 „ vanilla
at least 9 cup flour
Boil honey & butter to gether
1 then cool
Sift then measure flour sift 3 times
with spices add beaten eggs to butter
Mixture
Then add flour Roll about ½in Thick
Frost with powdered sugar frost or
7 min frost

I made only halve of it for me

A copy of Grandma Emma's own handwritten cookie recipe.

It Takes a Mother

It takes a mother's love to make a house a home,
A place to be remembered, no matter where we roam…
It takes a mother's patience to bring a child up right,
And her courage and cheerfulness to make a dark day bright…
It takes a mother's thoughtfulness to mend the heart's deep hurts,
And her skill and her endurance to mend little socks and shirts…
It takes a mother's kindness to forgive us when we err,
To sympathize in trouble and bow her head in prayer…
It takes a mother's wisdom to recognize our needs
And to give us reassurance by her loving words and deeds…
It takes a mother's endless faith, her confidence and trust
To guide us through the pitfalls of selfishness and lust…
And that is why in all this world there could not be another
Who could fulfill God's purpose as completely as a mother!

Simple pleasures are life's treasures!

The first cookbook I remember using was a small notebook with written recipes. I still have this notebook and will include a few of the recipes. The first printed cookbook I remember was the Walnut Creek Cookbook. Later a different one was printed from Walnut Creek.

I remember how pork was kept for winter use. Ribs and pork chops were cooked and put in large crocks. Lard was poured on top to seal it. After getting a meal's supply, lard was again poured on top. Ham was cured and smoked. After cutting off enough for a meal, it was again wrapped for later use. No canning or freezing was done. Ham bone was cooked, which made for dumplings, or "knepp." After lard was rendered on butchering day, a kettle full of popcorn was made, which made a delicious ending

The Schlabach family homestead in eastern Holmes County, the place of many cherished memories for the Andrew C.C. and Emma Schlabach family of eight children and many grandchildren.

for the day.

A busy day was the making of cider apple butter in the kettle on the furnace in the washhouse. All was put in gallon crocks, wax paper on top of apple butter and newspaper on top of crocks, and tied with cloth strips from white feed bags. Then it was stored upstairs in a closet for a year's supply of good spreading.

Homemade bread was ready to thoroughly clean the shining copper kettle. On a cold winter day corn hominy was also cooked in the kettle, which also made for good eating. Hominy and sausage, lightly fried, was eaten with applesauce.

Feed came in cloth bags with writing on them (Bob White Feeds) and a picture of a quail. These were soaked to get prints out, washed, and used for Dad's everyday shirts and sometimes dyed for everyday dresses. Later the feed came in nice white bags. Some had borders for pillowcases, others had nice prints of flowers, fruits, etc., and could be used for tea towels, tablecloths, etc. Usually no time was wasted to go and see what kind the feed truck would bring.

> Just a thought of sweet remembrance,
> A memory fond and true,
> Memories of my mother
> That time cannot erase.

··· *Mrs. Emanuel Nisley*

One memory of Grandma's cooking is corn mush in the evening. We would eat it with milk, then the rest was fried in the mornings. I remember she filled the frying pan with mush and set it on the back of the stove for a slow brown. Then she would go out to the barn and milk a cow, then come back in and turn the mush, and sometimes she came back out again. The fried mush was delicious!

··· *Andy Schlabach*

I remember making apple butter. Dad would gather apples from our own orchard here on the farm. Early the next morning he took them to a cider press and got twenty gallons of cider made, two milk cans full. In the evening the family sat together to peel and slice apples to cook with the cider to make apple butter.

The next morning Mom had the copper kettle all cleaned and Dad put it on the furnace in the woodhouse. He started a fire under it and poured the cider in the shiny kettle. The cider was cooked down and skimmed off. They knew just when to add the sliced apples, and continued stirring to keep it from burning.

There was a large hoist with a rope and hook to take the kettle off the fire when it was ready. No children were allowed to come close, as this was extremely hot. They would ladle it into crocks and let it cool. Mom put waxed paper on top and tied a cloth over it. It was then stored on shelves upstairs in a closet where it was cool and dark. This was ten gallons of apple butter for our winter use.

··· *Mrs. Lloyd (Bena) Miller*

One of my most vivid memories is how sister Leona and I carried firewood to fill Grandma's woodbox during the winter. From the woodshed, through the snow, in through her kitchen we'd march with our arms full of firewood.

What a treat when she rewarded us with her delicious homemade candy, opera cremes (similar to butter cremes), in the candy section of this cookbook. The times when she didn't come out from her living room to get our treat, we'd carry an extra load, making extra noise as we dropped it into the woodbox, so she'd be sure to know we were there.

In looking back now, I realize she knew it wasn't good for us to always get a treat. I have also wondered who cleaned up our snow tracks after us . . . perhaps we didn't always deserve a reward.

One of her favorite sayings was, "Die Morgenstund hat Gold im Mund" (The morning hours are golden).

··· *Mrs. Mary Esta Yoder*

I can remember going to Grandma's (Mommie's) overnight a few times. For supper we'd have fried potatoes and tomato gravy. (I still love it to this day.) Then on Saturday evenings Bena would braid all her girls' hair real tight and secure the ends with string.

Sundays in church she had "goodies"—pretzels, etc.—hidden in her pockets under her apron!

I also remember the pink candy she would get out each time we visited.

And it was always fun to pump water with that pump in the small room off the kitchen!

··· *Mrs. Linda Beachy*

SCHLABACH FAMILY CONTRIBUTORS

Ralph and Sarah Schlabach. . . . . Sugarcreek, Ohio

Robert and Audrey Schlabach (Sarah, Rachel) . . . . . . Sugarcreek, Ohio

Mike and Ruby Sommers . . . . .Sarasota, Florida

Dave and Mary Kaufman (Erica). . . . . Sugarcreek, Ohio

Willis and Ruth Schlabach (Michelle). . . . . Sugarcreek, Ohio

Willard and Naomi Schlabach (Zak, Jordan) . . . . . . .Sarasota, Florida

James and Ruth Schlabach (Jeremy). . . . . Sugarcreek, Ohio

Larry and Cindy Schlabach . . . . Hixson, Tennessee

Dave and Linda Beachy. Sugarcreek, Ohio

Jason and Fern Schlabach . . . . Sugarcreek, Ohio

Ken and Kris Miller (Kari). . . . . .Middlebury, Indiana

Mose A. (and the late Freda) Schabach. . . . . Millersburg, Ohio

Jonas and Katie Raber (Edward, Daniel, Ruth) . . . . . Millersburg, Ohio

Roy and Freda Miller. . . . . Millersburg, Ohio

Steve and Bena Yoder . . . . Apple Creek, Ohio

Paul and Wilma Schlabach (Lori, Regina, Rachel). . . . Millersburg, Ohio

Wayne and Emma Yoder . . . . Bremen, Indiana

Reuben and Sara Etta Schlabach . . . . Millersburg, Ohio
(Stephen, Rita, Martha Jean)

Pete Jr. and Ruth Miller (Reuben, Christina) . . . . Millersburg, Ohio

Roy M. Schlabach

Brenda Hostetler

Owen and Ada Schlabach (Owen Jr., Ruth Ann). . . . .Trenton, Kentucky

Freeman and Marie Schlabach (Ellen, Linda) . . . . . . .Trenton, Kentucky

Mervin and Rhoda Hilty. Holmesville, Ohio

Richard and Wilma Schlabach. . . . . .Trenton, Kentucky

Leroy and Betty Lou Schlabach . . . . Guthrie, Kentucky
       (Marlene, James, Norman, Jeremiah, Willard)

Paul and Linda Schlabach . . . . Bedford, Pennsylvania

Ammon and Esta Brenneman (Emanuel, Andrew) . . . . Guthrie, Kentucky

Emanuel and Mary Nisley . . . . Baltic, Ohio

Henry and Emma Troyer (Verna, Sara) . . . . Baltic, Ohio

David and Susan Nisley (Rosanna, Iva) . . . . Millersburg, Ohio

Alton and Nora Nisley (Paul, Dora, Norman) . . . . Millersburg, Ohio

Albert and Verna Yoder (Owen, Marlin, Mary Esther) . Millersburg, Ohio

Owen and Elsie Nisley . . . . Baltic, Ohio

Paul and Rebecca Nisley . . . . Millersburg, Ohio

Andrew Jr. and Elsie Schlabach . . . . Millersburg, Ohio

Marvin and Martha Mast (Melissa, Monica, Marita) . . Millersburg, Ohio

Stephen and Ruth Schlabach . . . . Berlin, Ohio

Philip and Denise Schlabach . . . . Millersburg, Ohio

Daniel and Lisa Schlabach . . . . Millersburg, Ohio

Lloyd and Bena Miller (Leona Sue) . . . . Sugarcreek, Ohio

David and Mary Esta Yoder . . . . Sugarcreek, Ohio
       (Julia, Hannah, Larisa, Jason, Lavern, Marnita)

Merlin and Linda Troyer (Derrick, Danita, Jared) . . . . . Sugarcreek, Ohio

Floyd and Marlene Yoder (Jessica, Rachel) . . . . Sugarcreek, Ohio

Mark and Ruth Miller (Bryan, Justin, Wendall, Kimberly) . Sugarcreek, Ohio

Freeman and Naomi Miller . . . . Sugarcreek, Ohio

Reuben and Betty Yoder (Kristine Joy) . . . . Sugarcreek, Ohio

Firman and Deborah Miller . . . . Sugarcreek, Ohio

Marion and Rachel Mullet . . . . Sugarcreek, Ohio

Atlee and Dorothy Schlabach . . . . Sarasota, Florida

Randal and Joyce Albritton (Aaron, Cody) . . . . Sarasota, Florida

Jarey and Ruth Davis Schlabach . . . . Hernando, Florida

Steve and Rhonda Rittenhouse . . . . Harrisonburg, Virginia

Appetizers,

Beverages

& Dips

Lord, place your hand upon our door,
and bless this home forevermore.

A Tea Party

I had a little tea party
 This afternoon at three;
  'Twas very small—
   Three guests in all—
    Just I, Myself, and Me.

   Myself ate all the sandwiches
    While I drank up the tea.
     'Twas also I
      Who ate the pie
       And passed the cake to Me.

Don't give up ~ look up!

ORANGE JEWLET
... Mrs. Linda Mae Troyer

1 - 6 oz. orange juice concentrate
1 cup milk
1 cup water
$1/4$ cup sugar
$1/2$ tsp. vanilla
10 ice cubes

Crush in blender until slushy. Jared's favorite summer refresher.

ELEPHANT'S JUG
... Monica Mast

1 cup milk
$1/4$ cup peanut butter
   (either crunchy or smooth)
1 ripe banana
2 tsp. sugar
4 ice cubes

Combine all ingredients, except ice cubes, in blender and blend until smooth. Add ice and blend just until ice is crushed. Pour into two glasses and serve immediately.

This makes a good after-school snack or a quick breakfast when time is short.

CITRUS SLUSH
... Mrs. Marion (Rachel) Mullet

$2^1/2$ cups sugar
3 cups water
1 - 12 oz. frozen orange juice
1 - 12 oz. frozen lemonade
1 - 46 oz. pineapple juice
3 cups cold water
4 qt. 7-Up, Sprite, or ginger ale

In 6-qt. saucepan over high heat, bring sugar and 3 cups water to a boil. Stir till sugar is dissolved. Remove from heat. Stir in frozen orange juice and lemonade. Stir until melted. Add pineapple juice and cold water. Stir till well blended. Pour into freezer boxes. Freeze till firm. When ready to serve, let thaw a little bit. Add 7-Up and serve.

PARTY PUNCH
... favorite of Rachel Joan Yoder, age 8

1 pkt. cherry Kool-Aid
1 pkt. strawberry Kool-Aid
1 - 6 oz. can frozen orange juice
1 - 6 oz. can frozen lemonade
   Makes 1 gal.
1 to 2 cups sugar
3 qt. water
ice and 7-Up

GOLDEN PUNCH
··· Mrs. Albert (Verna) Yoder

Prepare as directed:
3 lg. cans frozen orange juice concentrate
2 lg. cans frozen lemonade concentrate
Stir in:
2 qt. pineapple juice   4 qt. 7-Up
1/2 cup sugar
Mix well. Chill.

HINT
*Muffin and cupcake tins can be used to make extra ice cubes
if you're having a big outdoor get-together.*

CRANBERRY PUNCH
··· Mrs. Philip (Denise) Schlabach

4 cups cranberry juice   1 Tbsp. almond extract
1 1/2 cups sugar   2 qt. ginger ale
4 cups pineapple juice

Combine first four ingredients. Stir until sugar is dissolved; chill. Add ginger ale just before serving.

HOT MULLED CIDER
··· Mrs. Philip (Denise) Schlabach

1/4 cup brown sugar   1 tsp. whole cloves
1/4 tsp. salt   3 inches of stick cinnamon
2 qt. cider   dash of nutmeg
1 tsp. whole allspice

Combine brown sugar, salt, and cider. Tie spices in small piece of cheese-cloth; add. Simmer, covered, 20 minutes. Remove spices. Serve hot with twist of orange peel; use cinnamon sticks as muddlers.

JOGGIN' IN A JUG
··· Mrs. Linda Mae Troyer

1 qt. apple juice, unsweetened   1 cup good vinegar, such as Heinz
1 qt. grape juice, unsweetened

Drink 2 oz. a day to help keep your cholesterol in check.

EAGLE BRAND FINGER JELLO ... *Mrs. Alton (Nora) Nisley*
... Mrs. Lloyd (Bena) Miller

4 small boxes jello	4 pkg. gelatin
1 1/3 cups cold water	4 cups boiling water

Use four different flavors of jello. Add 1 pkg. of gelatin dissolved in 1/3 cup cold water to each box of jello with 1 cup boiling water. Dissolve.

WHITE LAYER

4 pkg. gelatin	3/4 cup cold water
1 can Eagle Brand milk	2 cups boiling water

Dissolve gelatin in cold water. Combine boiling water and Eagle Brand milk. Add to dissolved gelatin. Layer 1 flavor of jello in pan. Chill until set, then cover with 1 1/3 cups of white layer and chill again. Repeat until you have 7 layers, ending with jello. Sometimes the white layer sets before the last layers are finished. Put in a dish of hot water until it is dissolved again.

FRESH FRUIT WITH HAWAIIAN FRUIT DIP
... Mrs. Linda Mae Troyer

strawberries	bananas
melons	apples
kiwis	orange sections

DIP

1/2 cup sour cream	1 - 8 oz. can crushed pineapple,
1 cup milk	undrained
1 pkg. instant vanilla pudding	1/3 cup shredded coconut

Combine sour cream, milk, and pudding until smooth. Add pineapple and coconut. Mix to combine. Refrigerate 1 hour before serving. Cut fruit into slices, balls, rounds, or wedges.

FRUIT DIP
... Mrs. Mary Esta Yoder

2 cups pineapple juice	8 oz. cream cheese
2 Tbsp. clear jel	9 oz. Cool Whip
1/2 cup sugar	

Cook juice, sugar, and clear jel till thickened. Cool. Add softened cream cheese and Cool Whip. Mix together until creamy.

Serve with fresh fruits of your choice.

FRUIT DIP
... favorite of Linda Schlabach

1 sm. container strawberry yogurt   1 sm. jar marshmallow creme
1 sm. container Cool Whip

Mix and dip your favorite fruit: strawberries, pineapple, grapes, bananas, melons.

CREAMY CARAMEL DIP
... Julia Yoder

8 oz. cream cheese
$3/4$ cup brown sugar
1 cup sour cream
2 tsp. vanilla

2 tsp. ReaLemon
1 cup milk
3 oz. instant vanilla pudding

Beat cream cheese and sugar until smooth. Add sour cream, vanilla, and ReaLemon; beat again. Add pudding and milk, beating very well. Serve with fresh fruit or angel food cake cubes. Delicious!

VEGETABLE ROLL-UPS
... Mrs. Roy (Freda) Miller

8 oz. sour cream
1 cup grated cheddar cheese
$1/2$ cup onion
1 - 8 oz. pkg. cream cheese

1 - 4 oz. chopped olives
seasoned salt and garlic powder
   to taste
5 - 10" flour tortillas

Mix everything together thoroughly. Divide filling and spread evenly over tortillas. Roll them up and cover tightly with plastic wrap, twisting ends. Refrigerate several hours. Then cut into $1/2$" slices. Discard ends. You can substitute other vegetables instead of olives.

NUTTY CHEESE BALL
... Mrs. Jr. (Ruth) Miller

2 - 8 oz. pkg. cream cheese
1 - $8^1/2$ oz. can crushed pineapple
1 cup finely chopped walnuts
$1/4$ cup chopped green pepper

2 tsp. chopped onion
1 tsp. seasoned salt
1 cup finely chopped walnuts

Cream cheese until soft and smooth. Slowly add drained pineapple; add 1 cup nuts, chopped pepper, onion and salt. Refrigerate until it is ready to form a ball. After forming a ball, roll in 1 cup walnuts. Simple to make and very good.

CHEESE BALL
··· Mrs. Firman (Deborah) Miller

1 jar Old English cheese
1 jar pimento cheese
1 - 8 oz. cream cheese

1 tsp. Worcestershire sauce
1 tsp. grated onions
1 tsp. celery flakes

Let cheese soften, then beat all ingredients real well. Form into ball and chill. Can put nuts on top.

CHEESE SPREAD
··· Mrs. Lloyd (Bena) Miller

ALMOST LIKE OLD-FASHIONED CROCK CHEESE

1 lb. white American cheese $3/4$ cup milk

Melt in double boiler until smooth. Pour into dish and cool. Serve with crackers or jelly sandwiches.

WARM TACO DIP
··· Mrs. Floyd (Marlene) Yoder
··· favorite of Danita Renea Troyer, age 10

1 lb. hamburger, browned
1 can tomato soup
1 can cream of mushroom soup
1 can green chilies, chopped
$1/4$ cup onion, chopped

1 tsp. garlic salt
1 tsp. onion salt
1 Tbsp. Worcestershire sauce
$1/2$ lb. Velveeta cheese

Heat and serve with nacho chips.

Variation: Danita's mother adds $1/2$ cup green peppers and $1/4$ cup onions, chopped. She also uses 2 lb. Velveeta cheese.

CHILI CON QUESO
··· Mrs. Linda Mae Troyer

2 Tbsp. butter
1 Tbsp. flour
1 cup milk
dash of salt
garlic powder

1 cup cheddar cheese
some Velveeta cheese
1 - 4 oz. can green chilies
1 or 2 jalapeño peppers

Melt butter and add flour, milk, salt, and garlic powder. Stir until smooth and add remaining ingredients. Serve with taco chips. Also good to serve on Easy Enchiladas on page 99.

NACHOS
··· *Mrs. Freeman (Marie) Schlabach*

1 lb. hamburger
$^1/_2$ cup onion, diced
1 lb. Velveeta cheese
$^3/_4$ cup milk
1 med. bag tortilla chips

Brown hamburger and onion. Melt milk and cheese in microwave till saucy. On a large plate, crush chips and sprinkle with meat. Drizzle the cheese sauce over all. Very good!

NACHO DIP
··· *Leona Sue Miller*

1 lb. Mexican mild Velveeta cheese
16 oz. sour cream
1 can nacho cheese soup
1 can cheddar cheese soup
nacho chips

Mix all together and heat until cheese is melted. This is good with nacho chips.

TRISCUIT DIP
··· *Mrs. Philip (Denise) Schlabach*

2 cups shredded Swiss cheese
2 cups Hellmann's mayonnaise
1 cup sweet onion, diced

Mix ingredients. Bake in dish with high sides at 350° for 20 minutes or until brown and bubbly on top. Serve with Triscuits or crackers of your choice.

BEAN DIP FOR CHIPS
··· *Mrs. Mike (Ruby) Sommers*

1 lb. hamburger
small onion and small pepper
1 pkg. taco seasoning
1 can refried beans
layer of sour cream
mozzarella cheese

Fry hamburger with onion and some green pepper. Drain grease. Add 1 pkg. taco seasoning and beans. Put in 9"x13" pan. Let set overnight.

Layer with sour cream and top with mozzarella cheese. Bake at 350° for 15 to 20 minutes. Serve with any kind of taco chips.

CHEESE CRISP
··· *Mrs. Linda Mae Troyer*

Warm large flour tortillas under broiler. Using pastry brush, spread tortillas lightly with melted butter. Sprinkle generously with grated Colby or cheddar cheese. Place under broiler until cheese melts. May be topped with chopped green onions, tomatoes, green chilies, or cooked Chaigo sausage. Cut into wedges to serve.

SPINACH DIP A LA SANAI

... Mrs. Jarey (Ruth Davis) Schlabach

2¹/₂ Tbsp. Salad Supreme
   (dry spice mixture available at
   supermarket)
1 box chopped spinach
¹/₄ cup mayonnaise

1 med. shallot, chopped fine
1 tsp. dill pickle juice
¹/₂ tsp. lemon juice
4 tsp. parsley, chopped fine

Mix all ingredients together and refrigerate 2 to 3 hours before serving. Great on lemon/garlic toast. Garnish with fresh lemon slices and parsley.

CRUNCHY HAM & SWISS APPETIZERS

... Mrs. Marion (Rachel) Mullet

2 cups very stiff mashed potatoes
2 cups finely chopped cooked ham
1 cup (4 oz.) shredded Swiss cheese
¹/₃ cup mayonnaise
¹/₄ cup minced onion (optional)

1 egg, well beaten
1 tsp. prepared mustard
¹/₂ tsp. salt
¹/₄ tsp. pepper
3¹/₂ cups corn flakes, crushed

Combine all ingredients except corn flakes; chill. Shape into 1" balls and roll in corn flakes. Place on greased cookie sheet and bake at 350° for 25 to 30 minutes. Serve while warm. Yield: 8 dozen.

HAM ROLLS

... Mrs. Larry (Cindy) Schlabach

³/₄ to 1 cup softened butter
3 Tbsp. mustard
3 Tbsp. poppy seeds
1 tsp. Worcestershire sauce
1 sm. minced onion

³/₄ lb. thinly sliced cheese
   (Swiss is good)
1 lb. ham, shaved
3 dozen Pepperidge Farm rolls in
   tin pans

Cream together first 5 ingredients. Keeping rolls together, slice whole sheet of rolls in half. Spread the butter mixture on both sides of the rolls. Arrange ham and cheese slices on bottom of rolls; cover with top half of rolls. Return rolls to tin pans and cover tightly with foil. Bake at 400° for 20 minutes. Cut the mini sandwiches apart and serve hot.

Use your head to save your heels ~ be organized!

SOFT PRETZELS

··· *Mrs. Freeman (Naomi) Miller*
··· *Ruth Raber*

2¹/₂ cups warm water
2 tsp. yeast
2 Tbsp. sugar
1 tsp. salt
6 to 6¹/₂ cups bread flour

Dissolve yeast in 2¹/₂ cups warm water. Stir in sugar, salt, and flour. Knead. Let rise 45 minutes. Divide into 16 to 20 portions. Roll and shape into pretzels and put on a floured, greased surface. In a saucepan, bring 1 qt. water to a boil; add 4 tsp. soda. Boil pretzels, one by one, for 1 minute. Remove and sprinkle with pretzel salt and place on greased jelly roll pans. Bake at 475° for 15 to 20 minutes, till golden brown. Brush with melted butter. Serve with pizza sauce, salsa, or cheese sauce.

SOFT PRETZELS

··· *Willard and Naomi Schlabach, Zak and Jordan*

1 Tbsp. yeast
¹/₃ cup brown sugar
1¹/₂ cups warm water
5 cups all-purpose flour
2 to 3 Tbsp. baking soda
¹/₂ cup melted butter or margarine

OPTIONAL DIP/TOPPINGS

pizza sauce
cheddar cheese, melted
salt
garlic powder
cinnamon and sugar

In bowl, mix brown sugar with warm water. Sprinkle yeast on top and let sit for 5 minutes.

Measure flour into large bowl and add above liquid and stir until dough no longer sticks to the sides. Knead until stretchy.

Put about 1¹/₂ inches of very warm water into pan and add 2 to 3 Tbsp. baking soda.

Shape dough into a pretzel shape and soak in water with baking soda until dough rises to top.

Bake on greased cookie sheets until raised, then grease tops with melted butter.

Finish baking until golden brown.

Serve with cinnamon sugar, garlic powder, salt, cheddar cheese dip, or pizza sauce.

GARLIC BREAD STICKS

... favorite of Danita Renea Troyer, age 10

Make a regular bread dough or dinner roll dough and let rise. Shape into $1/2"$ wide x 7" long sticks and bake. Don't let rise much. When done baking, dip in butter, then sprinkle with Parmesan cheese and garlic salt. Delicious.

QUICK BREAD STICKS

... Mrs. Mark (Ruth) Miller

For quick bread sticks, slice bread 1 inch thick and cut into strips. Toast in broiler, then brush with butter and top with Parmesan cheese, garlic salt, etc. Serve with warm pizza sauce.

Fondue Meals *... Mrs. Mary Esta Yoder*

Want to treat your family or friends to something special, not just the "same old grind" menus? I have used a double boiler to keep the fondue warm while serving. Non-electric fondue pots are reasonably priced; however, electric fondue pots have a more even heat distribution. Have fun and make memories!

PIZZA FONDUE

... Mrs. Linda Mae Troyer

2 Tbsp. cornstarch
2 - $10^1/2$ oz. cans pizza sauce
  with cheese
$1/4$ lb. pepperoni, finely chopped
1 Tbsp. minced onion
1 tsp. oregano
1 - 16 oz. pkg. pasteurized process
  cheese
1 Tbsp. parsley

Mix cornstarch and $1/2$ cup pizza sauce. Stir in remaining pizza sauce. Add pepperoni, onion, and oregano. Heat to boiling. Boil for 1 minute, stirring constantly. Remove from heat. Stir in cheese; melt. Add parsley. Pour into fondue pot to keep warm. Spear dippers (cherry tomatoes, green peppers, bread sticks, mushrooms, etc.) and swirl them in fondue.

CHEESE SAUCE   *... Leona Sue Miller*

2 Tbsp. butter $^1/_2$ tsp. salt
2 Tbsp. flour $^1/_4$ tsp. pepper
1 cup milk $^1/_4$ tsp. paprika
1 cup Velveeta cheese

Make white sauce; add cheese to melt. This is our favorite fondue sauce. Serve with potato cubes, cauliflowerets, Tater Tots, carrots, Trail bologna, toast, or bread cubes as dunkers.

This is also good to use as a cheese sauce to serve over vegetables.

CARAMEL FONDUE   *... Mrs. Mary Esta Yoder*

$^1/_2$ cup butter   2 Tbsp. water
2 cups brown sugar   15 oz. can sweetened condensed milk
1 cup light corn syrup   1 tsp. vanilla

Melt butter in double boiler. Stir in sugar, corn syrup, and water. Bring to a boil. Stir in milk and simmer, stirring constantly, till mixture reaches 230° (thread stage). Add vanilla.

Place in heated fondue pot and serve with your choice of dunkers: angel food cake cubes, marshmallows, wedges or chunks of fresh fruits, doughnuts, or popcorn.

Roll dipped dunkers in toasted coconut, finely chopped nuts, or granola, if desired.

CHOCOLATE FONDUE   *... Mrs. Mary Esta Yoder*

2 bags Hershey's kisses   1 pt. half and half
1 - 8 oz. cream cheese

Melt kisses in double boiler; add cream cheese and half and half. Stir till mixture is smooth and creamy.

Place warm mixture in fondue pot and serve with your choice of fresh fruits in chunks, cake cubes, or marshmallows.

The seven ages of men:
Spills, drills, thrills, bills, ills, pills, wills...

Breads & Rolls

*Blessed are the peacemakers;
for they shall never be unemployed.*

The Crust of Bread

I must not throw upon the floor
The crust I cannot eat,
For many little hungry ones
Would think it quite a treat.

My parents labor very hard
To get me wholesome food,
So I must never waste a bit
That would do others good.

For willful waste makes woeful want,
And I might live to say,
"Oh, how I wish I had the bread
That I once threw away."

*To make your morning go well,
make sure everything is in place the night before.*

LIGHT WHEAT BREAD   ... *Mrs. Mark (Ruth) Miller*

1 cup brown sugar or honey
$3/4$ cup cooking oil
3 Tbsp. salt
3 Tbsp. yeast

6 cups warm water
2 cups wheat flour
$14^1/2$ cups Thesco flour

Dissolve yeast in warm water. Mix together cooking oil, salt, and sugar. Add water and yeast. Let set for 10 minutes. Gradually add flour, kneading well. Let rise until double; punch down. Let rise again, then form loaves. Let rise. Bake at 350° for 35 minutes. Makes 6 loaves.

WHEAT BREAD   ... *Mrs. Reuben (Betty) Yoder*

$1/3$ cup white sugar
$1/3$ cup brown sugar
3 Tbsp. flour
1 Tbsp. salt
2 cups hot water

1 cup lukewarm water
2 Tbsp. yeast
$3/4$ cup oil
8 cups flour (3 whole wheat and
    5 white)

Mix sugars, salt, and 3 Tbsp. flour. Add 2 cups hot water; stir to dissolve. Dissolve yeast in 1 cup lukewarm water. Add it to the sugar mixture once dissolved. Add half of flour, then add some oil, then the remaining flour, and oil last. Let rise 30 minutes and work down. Repeat, then shape loaves and let rise. Put in pans. Bake at 325° approx. 30 to 35 minutes.

I like to use $1/4$ cup peanut oil and $1/2$ cup oil; it makes a good taste.

BREAD   ... *Mrs. Steve (Bena) Yoder*

1 cup warm water
2 tsp. white sugar
6 tsp. yeast
$1/4$ cup brown sugar
$1/4$ cup white sugar
$1/4$ cup honey

$1/2$ cup oil
3 tsp. salt
2 cups hot water
$1^1/2$ cups whole wheat flour
$6^1/2$ cups Robin Hood flour

Combine first 3 ingredients. Let yeast rise. Meanwhile, combine sugars, honey, oil, salt, and hot water. Now add yeast mixture and the flour. Let rise, knead, let rise again, knead, and form loaves. Bake at 350° for 35 to 40 minutes.

SPELTZ OR WHOLE WHEAT BREAD

··· Mrs. Paul (Rebecca) Nisley

3 cups hot water	2 Tbsp. salt
2 cups quick oats	$3/4$ cup oil
1 cup honey	3 Tbsp. yeast in 1 cup warm water
4 eggs	2 cups flour (your choice)

Pour hot water over oatmeal and set aside to cool. Beat all other ingredients together, making sure everything is just lukewarm before adding yeast mixture. Work in 9 cups more flour to make a nice, spongy dough (not sticky). Grease top and let rise twice after kneading it. Bake at 325° for 30 to 40 minutes.

Can also be made using a few cups of white bread flour, if so desired.

GRANNY BREAD

··· Mrs. Mary Esta Yoder

Dissolve:

2 pkt. yeast	$1/2$ cup lukewarm water
1 tsp. sugar	

Let stand 10 minutes. Add:

2 cups warm water	$3/4$ cup oatmeal
$1/2$ cup sugar or $1/3$ cup honey	$3/4$ cup wheat flour
1 Tbsp. salt	6 to 7 cups bread flour
$1/2$ cup vegetable oil	

Knead 10 minutes. Let rise in a warm place till double. Punch down and let rise again. Shape into loaves. Let rise. Bake at 350° for 30 minutes. Yield: 3 loaves.

RICH EGG BREAD

··· Mrs. Lloyd (Bena) Miller
··· Mrs. Mary Esta Yoder

2 pkg. yeast	$1 1/2$ cups scalded milk
$1/2$ cup warm water	$1/2$ tsp. salt
$1/2$ cup sugar	$1/4$ cup oleo
3 eggs, beaten	$7 1/2$ cups flour

Dissolve yeast in warm water. Cool milk to lukewarm; add beaten eggs, sugar, salt, and oleo. Blend into yeast mixture and add flour. Knead 8 to 10 minutes. Let rise to double in size. Shape into 3 loaves; let rise till light. Bake at 350° for 25 to 30 minutes.

CORNMEAL BREAD   *... Mrs. Mike (Ruby) Sommers*

2 cups yellow cornmeal

2 cups flour

4 tsp. baking powder

2 tsp. baking soda

1$^1/_2$ tsp. salt

8 Tbsp. sugar

2 eggs, beaten

2$^1/_2$ cups sour cream

2$^1/_2$ cups melted shortening

Combine first 6 ingredients in large bowl. Make a well in center of mixture. Combine eggs, sour cream, and shortening. Add to dry ingredients. Stir just until moistened. Bake at 350° until set or golden brown, about 15 minutes.

BANANA BREAD   *... Mrs. Mike (Ruby) Sommers*

2 cups sugar

$^1/_2$ cup butter or oleo

2 eggs

3 ripe bananas
   (mash before adding)

5 Tbsp. sour cream

3 cups flour

1 tsp. baking soda

$^2/_3$ cup chopped nuts

Mix sugar and butter; add eggs and mix well. Add soda, sour cream, bananas, and flour. Mix. Add nuts last. Bake in loaf pans at 350° for 45 minutes.

POPPY SEED BREAD   *... Mrs. Linda Beachy*

3 cups flour

1$^1/_2$ tsp. salt

1$^1/_2$ tsp. baking powder

3 eggs

1$^1/_2$ cups milk

1 cup oil

2$^1/_4$ cups white sugar

1$^1/_2$ Tbsp. poppy seeds

1$^1/_4$ tsp. vanilla

1$^1/_2$ tsp. almond extract

1$^1/_2$ tsp. butter flavoring

Mix all ingredients and pour into two greased 9"x5" pans. Bake 1 hour at 350°. Top with glaze after baked.

GLAZE

$^1/_2$ tsp. butter flavoring

$^1/_2$ tsp. almond extract

$^1/_2$ tsp. vanilla

$^1/_4$ cup orange juice

$^3/_4$ cup sugar

DINNER ROLLS
··· Mrs. Paul (Wilma) Schlabach

2 eggs, well beaten
$^1/_3$ cup white sugar
$^1/_2$ cup margarine, melted
1 tsp. salt

4 cups all-purpose flour
1 pkg. dry yeast
1 cup lukewarm water

Dissolve yeast in warm water. Beat eggs until very light. Mix ingredients in order given. Blend well. Let dough rise once. Shape into balls, 2 dozen in 13" x 9" cake pan. Let rise until double. Bake at 325° for 15 minutes, or until done.

DINNER ROLLS
··· Leona Sue Miller

$1^1/_2$ cups milk, scalded and cooled
1 cup lukewarm water
2 pkg. yeast
2 eggs, beaten
2 Tbsp. lard

$^3/_4$ cup sugar
2 tsp. salt
7 cups Thesco flour
  (may use part wheat)

Mix warm water, lard, sugar, salt, and yeast together. Soak until yeast is dissolved. Add eggs, milk, and flour. Knead 10 minutes. Put in warm place. Let rise until double. Shape into buns. Let rise again until nice and fluffy. Bake at 325° for 15–20 minutes or until nice and browned.

GOLDEN PUMPKIN ROLLS
··· Mrs. Mike (Ruby) Sommers

1 Tbsp. yeast dissolved in $^1/_4$ cup
  water
1 cup milk, scalded
2 Tbsp. shortening
2 Tbsp. sugar

1 tsp. salt
$^1/_2$ cup canned pumpkin
5 cups flour
1 egg, beaten

Dissolve yeast in warm water and set aside. Scald milk, then stir in next ingredients—shortening, sugar, salt, and pumpkin. Cool mixture to lukewarm and add 2 cups flour and beat until smooth; add yeast mixture and 1 beaten egg, then 3 cups flour. Knead 8–10 minutes. Let rise. Punch down. Let rest 10 minutes. Shape and put in pans to rise. Bake at 375° for 15 minutes.

The best vitamin for making friends is B~1.

BUTTERHORNS
... Mrs. Mike (Ruby) Sommers

1 Tbsp. active dry yeast
2 Tbsp. warm water (110°–115°)
2 cups warm milk (110°–115°)
1/2 cup sugar

1 egg, beaten
1 tsp. salt
6 cups flour
3/4 cup butter or oleo, melted

Dissolve yeast in water; add milk, sugar, egg, and 3 cups flour; beat and add butter and remaining flour; put in greased bowl. Cover and refrigerate overnight. Next a.m. divide into two balls. Roll into 12" circle and cut into 12 pie-shaped wedges. Roll from large end to point and place on greased cookie sheet. Let rise. Bake at 350° for 15–20 minutes.

BUTTERHORNS
... Mrs. Marion (Rachel) Mullet

Mix together:
1 pkg. yeast
1 Tbsp. sugar

Beat in 3 eggs with 1 cup warm water. Let stand 15 minutes.
Add:
1/2 cup sugar
1/2 cup shortening
1/2 tsp. salt
5 cups Thesco flour

Knead well. Cover and let stand in refrigerator overnight. Divide in 2 parts and roll out in a 12" circle. Cut into 16 wedges; roll up starting with wide side. Let rise 3–4 hours. Bake at 350° for 10–12 minutes. Brush with butter. Serve while warm. Yield: 32 dinner rolls.

BLUEBERRY MUFFINS
... Mrs. Ralph (Sarah) Schlabach

2 cups all-purpose flour
2/3 cup sugar
1 Tbsp. baking powder
1/2 tsp. salt
2 eggs

1 cup milk
1/3 cup butter or margarine, melted
1 tsp. ground nutmeg
1 tsp. vanilla
2 cups fresh or frozen blueberries

In mixing bowl, combine flour, sugar, baking powder, and salt. In another bowl, beat eggs and blend in milk, butter, nutmeg, and vanilla. Pour into dry ingredients and mix just until moistened. Fold in blueberries. Fill greased or paper lined muffin cups. Bake at 375° for 20–25 minutes. Brush tops with butter and sprinkle with sugar.

APPLE STREUSEL MUFFINS ··· Mrs. Willis (Ruth) Schlabach

2 cups flour
1 cup brown sugar
1 Tbsp. baking powder
1 1/4 tsp. cinnamon
1/2 tsp. salt

1/2 tsp. baking soda
2 large eggs, beaten
1 cup sour cream
1/4 cup butter, melted
1 1/2 cups diced apples

STREUSEL TOPPING

1/3 cup brown sugar
2 Tbsp. flour
1/2 tsp. cinnamon

2 Tbsp. butter
1/3 cup chopped pecans (optional)

In large bowl, stir together flour, sugar, baking powder, cinnamon, salt, and baking soda. Set aside. In small bowl, beat eggs, sour cream, and butter. Add all at once to dry ingredients along with apples. Stir just until moistened. Fill well greased muffin tins 2/3 full. Combine topping ingredients; sprinkle on top. Bake at 400° for 20–25 minutes. Yield: 18 muffins.

FEATHER LIGHT MUFFINS

··· Mrs. Jr. (Ruth) Miller
··· Daniel Raber

1/3 cup shortening
1/2 cup white sugar
1 egg
1 1/2 cups flour

1 1/2 tsp. baking powder
1/2 tsp. salt
1/2 cup milk

TOPPING

1/2 cup white sugar
1 tsp. cinnamon

1/2 cup melted butter

In mixing bowl, cream shortening, sugar, and egg. Mix dry ingredients; add slowly to creamed mixture along with milk. Fill greased muffin pans 2/3 full. Bake at 325° for 25 minutes. Let cool 4 minutes. Roll warm muffins in melted butter, then in sugar mixture. Makes 8 to 10 muffins.

BRAN MUFFINS

··· Mrs. Mike (Ruby) Sommers

3 cups bran
1 cup boiling water
1/2 cup oil
2 eggs

2 1/2 cups whole wheat flour
1 1/2 cups sugar
2 1/2 tsp. baking soda
2 cups buttermilk

Combine bran and boiling water in large mixing bowl. Let stand 5 minutes. Beat in oil and eggs. Stir in remaining ingredients until well mixed. Fill muffin cups 3/4 full. Bake at 400° for 15–20 minutes.

ENGLISH TEA MUFFINS   *··· Mrs. Steve (Ruth) Schlabach*

2 cups flour
$^3/_4$ cup sugar
2 tsp. baking powder
$^1/_2$ tsp. salt
$^1/_2$ tsp. ground cinnamon

$^3/_4$ cup raisins
$^1/_2$ cup vegetable oil
1 cup milk
1 egg

TOPPING

$^1/_2$ cup packed brown sugar
1 tsp. cinnamon

$^1/_4$ cup finely chopped walnuts

Preheat oven to 400°. Combine dry ingredients and raisins in large bowl. In separate bowl, combine oil, milk, and egg; mix well. Add to dry ingredients; stir only until dry ingredients are moistened. Fill greased muffin pans $^3/_4$ full. Combine topping ingredients and spoon over top of each muffin. Bake 17–20 minutes. Yield: 18 muffins.

KENTUCKY BISCUITS   *··· Mrs. Linda Mae Troyer*
··· Mrs. Richard (Wilma) Schlabach

2 cups all-purpose flour
$2^1/_2$ tsp. baking powder
$^1/_2$ tsp. soda
dash of salt

1 Tbsp. white sugar
$^1/_2$ cup butter or shortening
$^3/_4$ cup buttermilk
1 Tbsp. melted butter

Mix flour, baking powder, soda, salt, and sugar. Cut in butter until mixture resembles coarse crumbs. Add buttermilk; mix quickly to make a soft dough. Turn out onto lightly floured surface. Knead a few times to make a soft dough. Don't overknead or the buscuits will turn hard and dry. Roll out to a 6" x 6" square. Place on ungreased baking sheet. With knife, cut dough into 12 even portions. Do not separate. Bake at 400° until golden, about 15 minutes. Serve with butter and jam. *You are off to a good start in the morning if you pass along a basket with hot biscuits.* Yield: 12 biscuits.

*A child is a person who passes through your life
and suddenly disappears into an adult.*

BUTTER ROLLS
··· *Mrs. Paul (Rebecca) Nisley*

2 cups flour

2 tsp. baking powder

GRAVY

1 qt. milk

4 Tbsp. flour

$^1/_2$ tsp. salt

milk or cream

sugar and cinnamon to taste

Add milk or cream to first 3 ingredients to make a stiff dough. Roll out and spread with butter, cinnamon, and brown sugar. Cut into approx. 4" square and roll up. When baked, unfold the rolls and spread the gravy over top.

MAPLE TWIST ROLLS
··· *favorite of Rachel Kay Schlabach, age 8*

$^3/_4$ cup milk

$^1/_4$ cup butter, melted

1 Tbsp. yeast dissolved in $^1/_4$ cup warm water

1 tsp. maple flavoring

FILLING

$^1/_4$ cup butter, melted

$^1/_2$ cup brown sugar

1 tsp. maple flavoring

FROSTING

1 cup powdered sugar

1 to 2 Tbsp. milk

$2^3/_4$ to 3 cups all-purpose flour

3 Tbsp. white sugar

1 egg

$^1/_2$ tsp. salt

$^1/_2$ cup nuts

1 tsp. cinnamon

1 Tbsp. margarine

$^1/_2$ tsp. maple flavoring

Combine dough ingredients, adding flour last, one cup at a time. Grease 13" x 9" pan. Divide dough into 3 parts, then roll out into rectangle. Spread half of filling on first layer, then cover with another layer of dough. Spread remainder of filling over second layer and top with last of dough. Cut into 8 pieces and twist each piece one time. Let rise and bake at 350°. Mix frosting ingredients and pour over rolls while they are still warm.

Pray to God, but row toward shore.

CINNAMON ROLLS   *··· Mrs. Owen (Elsie) Nisley*

Beat together well:

3 eggs $^1/_2$ tsp. salt
$^3/_4$ cup sugar

Add:

$^3/_4$ cup oil $^3/_4$ cup cold milk
1$^1/_2$ cups boiling water

Add 3 pkg. dry yeast, dissolved in $^1/_2$ cup lukewarm water. Add 4–5 cups flour, just enough to make it thick enough to really beat it. Now add more flour, enough to make a soft but not sticky dough. Knead until like satin. Grease sides of bowl and let rise till double. Work down and let rise again. Divide dough in half and roll about $^1/_2$" thick. Spread a little cream and butter on this; add sugar and cinnamon. Roll up. Slice off and let rise in pans for 1 hour. Bake at 325°.

FOR PECAN ROLLS, MIX IN PAN:

$^1/_3$ cup butter, melted   2 Tbsp. water
$^1/_2$ cup brown sugar $^1/_2$ cup pecans
1 Tbsp. corn syrup or maple syrup

Place roll slices on top of sugar–pecan layer; let rise. Bake. Invert while warm.

CINNAMON ROLLS   *··· Mrs. Jr. (Ruth) Miller*
                                  ··· Mrs. Steve (Bena) Yoder

2 pkg. or Tbsp. yeast   6 eggs, well beaten
1$^1/_3$ cups warm water   1 cup Wesson oil
$^2/_3$ cup white sugar   7 cups flour (Gold Medal)
1$^1/_2$ tsp. salt

Mix ingredients in order given. Let rise until double in size. Divide dough in half and roll out to 1" thick. Spread on some butter, softened at room temperature, and sprinkle with brown sugar and cinnamon. Roll up and cut with thread. I have always had better luck baking these in tinfoil pans. Dough is very soft, but do not add more flour. Use flour when rolling out dough. Bake at 350° for 20–25 minutes. Do not overbake. Ice with Caramel Icing (page 161).

This is a hearty "welcome home" for the school children!

CINNAMON ROLLS
··· Mrs. Mike (Ruby) Sommers

2 cups scalded milk
2 cups warm water
2 Tbsp. yeast dissolved in part
 of water
1 cup melted shortening (I use Crisco)

1 $^1/_2$ cups sugar
2 eggs, beaten
3 tsp. salt
approx. 11 cups flour

Mix together milk, sugar, salt, shortening, eggs, and remaining water. Add yeast and stir. Add half of flour and mix well, then add remaining flour. Mix well and let rise 1 hour or until double in bulk. Work down and let rise again. Roll out and top with butter, brown sugar, and cinnamon. Roll into jelly roll and cut; place on cookie sheets or cake pans and let rise. Bake at 350° for 15–20 minutes. Top with favorite icing.

OVERNIGHT CINNAMON ROLLS
··· Mrs. Mary Esta Yoder

$^1/_2$ cup warm water
2 Tbsp. sugar
2 Tbsp. yeast
4 cups warm water
1 cup vegetable oil

1 $^1/_2$ cups sugar
2 eggs, beaten
2 tsp. salt
14 cups flour

Mix first 3 ingredients and let stand 10 minutes. Add next 5 ingredients; mix well, then add flour, beating as long as possible. Let rise 2 hours. Punch down and let rise again. Roll out $^1/_2$" thick; spread with butter and sprinkle with brown sugar and cinnamon. Roll up jelly roll fashion and slice. Place on greased baking sheets and let stand overnight in a cool place. Bake at 350° for 15–20 minutes. Frost with your favorite icing.

Plan ahead...have fresh, warm rolls to serve to your family for breakfast or at a special tea party!

CHOCOLATE ROLLS
··· Mrs. Mary Esta Yoder

$^1/_2$ cup butter
1 cup brown sugar

$^1/_4$ cup light corn syrup
3 Tbsp. cocoa

Combine and cook 1 minute. Pour into two 9" round pans. Sprinkle pecans over top. Use your favorite cinnamon roll dough. Roll out and spread with butter and a mixture of:

1 cup sugar

2 Tbsp. cocoa

Roll up and cut into slices. Place slices on chocolate pecan layer. Let rise; bake. Invert to serve.

CREAM STICKS   *··· favorite of Emanuel Andrew Brenneman*

2 Tbsp. yeast	1 tsp. vanilla
1 cup warm water	1 tsp. lemon flavor (if desired)
2 eggs	$1/2$ cup oleo
1 cup scalded milk	$2/3$ cup sugar
1 tsp. salt	6 cups flour

Soak yeast in water. Mix the remaining ingredients except flour. Beat well. Add dissolved yeast and 2 cups flour. Beat well. Add the rest of the flour. Let rise to twice its bulk, then roll out $1/2$" thick and cut 1" x 4". Let rise again. Fry in hot deep fat at 375°. Fill with cream stick filling and frost with caramel icing.

FILLING

1 cup milk	3 Tbsp. flour

Cook over low heat till very thick. Cool, then beat well.

$1/2$ cup shortening	1 cup powdered sugar

Cream together.

Beat flour mixture, shortening, and powdered sugar together. Add 2 tsp. vanilla and $2^1/2$ cups or more powdered sugar to desired consistency.

RASPBERRY CREAM-FILLED COFFEE CAKE

··· Mrs. Mary Esta Yoder

3 lb. doughnut mix	2 Tbsp. yeast
3 cups lukewarm water	pinch of salt
2 Tbsp. white sugar	redi-tube cream cheese
$1/2$ cup bread flour	pie filling – red or black raspberry

Mix dough and knead 5–8 minutes. Cover and let rise. Roll out on floured surface; spread with softened oleo, sugar, and cinnamon (cinnamon is optional). Roll up like cinnamon rolls. Slice off in 1"–2" slices. Chop up slices into small pieces. Place pieces into a greased round cake pan, just to cover bottom. Spread softened cream cheese over this, then add your choice of pie filling. Put more dough pieces on top and let rise. Bake at 350°. Drizzle icing on top. Yield: 3 to 4 coffee cakes, depending on pan size used.

CORN PONE
··· *Mose A. Schlabach*

1 cup cornmeal
3 Tbsp. sugar
1 tsp. soda
1 stick oleo or butter
1 cup milk

1 cup flour
1 tsp. salt
1 tsp. baking powder
1 egg

Turn oven to 350°. Put oleo in 10" pie pan and set in the oven to melt while you mix the other ingredients together. Then add the melted oleo; now pour all back into pie pan and bake approximately 25–30 minutes.

By experience, I know this is easy to make and a tasty, nutritious meal. Serve with fruit or berries and milk.

GOOD EASY PIZZA DOUGH
··· *Mrs. Roy (Freda) Miller*

1 Tbsp. yeast
1 cup warm water
1 tsp. sugar

1 tsp. salt
2 Tbsp. salad oil
$2^1/_2$ cups flour

Dissolve yeast in warm water. Stir in remaining ingredients, beating vigorously. Set aside 5 minutes. Bake at 425°. Makes two 10" pizzas.

PIZZA CRUST
··· *Mrs. Paul (Wilma) Schlabach*

$1^1/_3$ cups warm water
1 Tbsp. yeast
1 tsp. white sugar

$1^1/_2$ tsp. salt
2 Tbsp. vegetable oil
$3^1/_4$ cups all-purpose flour

Mix and let rise. Press into pizza pan. Bake for 7 minutes at 350°. Add all your favorite toppings and bake for 12–15 minutes more.

PIZZA CRUST
··· *Mrs. Jason (Fern) Schlabach*

1 Tbsp. yeast   1 cup warm water
    Dissolve yeast in water. Let rise 5–10 minutes.
1 tsp. sugar $2^1/_2$ Tbsp. oil
1 tsp. salt   approx. $2^1/_2$ cups flour
    Mix all together. Let set to rise 5–10 minutes.

Breakfast

Delights

*Today will never return;
use it well.*

The Letter "E"

Did you know the little letter "e" is the most used letter in the alphabet? It is also the most unfortunate letter because it is always out of cash, always in debt, never out of danger, and in torment all the time. All this is true; still it is never in war, always in peace, and always in something to eat.

It is the beginning of existence, the commencement of ease, and the end of trouble. Without it there would be no heaven. It is the center of honesty and always in love.

Take Your Smile with You

Take your smile with you
Wherever you go—
Keep it bright, use it,
For you never know
Who's tired and discouraged
And sad-hearted, too,
And waiting for sunshine
And friendship from you!
Keep your smile handy
And pass it along—
You'll find in return
You've a heart full of song.

BREAKFAST WAKE-UP   *··· Mrs. Freeman (Marie) Schlabach*

12 eggs, beaten
1 lb. sausage, cooked

1 can cream of mushroom soup
1 lb. cheese

Layer in 9" x 13" pan in order given. Refrigerate overnight. Bake at 350° for 30 minutes or till done.

MORNING MIX-UP   *··· Mrs. Willis (Ruth) Schlabach*

2 cups frozen hash browns
1 cup cooked ham
$1/2$ cup onions
2 Tbsp. cooking oil

6 eggs
salt and pepper
1 cup shredded cheddar cheese

In large skillet, sauté potatoes, ham, and onions in oil for 10 minutes or until potatoes are tender. In a small bowl, beat eggs, salt, and pepper. Add to the skillet. Cook, stirring occasionally, until eggs are set. Remove from heat and gently stir in cheese.

BREAKAST CASSEROLE   *··· Mrs. David (Susan) Nisley*

3 cups cubed bread
3 cups cubed ham or bacon
3 cups shredded cheddar or
   Colby cheese
1 Tbsp. flour

1 tsp. dry mustard
2 Tbsp. melted butter
6 eggs, beaten
3 cups milk

Place first 3 ingredients in large 9" x 13" pan. Combine flour and mustard; sprinkle over bread mixture. Beat eggs, milk, and butter; pour over bread, cheese, and meat mixture. Refrigerate for at least 8 hours. Bake uncovered at 350° for 1 hour.

BREAKFAST CASSEROLE   *··· Mrs. Wayne (Emma) Yoder*

6 eggs
$1^1/2$ cups milk
3 slices diced white bread
1 tsp. dry mustard

1 tsp. salt
1 lb. sausage, browned
1 cup grated cheese

Brown sausage and drain well. Beat eggs, milk, mustard, and salt together. Add bread, cheese, and sausage. Chill overnight. Bake at 350° for 50 minutes. Ham or bacon may also be used.

CHEESE SOUFFLÉ   ··· Mrs. Kris Miller ··· Mrs. Linda Beachy

8 slices bread   cubed ham or bacon
1 lb. shredded cheese   salt
6 eggs, beaten   pepper
2 cups milk

Cube bread, put in bottom of casserole. Combine cheese and meat. Sprinkle over bread cubes. Mix eggs, milk, and seasonings. Add over top of other ingredients. Refrigerate overnight. Bake at 325° for 45 minutes.

HAM & CHEESE STRATA   ··· Mrs. Philip (Denise) Schlabach

10 slices bread

Arrange 5 slices on the bottom of a buttered baking dish and layer:

$^1/_2$ cup ground cooked ham or   4 oz. American or cheddar cheese
        Canadian bacon

Cover with remaining 5 slices of bread and repeat layers of:

$^1/_2$ cup ground cooked ham or   4 oz. American or cheddar cheese
        Canadian bacon

Mix:

3 eggs, slightly beaten $^1/_2$ tsp. dry mustard
$2^3/_4$ cups milk

Pour over layers in casserole dish and cover. Refrigerate overnight. Bake for 1 hour at 350°. Slice in squares and serve. Serves 6 to 8.

APPLE SAUSAGE BREAKFAST   ··· Mrs. Mary Esta Yoder
··· Mrs. Linda Mae Troyer ··· Mrs. Marion (Rachel) Mullet

2 lb. lean bulk sausage   1 cup grated apple
$^1/_2$ cup minced onion $1^1/_2$ cups crushed Ritz crackers
2 lg. eggs, beaten $^1/_4$ cup milk

Line a $2^1/_2$-qt. ring mold with plastic wrap. Combine all ingredients; mix well and press firmly into mold. Chill several hours or overnight. Unmold, removing plastic wrap onto a baking sheet with raised edges. Bake at 350° for 1 hour. Transfer onto serving platter; fill ring with scrambled eggs. Serve with cheese sauce. Makes 8 servings. Delicious!

CREAMED EGGS ··· Mrs. Reuben (Betty) Yoder

Sauté 1 Tbsp. chopped onion in $^1/_3$ cup butter. Add $^1/_4$ cup flour; cook until bubbly. Add enough milk to make a med. white sauce. Season with chicken or ham bouillon and seasoned salt to taste. Grate 4 to 6 hard-boiled eggs. Add to sauce and heat thoroughly. Serve with toast.

BRUNCH PIZZA ··· Mrs. Linda Mae Troyer
CRUST

1 pkg. (24 oz.) frozen hash browns, thawed

1 egg

EGG TOPPING

7 eggs

$^1/_2$ cup milk

$1^1/_2$ cups shredded cheddar cheese

OPTIONAL TOPPINGS

chopped onions
chopped green pepper
sliced mushrooms

bacon, crumbled
chopped ham

Preheat oven to 400°. Combine potatoes and egg and put in 14" pan. Pat down with spoon; bake 20 minutes. Whisk eggs and milk; cook for 3 minutes and stir. Cook an additional 3 minutes and stir again. Spread cooked eggs evenly over baked potato crust. Top with optional toppings. Sprinkle with cheese and bake for 10 minutes. Cut into wedges.

BREAKFAST BURRITOS Mrs. Linda Mae Troyer

1 lb. pork sausage
$^1/_4$ cup diced onion
$^1/_4$ cup diced green and red peppers
$1^1/_2$ cups hash brown potatoes
4 eggs, beaten

12 flour tortillas
$^1/_2$ cup shredded cheddar cheese or Velveeta cheese
taco sauce
sour cream

Brown sausage in a large skillet. Add onion and peppers; cook until tender. Add potatoes; cook until tender. Add eggs; stir. Cook until eggs are set. Divide filling mixture between 12 tortillas. Sprinkle with cheese. Fold tortillas; serve with taco sauce and sour cream. (Burritos can be made in advance and refrigerated or frozen. Reheat.)

BREAKFAST PIZZA   ··· *Mrs. Freeman (Marie) Schlabach*

2 cups biscuit mix
milk to make a dough like cake
   batter
16 eggs, scrambled in butter

1 can cream of mushroom soup
American cheese slices or shredded
   cheddar cheese

Mix biscuit mix and milk. Bake in sheet cake or pizza pan at 400° till done. Put scrambled eggs on top, next soup or sausage gravy, and top with plenty of cheese. Can be varied any way with bacon, etc. Serve with orange juice. Always delicious!

BREAKFAST SANDWICHES   ··· *Mrs. Marion (Rachel) Mullet*

1 lb. hamburg
1 lb. sausage

1 lb. Velveeta cheese
1 tsp. oregano

Brown hamburg and sausage. Add cheese and oregano. Heat until cheese is melted. Serve warm on toasted split buns or muffins.

PANCAKE MIX   ··· *Leona Sue Miller*

10 cups flour
3 cups whole wheat flour
2 cups quick-cooking oatmeal
3 cups crushed corn flakes

$1/4$ cup white sugar
5 heaping Tbsp. baking powder
3 Tbsp. soda
1 Tbsp. salt

Mix well and store in airtight container.

TO MAKE PANCAKES

1 cup mix
1 cup milk (sweet or sour) or
   buttermilk

1 egg
1 Tbsp. melted shortening

Mix and bake.

PANCAKES ··· *favorite of Aaron (age 10) and Cody (age 7) Albritton*

2 cups flour
3 Tbsp. warm milk

2 Tbsp. butter
pinch of salt

Mix ingredients together. Make your pancakes. Enjoy! Great recipe for children. Aaron and Cody love to cook pancakes.

FLANNEL PANCAKES   *... Mrs. Albert (Verna) Yoder*

2 cups flour

4 tsp. baking powder

2 Tbsp. sugar

2 eggs, beaten

$^1/_4$ cup vegetable oil

$^1/_4$ tsp. salt

sweet milk to make a fairly thin batter

Just mix with a fork. Do not overbeat. Fry in butter on a hot skillet. Delicious served with maple syrup or chicken gravy! Pile 'em high—set on table and see what happens!

OATMEAL PANCAKES   *... Mrs. Henry (Emma) Troyer

Mix:

$1^1/_2$ cups rolled oats

Beat in:

$^1/_2$ cup flour

1 tsp. sugar

1 tsp. soda

2 cups buttermilk or sour milk

1 tsp. salt

2 beaten eggs

FINNISH PANCAKES   *... Ellen Schlabach*

$^1/_4$ cup butter

4 eggs, well beaten

$^2/_3$ cup flour

$^1/_2$ tsp. salt

1 Tbsp. butter

$^1/_4$ cup sugar

2 cups milk

Place $^1/_4$ cup butter on 9" x 13" pan. Heat in oven at 400° while you mix remaining ingredients and pour into warm greased pan. Bake at 400° for 20 minutes. Will be brown and bubbly. Serve with syrup. We beg Mom to fix this for breakfast. She has been fixing it for years!

FRENCH TOAST   *... favorite of Jason David Yoder, age 7*

6 eggs

$^1/_2$ cup flour

$^1/_4$ tsp. salt

$1^1/_2$ Tbsp. sugar

2 cups milk

Beat flour, eggs, sugar, salt, and milk until smooth. Soak bread in egg mixture, then fry in buttered skillet until golden brown. Serve with peanut butter and maple syrup.

For a special treat, I make peanut butter and jelly sandwiches, dip in egg mixture, and fry to a golden brown.

OVEN-BAKED FRENCH TOAST   ··· Mrs. Mary Esta Yoder

6 slices wheat bread   3 eggs
$^1/_4$ cup butter $^1/_2$ cup orange juice
2 Tbsp. honey $^1/_8$ tsp. salt
$^1/_2$ tsp. cinnamon

Combine and melt butter and honey in a 13" x 9" x 2" pan, spreading to sides of pan. Sprinkle with cinnamon. Combine eggs, juice, and salt in a bowl; beat well. Dip bread slices, one at a time, into egg mixture, coating well. Arrange on top of honey mixture. Bake at 400° for 20 minutes, or until browned. Invert to serve with additional honey.

FLUFFY SYRUP   ··· Mrs. Mary Esta Yoder

2 sticks margarine, softened   1 egg
$^1/_2$ cup pancake syrup   1$^1/_2$ cups powdered sugar

Beat all together on high for several minutes. Serve on pancakes, French toast, zucchini bread, etc.

FRIED CORN MUSH   ··· Mrs. Marvin (Martha) Mast

Bring 2$^1/_2$ cups water to a boil. Add mixture of:

1 cup cold water $^1/_4$ cup flour
1 cup cornmeal   1 tsp. salt

Bring to a boil, then simmer for 30 minutes. Pour into pan. When cooled, cut and fry.

CREAMED TOMATOES   ··· Mrs. Mary Esta Yoder

1 cup tomato juice   1 tsp. salt
$^1/_2$ cup water   2 cups milk
$^1/_2$ cup brown sugar $^1/_3$ cup flour

Bring tomato juice, water, sugar, and salt to a boil. Mix milk and flour till smooth; add to juice and cook until thickened, stirring constantly. Serve over fried corn mush, home fries, or scrambled eggs.

SAUSAGE GRAVY   ··· Mrs. Linda Mae Troyer

Fry 4 lb. fresh sausage. Then add 3 cups flour and brown. (If sausage is dry, you may need to add some butter when adding flour.) Add 2 Tbsp. salt and $^1/_2$ Tbsp. pepper. Stir well and add 18 cups milk. Heat to boiling point; reduce heat and simmer a few minutes. Makes approx. 5 qt. of gravy.

BAKED OATMEAL
··· *Mrs. Mike (Ruby) Sommers*

1 cup brown sugar
$^1/_2$ cup melted butter
2 beaten eggs
3 cups oatmeal

2 tsp. baking powder
1 tsp. salt
1 cup milk

Mix brown sugar, butter, and eggs. Then add remaining ingredients. Pour into 9" x 13" pan. Bake at 350° for 30 minutes. Serve with milk and canned peaches.

BAKED OATMEAL
··· *Mrs. Reuben (Betty) Yoder*
··· *Michelle Schlabach*

$^1/_2$ cup melted butter
$^3/_4$ cup brown sugar
2 beaten eggs
1 tsp. salt

3 cups rolled oats
$1^1/_2$ tsp. cinnamon
2 tsp. baking powder
1 cup milk

Mix everything together and pour into a greased 8" square pan. Bake at 350° for 30 minutes. Serve warm with milk. We like to add some fruit, like raspberries or slightly thawed strawberries. Good for breakfast or for dinner on a cold winter evening! Yield: 6–8 servings.

GRANOLA BREAKFAST CEREAL
··· *Mrs. Freeman (Naomi) Miller*

8 cups quick oats
1 cup whole wheat flour
1 cup brown sugar
2 cups coconut
1 tsp. salt
$1^1/_2$ tsp. soda

1 Tbsp. cinnamon
1 cup butter or oleo
1 tsp. vanilla
$^1/_2$ cup honey
1 cup raisins or chocolate chips

Combine dry ingredients. Melt butter (I use $^1/_2$ cup butter and $^1/_2$ cup oleo) and add vanilla and honey to melted butter. Pour over dry ingredients and mix well. Spread on jelly roll pans and toast in 250° oven until nicely browned, approximately 1 hour. When still warm, add raisins or chocolate chips.

GRANOLA CEREAL
··· Mrs. Reuben (Betty) Yoder
··· Mrs. Linda Mae Troyer

1 1/4 cups brown sugar
8 cups oatmeal
4 cups whole wheat flour
4 cups coconut
2 pkg. graham crackers, coarsely
    broken

2 tsp. salt
3 tsp. soda
2 cups melted butter
1 lb. chocolate chips (optional)
1 lb. butterscotch chips (optional)

Mix all together and bake at 250° for 45 minutes, stirring every 15 minutes. After cereal is slightly cooled, add the chocolate or butterscotch chips if desired.

GRANOLA MIX
··· Mrs. Reuben (Sara Etta) Schlabach

12 cups rolled oats
2 cups wheat germ
2 cups coconut

2 cups nuts, chopped
    (almonds, walnuts, etc.)

Mix this together, then heat the following and add to the above mixture:

2 cups melted butter
1/2 cup honey
1/2 cup molasses
2 cups brown sugar

2 tsp. vanilla or maple flavoring
2 tsp. cinnamon
1 1/2 tsp. salt

Spread on 4–6 cookie sheets and toast at 250° for 1 hour. Stir every 10–15 minutes. Cool.

After cool and crisp, put in airtight container. Can also be frozen. Delicious cereal—we're never out of it. It's a must on the breakfast table. Also good on ice cream.

Each time you turn the pages
Looking for something new to cook,
Fondly remember each person
Who makes possible this book.

Salads
& Soups

Home is where Love surrounds you.

Be

If you can't be a wave, be a ripple;
If you can't be a forest, be a tree.
If you can't be a rock, be a pebble;
But the most important thing is to "Be."

If you can't be a king, be a peasant;
If you can't be an "A," be a "Z,"
For the joy, after all, is not lessened
If you are just the best that you can be.

Live and Learn

I've learned that young people need older people's love,
respect, and knowledge of life.
Older people need the love, respect, and strength
of young people.

WE NEED EACH OTHER

GRANDMA'S GELATIN FRUIT SALAD

··· Mrs. Atlee (Dorothy) Schlabach

2 cups boiling water, divided
1 pkg. (3 oz.) lemon flavored
    gelatin
2 cups ice cubes, divided
1 pkg. (3 oz.) orange flavored
    gelatin

1 can (20 oz.) crushed pineapple
    liquid, drained
2 cups miniature marshmallows
3 large bananas, sliced
1/2 cup finely shredded cheddar
    cheese

COOKED SALAD DRESSING

1/2 cup sugar
1 cup reserved pineapple juice
1 egg, beaten

2 Tbsp. cornstarch
1 cup whipped topping
1 Tbsp. butter or margarine

In a mixing bowl, combine 1 cup water and lemon gelatin. Add 1 cup ice cubes, stirring until melted. Add pineapple. Pour into a 13" x 9" x 2" baking pan. Refrigerate until set. Repeat with orange gelatin, remaining water, and ice. Stir in marshmallows. Pour over lemon layer. Refrigerate until set.

TO MAKE DRESSING: Combine pineapple juice, sugar, egg, cornstarch, and butter in saucepan. Cook over med. heat until thick. Cover and refrigerate overnight.

On the following day, arrange bananas over gelatin. Combine dressing with topping. Spread over bananas. Sprinkle with cheese. Yield: 12–15 servings.

MANDARIN ORANGE SALAD   ··· Mrs. Mary Esta Yoder

1 - 6 oz. box orange jello
2 cups boiling water
1 - 3 oz. can frozen orange juice
    concentrate (undiluted)
1 1/2 cups 7-Up
2 - 11 oz. cans mandarin oranges, drained

1 cup pineapple juice
1/2 cup white sugar
1 egg, beaten
3 Tbsp. flour
8 oz. Cool Whip

Dissolve jello in boiling water. Add 7-Up and orange juice. When starting to jell, add 1 can oranges. Pour into ring mold. Refrigerate. Mix together sugar and flour; add pineapple juice and beaten egg. Heat till thickened. Cool, then add Cool Whip and 1 can drained mandarin oranges. To serve, unmold jello and place pineapple sauce in center of ring. Drained crushed pineapple may also be added to the pineapple sauce if you prefer.

APRICOT GELATIN SALAD ··· *Mrs. Ralph (Sarah) Schlabach*

1 pkg. orange or apricot gelatin
2 cups boiling water
1 can crushed pineapple
1 - 8 oz. pkg. cream cheese, softened

1 - 15 oz. can apricots, drained and chopped
1/2 cup chopped walnuts
8 oz. whipped topping

Dissolve gelatin in bowl. Drain pineapple, reserving juice. Add pineapple and apricots to gelatin; set aside in bowl. Beat cream cheese and pineapple juice until smooth. Stir in gelatin mixture. Chill till partly set. Fold in whipped topping. Pour into dish; sprinkle with chopped nuts.

CIRCUS PEANUT JELLO   ··· *Mrs. Wayne (Emma) Yoder*

2 sm. boxes orange jello
25 circus marshmallow peanuts

3 cups boiling water

Mix together until peanuts are dissolved. Chill until it starts to thicken, then add 1 can crushed pineapple and 1 bowl of Cool Whip. Stir and pour into mold or bowl.

FIVE CUP SALAD   ··· *Leona Sue Miller*

1 cup crushed pineapples (partially drained)
1 cup mandarin oranges (drained)

1 cup coconut
1 cup small marshmallows
1 cup sour cream

Mix all together and leave set for several hours or overnight.

WALDORF SALAD   ··· *Mrs. Lloyd (Bena) Miller*

2 cups chunk pineapple, drained
1/2 cup chopped celery
2 cups seeded grapes

6 diced apples
nuts may be added if desired

DRESSING

1 cup pineapple juice
2/3 cup sugar
1 Tbsp. cornstarch

1/2 tsp. salt
1 egg

Bring 1 cup pineapple juice to a boil. Stir together the sugar, cornstarch, salt, and egg and blend. Stir in 3 or 4 Tbsp. hot pineapple juice. Add this mixture to the hot pineapple juice. Cook over low heat until thoroughly cooked, but do not overcook. Cool and add dressing to salad.

SOUR CREAM JELLO   ⋯ Mrs. Marion (Rachel) Mullet

16 oz. sour cream
5 different flavors jello, 3 oz. each (cherry, lemon, lime, orange, black cherry,
    or whatever kind desired)

Dissolve 1 - 3 oz. pkg. jello in 1 cup hot water. Divide jello in half; add 3 Tbsp. cold water to one half, and $1/3$ cup sour cream to other half. Pour jello into bowl (starting with the one to which the cold water has been added). Let each layer set before putting on another. Repeat for each box of jello. Very colorful to serve in a glass bowl (10 layers).

INDIANA SALAD   ⋯ Mrs. Marion (Rachel) Mullet

2 boxes (3 oz. each) lime jello
4 cups hot water
1 can crushed pineapple, drained
    (save juice – optional)
2 cups Rich's Topping, whipped
1 - 8 oz. pkg. cream cheese
$1^1/2$ cups pineapple juice
    (add water to make enough)
1 cup sugar
3 egg yolks
1 heaping Tbsp. flour
pinch of salt

Dissolve jello in hot water. When the jello has started to set, add pineapples. Pour into an oblong cake pan. Mix together cream cheese and topping till smooth. Put on top of jello when it is firm. Cook the last five ingredients until thick. Cool. Spread on top of second layer when it is firm. Refrigerate.

UNDER-THE-SEA SALAD   ⋯ Leona Sue Miller

3 - 16 oz. cans pear halves,
    drained (reserve $2^1/4$ cups juice)
3 - 3 oz. pkg. lime jello
3 cups boiling water
3 Tbsp. lemon juice
2 - 8 oz. and 1 - 3 oz. pkg. cream
    cheese

Drain pears, reserving $2^1/4$ cups syrup. Dice pears and set aside. Dissolve gelatin in boiling water; add reserved syrup and lemon juice. Pour $3^3/4$ cups into oblong Tupperware. Chill until set, but not firm, about 1 hour. Meanwhile, soften cheese until creamy. Very slowly blend in remaining gelatin, beating until smooth. Add pears and spoon into pan. Chill until firm, about 4 hours. Unmold. Yield: 18 servings.

Hint: This is a nice salad to put into a mold.

LAZY DAY SALAD
··· Mrs. Philip (Denise) Schlabach

30 oz. can mixed fruit, drained
2 cans mandarin oranges, drained
1 lg. can crushed pineapple with juice
1 box dry instant lemon pudding
1 box dry instant vanilla pudding
8 oz. whipped cream

Mix ingredients in order given. Fold in whipped cream last. Cover and chill for two hours. Good for 1 week.

COTTAGE CHEESE SALAD
··· Mrs. Freeman (Marie) Schlabach

$^1/_2$ cup milk
1 lb. marshmallows
8 oz. cream cheese
1 lb. cottage cheese
1 cup whipping cream
1 cup crushed pineapple

Melt marshmallows in milk. Beat in cream cheese and cottage cheese. Chill, then add whipped cream and pineapple. Add sugar if needed. Finish chilling.

PINEAPPLE COOL WHIP SALAD
··· Mrs. Mary Esta Yoder

In large bowl, mix:
1 cup white sugar
1 - 20 oz. can crushed pineapple

In saucepan:
6 Tbsp. cold water
2 Tbsp. Knox gelatin

Dissolve gelatin, then bring to a boil. Pour over sugar and pineapples and stir. Set in refrigerator to cool. When slightly set, add:

2 large carrots, shredded
1 cup chopped celery
1 cup cottage cheese
1 large container Cool Whip
$1^1/_2$ cups Hellmann's mayonnaise

Mix all together and let set.

CHEESE, BROCCOLI, AND CAULIFLOWER SALAD
··· Mrs. Mark (Ruth) Miller

$^1/_2$ head cauliflower
1 head broccoli
$^1/_2$ cup chopped onion
1 - 8 oz. pkg. cheddar cheese
1 lb. bacon
1 cup Miracle Whip
$^1/_2$ pkg. Hidden Valley Ranch dressing mix
$^1/_4$ cup sugar
1 Tbsp. vinegar

Thoroughly toss vegetables, cheese, and bacon. Combine Miracle Whip, dressing mix, sugar, and vinegar. Pour over salad. Mix lightly and chill.

BROCCOLI AND CAULIFLOWER SALAD

... Joyce (Schlabach) Albritton

1 head broccoli
1 head cauliflower
1 cup raisins

$^1/_2$ cup dry roasted, unsalted peanuts
1 small onion, diced

SAUCE

1 cup mayonnaise
1 Tbsp. vinegar

2 Tbsp. sugar

Chop broccoli and cauliflower into bite size pieces. Add raisins, peanuts, and onions. Add the sauce and mix well.

LETTUCE AND CAULIFLOWER SALAD

... Mrs. Andy (Elsie) Schlabach

Put in layers as follows:
1 head of lettuce, broken up fine
1 small head of cauliflower,
    chopped fine
1 sweet onion
1 lb. bacon, fried and crumbled

$1^3/_4$ cup salad dressing – spread
    over ingredients like icing on a cake
$^1/_4$ cup white sugar – sprinkle on top
    of salad dressing
$^1/_3$ cup grated cheese

Prepare in round Tupperware bowl and seal. Can be refrigerated overnight. Mix very thoroughly just before serving. A very delicious salad.

SUPER GARDEN SALAD

... Mrs. Mary Esta Yoder

$^1/_2$ head cabbage, shredded
1 head lettuce
carrots
shredded cheese
bacon, fried and crumbled

$2^1/_2$ cups salad dressing
$^1/_2$ tsp. mustard
$^1/_2$ cup white sugar
milk

Fix this salad in layers on a tray or loaf pan. Make several holes in the salad, then pour over all. Top with slices of tomatoes and sprouts if you wish.

TACO SALAD

... favorite of Stephen R. Schlabach, age 9

1 head lettuce
1 lb. hamburger, browned with
    onion
$^1/_2$ can kidney beans
4 chopped tomatoes
$^1/_2$ pkg. taco seasoning

6 oz. grated cheddar cheese
1 pkg. taco chips
1 cup Thousand Island dressing
$^1/_2$ cup Miracle Whip
$^1/_3$ cup sugar
$^1/_2$ pkg. taco seasoning

TACO SALAD
··· Mrs. Jr. (Ruth) Miller

1 head lettuce
1 lb. hamburger
1 onion, chopped
1 pkg. taco seasoning

8 oz. cheddar cheese
1 small can kidney beans
4 medium tomatoes
1 pkg. taco chips

DRESSING

8 oz. Thousand Island dressing
$1/3$ cup sugar

1 Tbsp. taco sauce
1 Tbsp. taco seasoning

Brown hamburger. Add taco seasoning, reserving 1 Tbsp. for dressing. Select large salad bowl, allowing enough room to toss salad at serving time. Layer salad in bowl, starting with lettuce and ending with cheese. Cover and refrigerate. Toss salad with dressing and taco chips.

PASTA SALAD
··· Mrs. Floyd (Marlene) Yoder

$1^1/2$ lb. spiral macaroni, cooked
8 oz. diced ham
$1/2$ cup chopped celery
2 medium tomatoes

1 small onion, minced
1 green pepper, chopped
1 cup ripe olives

Mix all these ingredients together and add the following dressing.

DRESSING

2 cups Miracle Whip
1 cup mayonnaise
$1/4$ cup Dijonnaise creamy blend
   mustard
$1/4$ cup salad oil

salt to taste
$1/2$ cup vinegar
$1^1/2$ cups white sugar
1 Tbsp. onion salt
$1/2$ Tbsp. celery seed

Mix well and pour over pasta and toss till it is mixed well.

PASTA SALAD
··· Mrs. Linda Mae Troyer

2 lb. rotini macaroni, cooked
1 green pepper
1 red pepper
1 cup celery

1 cup carrots
$1/4$ cup onion
$1/2$ cup chopped radishes
1 cup grated cheese

DRESSING

$1/2$ cup Sweet and Sour dressing
1 cup salad dressing
$1/2$ cup Creamy Italian dressing (Kraft)

$1/8$ to $1/4$ cup vinegar
$3/4$ cup white sugar

Cook macaroni according to directions on box. Drain and cool; add remaining ingredients. Mix dressing ingredients and combine with macaroni mixture until well covered. Chill 1 hour before serving.

BEAN SALAD
··· Mrs. Mary Esta Yoder

1 qt. green or yellow beans

1 qt. cooked carrots

1 can kidney beans, drained

1 onion, chopped

2 cups celery, diced

cauliflower (optional)

DRESSING

1 cup sugar

1 tsp. salt

$^1/_2$ tsp. pepper

1 tsp. celery seed

3 tsp. mustard

$^1/_3$ cup vinegar

1 cup vegetable oil

2 Tbsp. salad dressing

Mix dressing ingredients till sugar is dissolved. Pour over vegetables and marinate.

BEAN SALAD
··· Mrs. Freeman (Marie) Schlabach

1 pt. Great Northern beans

1 head lettuce, shredded

1 stalk celery, diced

a bit of onion, chopped

6 to 8 hard-boiled eggs

mayonnaise

sugar

vinegar

salt

Mix all together; add onions last. Make dressing with mayonnaise, sugar, salt, and vinegar. I never measure. Taste when mixed and add what it still needs. Toss with lettuce, beans, etc. Let sit a while. Very good!

DANDELION
··· Mrs. Mary Esta Yoder

IF YOU CAN'T BEAT 'EM, EAT 'EM!

Toss together:

4 cups dandelion greens, cut up

3 hard-boiled eggs, chopped

2 Tbsp. minced onion

Fry 3 slices bacon. Remove bacon slices and add 2 Tbsp. flour to drippings. Stir until browned. Blend in:

$^3/_4$ cup water

$^3/_4$ cup milk

2 Tbsp. vinegar

1 tsp. salt

Add crumbled bacon. Cook 3–5 minutes. Pour over greens; serve immediately.

DANDELION GRAVY   ⋯ *Mrs. Emanuel (Mary) Nisley*
THE KIND MOTHER USED TO MAKE

In a frying pan, heat butter or oil and add enough flour to make a smooth paste. Brown nicely. Add some cold water, stirring briskly until smooth. Add milk gradually and cook to thicken. Remove from heat and add salt to taste and some vinegar and honey. Pour over prepared chopped fresh young dandelion greens to suit your taste. Add a few hard-boiled eggs and onions. Also good for endive. Eat with potatoes cooked in their jackets.

BEST POTATO SALAD   ⋯ *Mrs. Freeman (Marie) Schlabach*

4 cups shredded, cooked potatoes
4 eggs, chopped
$1/4$ cup onion, minced
$3/4$ cup clelery, minced
$1 1/4$ tsp. salt

1 cup mayonnaise
1 Tbsp. mustard
$1/4$ cup sugar
$1 1/4$ Tbsp. vinegar

Mix dressing made of 5 last ingredients to potatoes, eggs, celery, and onion. Let sit several hours in refrigerator before serving to blend flavors.

POTATO SALAD   ⋯ *Mrs. Mary Esta Yoder*
                            ⋯ *Mrs. Paul (Wilma) Schlabach*

12 cups potatoes
12 eggs, hard-boiled

1 medium onion
2 cups celery

DRESSING

3 cups salad dressing
6 Tbsp. mustard
$1 1/2$ cups white sugar

$1/2$ cup milk
2 tsp. salt
$1/4$ cup vinegar

Boil potatoes in jackets. When cold, peel and put through Salad Master. Use potato masher to do eggs, down only once. Mix dressing and pour over all. Stir gently. Refrigerate till ready to serve. Will keep 3–5 days. Yield: 20 servings.

*Even a woodpecker has found the way to progress
is to "use your head."*

POTATO SALAD
··· *Mrs. Marvin (Martha) Mast*

4 lb. potatoes

1 1/2 cups macaroni, uncooked

1/2 cup onion

12 eggs, hard-boiled

2 cups celery, chopped

DRESSING
3 cups salad dressing

3 tsp. mustard

1 1/2 cups sugar

1/2 cup milk

1/8 cup vinegar

salt and Lawry's seasoned salt to taste

Cook and dice potatoes. Cook macaroni. Mix dressing. Mix all together. Makes 1 gallon.

COOKED POTATO SALAD DRESSING
··· *Mrs. Paul (Linda) Schlabach*

1/4 cup vinegar

1/4 cup water

1/4 cup sugar

1/4 tsp. salt

dash of pepper

1 tsp. prepared mustard

2 eggs, well beaten

1 cup salad dressing or mayonnaise

Combine all ingredients except eggs and salad dressing or mayonnaise, and cook. Bring to a boil. Reduce heat and gradually add 2 well beaten eggs. Cook, stirring constantly, till slightly thickened, about 5 minutes. Beat in salad dressing or mayonnaise. Cool and pour over potato salad.

VEGETABLE PIZZA
··· *Rosanna Nisley*

1/4 cup margarine

2 Tbsp. white sugar

1/4 cup boiling water

1 pkg. active dry yeast

1/4 cup very warm water

1 egg, beaten

1 1/2 cups all-purpose flour

1 tsp. salt

1 pkg. Hidden Valley Ranch dressing

1 pt. sour cream

vegetables: carrots, celery, green
peppers, broccoli, cauliflower,
shredded cheddar or Velveeta cheese

Combine the first 3 ingredients in a large bowl. Cool to lukewarm. Put yeast into warm water and let stand a few minutes, then stir until dissolved. Add yeast and egg to butter mixture; add flour and salt. Mix well and cool. Pour onto well greased sheet pan; press evenly. Fingers need to be greasy. Bake at 325° till done, golden brown. Cool. Add dressing to sour cream and spread on dough. Top with vegetables. You can use 2 pkg. cream cheese and 1 cup salad dressing instead of sour cream.

SIMPLE TACO SALAD
··· Mrs. Mary Esta Yoder

2 cups flour
2 tsp. sugar
$1/2$ tsp. salt
$2/3$ cup milk
4 tsp. baking powder
$1/2$ tsp. cream of tartar
$1/2$ cup shortening
$1^1/2$ lb. hamburger
1 pkg. taco seasoning

1 pt. pizza sauce
16 oz. sour cream
8 oz. cream cheese
lettuce
tomatoes
grated cheese
taco chips, crushed
hot sauce

Combine first 7 ingredients and spread in an 11" x 17" cookie sheet with sides. Bake at 350°. Mix sour cream and cream cheese and spread on cooled crust. Brown hamburger and season with taco seasoning and pizza sauce. When cooled, spread on top of sour cream layer. Top with shredded cheese. Serve with lettuce, tomatoes, taco chips, and hot sauce. Cut into squares before adding lettuce and tomatoes on top.

MOCK TUNA SALAD
··· Mrs. Owen (Elsie) Nisley

1 qt. shredded cabbage
1 cup ground sunflower seeds
$1/2$ cup peppers, chopped (optional)
1 cup celery, diced

$1/4$ tsp. celery seed (optional)
$1/4$ tsp. sweet basil
$1/2$ tsp. thyme

Mix all ingredients thoroughly and serve. It is delicious stuffed in peppers.

FRENCH DRESSING
··· Mrs. Linda Mae Troyer

2 cups sugar
2 cups vegetable oil
$1/2$ cup salad dressing

$1/2$ cup vinegar
$3/4$ cup catsup
$1/4$ tsp. Worcestershire sauce

Blend until mixed well.

CHEF ADLER DRESSING
··· Mrs. Linda Mae Troyer
··· Leona Sue Miller

3 cups salad dressing
$1/4$ cup mustard
$3/4$ cup oil
$1/2$ cup vinegar

$1^1/2$ cups sugar
1 tsp. onion salt
1 tsp. celery seed
$1/2$ tsp. salt

Mix together, adding oil last. Beat well. This dressing keeps well.

EAT'N HOUSE FRENCH DRESSING

··· Mrs. Lloyd (Bena) Miller ··· Mrs. Linda Mae Troyer

1 pt. salad dressing	$1/2$ tsp. pepper
1 cup sugar	$1/2$ tsp. Worcestershire sauce
$1/3$ cup vinegar	$1/2$ tsp. mustard
1 small onion, chopped	$1/3$ cup salad oil
$1/3$ cup catsup	$1/2$ tsp. paprika
$1/2$ tsp. salt	

Combine all ingredients and mix well. Add oil last. Makes 1 qt. A Miller family favorite.

BREAD CROUTONS   ··· Mrs. Mary Esta Yoder

Toast on cookie sheet about 20 minutes:

6 cups bread cubes

Sprinkle with:

$1/2$ tsp. poultry seasoning	$1/2$ tsp. seasoned salt
$1/2$ tsp. salt	$1/2$ tsp. chicken base

Pour $1/2$ cup melted butter over all and toss till well mixed. Continue to toast till a nice golden brown.

BROCCOLI SOUP   ··· Mrs. Mary Esta Yoder

10 oz. frozen or 1 bunch chopped broccoli	2 cups chicken broth or 2 cups water plus 1 Tbsp. chicken bouillon
6 Tbsp. butter	dash of black pepper
5 heaping Tbsp. flour	1 can cream of celery or
1 Tbsp. chopped onion	cream of chicken soup
2 cups milk	Velveeta cheese
$3/4$ tsp. salt	

Bring chicken broth or bouillon to a boil; add broccoli and simmer till soft. Sauté onions in butter. Add flour and stir to a paste. Slowly add milk and heat, stirring constantly. Add salt and pepper. Add broccoli mixture, soup, and a few slices of cheese. Heat till completely hot. Do not boil.

Our family prefers peas instead of broccoli in this soup. You can also add potatoes to peas...mash when soft, then omit the soup.

POTATO SOUP   ··· Mrs. Mary Kaufman

4 large potatoes, diced   1 can celery soup
1 small onion (optional)   butter
1 carrot   Velveeta cheese

Cook vegetables until tender. Partly mash them and add a chunk of butter, celery soup, and some Velveeta cheese. Then add milk as you like. I also like to add some diced ham after potatoes are mashed.

HEARTY HAM SOUP   ··· Mrs. Paul (Rebecca) Nisley

4 cups carrots   4 cups potatoes
3 cups onions   3 cups celery

Cover with water; add 2 Tbsp. chicken base. Cook until tender. Add 4 qt. milk and 6 cups ham. Thicken with clear jel. Add American or Velveeta cheese.

HEARTY HAMBURGER SOUP   ··· Mrs. Jr. (Ruth) Miller
··· Mrs. Alton (Nora) Nisley

2 Tbsp. butter   1 tsp. seasoned salt
1 cup carrots, cubed $1^1/_2$ tsp. salt
1 cup potatoes, cubed $^1/_2$ cup flour
1 lb. hamburger   4 cups milk
2 cups tomato juice

Fry hamburger with some onions. Add flour to hamburger. Cook carrots and potatoes. Melt butter in 6 qt. kettle. Add milk, tomato juice, and seasonings. Add hamburger, carrots, and potatoes. Heat thoroughly; do not boil.

Variation: Nora adds $^1/_2$ cup green pepper and 3 Tbsp. brown sugar.

CREAMY BARLEY SOUP   ··· Mrs. Owen (Elsie) Nisley

$^1/_3$ cup barley (dry grain) $^1/_2$ cup chopped carrots
5 cups water $^1/_2$ tsp. parsley flakes
1 cup chopped celery $^1/_2$ tsp. dried celery leaf flakes
1 cup chopped onion   salt to taste

Soak barley in water all day until about 3 hours before supper time. Add other ingredients and bring to a boil. Simmer for $2^1/_2$–3 hours.

NOTE: This tastes better the next day, for then it is marinated.

EXCELLENT CREAM SOUP ··· *Mrs. Philip (Denise) Schlabach*
1 stick oleo melted in a pan
$^1/_2$ cup flour

Make a paste with this as for white sauce. Add a 13 oz. can of chicken broth, or you can use your own broth. Chop in blender either about 10 oz. California Blend vegetables or 10 oz. thawed broccoli or 10 oz. thawed cauliflower. Cook gently 5 minutes. Take from heat and add 4 oz. Velveeta cheese cut in small chunks. Stir until melted. Put back on heat and add half and half. Salt and pepper to taste.

You can also use plain milk instead of half and half.

MIDWEST CHOWDER   ··· *Mrs. Robert (Audrey) Schlabach*
2 cups diced potatoes $^1/_4$ cup margarine
$^1/_2$ cup chopped carrots   2 cups milk
$^1/_2$ cup chopped celery $^1/_2$ to 1 lb. Velveeta cheese
$^1/_4$ cup chopped onions   2 cups cream style corn
$^1/_4$ cup flour

In 2 cups boiling salted water, simmer potatoes, carrots, celery, and onion for 10 minutes. Make cream sauce with flour, margarine, and milk. Stir in shredded Velveeta cheese. Add to vegetables. Add cream style corn. Heat thoroughly. Diced ham can be added if desired.

HAM CHOWDER   ··· *Mrs. Firman (Deborah) Miller*
$^1/_4$ cup butter   3 Tbsp. flour
$^1/_2$ cup minced onion $^1/_2$ tsp. black pepper
$^3/_4$ cup diced ham $4^1/_2$ cups milk
$1^1/_2$ cups diced raw potatoes $1^1/_2$ tsp. salt
$^1/_2$ cup finely chopped celery

Add onion, ham, and celery to melted butter. Sauté till vegetables are tender. Add potatoes and cook over low heat 10 minutes. Stir in flour, salt, and pepper (let brown a little bit). Add milk and cook over low heat 15 minutes.

Patience is a virtue that carries a lot of wait!

CLAM CHOWDER   ··· Mrs. Freeman (Marie) Schlabach

2 cups water   4 Tbsp. butter
2 cans clam chowder   1/2 lb. Velveeta cheese
2 cups diced potatoes   2 Tbsp. flour
2 cups diced celery   1 cup milk
1 onion, diced   dash of salt and pepper

Cook vegetables in water till tender. Add chowder and thickener made of flour and milk. When cooked, add cheese last.

Our family eats large quantities of this during the winter.

TACO SOUP   ··· Mrs. Reuben (Betty) Yoder

1 1/2 lb. hamburger, browned   1 qt. water
1 pkg. taco seasoning mix   1 qt. pizza sauce
1 small onion, chopped   1/2 cup white sugar
1 pt. corn   1 - 15 oz. can chili beans

Brown hamburger and onion. Add the remaining ingredients and simmer 15 minutes. Serve with shredded cheddar cheese, sour cream, and taco chips.

I like to can this soup for a quick meal. Double the recipe and cold pack for 2 1/2 hours.

TACO SOUP   ··· Mrs. Floyd (Marlene) Yoder

2 lb. hamburger   1 qt. corn
2 pkg. taco seasoning   corn chips, crushed
1 small onion, chopped   cheddar cheese, grated
2 qt. tomato juice   sour cream
3/4 cup sugar   lettuce
1 can pork and beans

Brown hamburger and onion. Add tomato juice, sugar, corn, beans, and taco seasoning. Bring to a boil, then simmer for 1 to 2 hours. Serve over crushed corn chips. Sprinkle cheese over top and add sour cream and lettuce.

CHILI SOUP
··· Mrs. Andy (Elsie) Schlabach

1 lb. lean ground beef
1/2 cup chopped onion
1/2 cup chopped celery
3 Tbsp. flour
1/4 cup brown sugar

1/4 cup catsup
4 cups tomato juice
2 tsp. chili powder
1 - 16 oz. can kidney beans
salt to taste

Brown ground beef, onions, and celery. Drain excess fat. Add flour and heat thoroughly, stirring constantly. Add all remaining ingredients and mix well. Cover and simmer 30 minutes. Makes 6 servings.

FREEMAN'S CHILI SOUP ··· Mrs. Freeman (Marie) Schlabach

1 1/2 lb. hamburger, browned
2 - 15 1/2 oz. cans kidney beans, mashed
2 - 6 oz. cans tomato paste
1 qt. whole tomatoes

2 cups water
2 pkts. mild McCormick chili seasoning
1/2 cup onions (scant)

Brown hamburger and add beans; cook a bit. Add remaining ingredients and simmer a while. I experimented for years till I came up with a chili that Freeman really liked! I like to make it in a large cast-iron pot and simmer it all afternoon. Serve with crusty toasted and buttered French bread.

VEGETABLE SOUP
··· Rhonda Rittenhouse

large can (32 oz.) V-8 juice
1 can mushroom soup
1 lb. hamburger
1 tsp. salt

1/4 tsp. pepper
1/2 tsp. garlic powder
1/2 tsp. onion powder
frozen mixed vegetables

Brown hamburger, drain, and add to mixture in crock pot. Let sit all day. Very easy. Very delicious.

Don't despise small things;
remember, a little lantern can do what a great sun
can never do ~ it can shine in the night.

Favorite Recipes

_____

_____

_____

_____

_____

_____

_____

_____

_____

_____

_____

_____

_____

_____

_____

_____

_____

_____

_____

_____

Meats &
Main Dishes

Christ is the Head of the Home;
The unseen Guest at every meal;
The silent Listener to every conversation.

I have only just a minute—
Only 60 seconds in it;
   Didn't choose it, can't refuse it,
   But it's up to me to use it.
I must suffer if I lose it,
Give account if I abuse it.
   I have only just a minute,
   But eternity is in it.

*A Christian
should be like a good watch:
open face, busy hands, pure gold, well regulated,
and full of good works.*

B - patient, B - prayerful, B - modest, B - mild,
   B - wise as Solomon, B - meek as a child.
B - studious, B - thoughtful, B - loving, B - kind,
   B - sure you always keep others in mind.

HOT BAR-B-QUE CHIP CHOP HAM SANDWICH

... *Mrs. Linda Mae Troyer*

1 lb. chipped ham
$^1/_2$ cup catsup
1 tsp. salt
1 tsp. celery salt

$^1/_3$ cup vinegar
1 tsp. lemon juice
$^1/_4$ cup brown sugar

Combine all ingredients except meat. Mix well and cook to dissolve sugar. Add meat and cook until hot. Sauce makes about 1$^1/_2$ cups.

BARBECUED BEEF SANDWICHES

... *Mrs. Linda Mae Troyer*

1 cup onions, chopped
    Brown onions in oil, then add:
1 cup water
1 cup catsup
1 tsp. garlic salt

$^1/_4$ cup vegetable oil

2 Tbsp. vinegar
2 Tbsp. Worcestershire sauce
1 beef bouillon cube

Heat to boiling, then simmer 30 minutes. Add beef stew meat.

SLOPPY JOE

... *Brenda Hochstetler*

2$^1/_2$ lb. hamburger
1 medium onion, chopped
2$^1/_2$ Tbsp. Worcestershire sauce
$^1/_3$ cup brown sugar

$^1/_2$ cup catsup
1 Tbsp. mustard
1 small can (10$^3/_4$ oz.) cream of
    mushroom soup

Fry hamburger with salt, pepper, and onions. Drain grease and add Worcestershire sauce, sugar, catsup, mustard, and mushroom soup. Heat and serve.

BEEF BURGERS

... *Mrs. Andy (Elsie) Schlabach*

2 lb. hamburger
1 small onion
1 can cream of mushroom or cream of chicken soup

$^1/_2$ lb. Velveeta cheese

Brown hamburger and onions; drain. Add soup and cheese. Heat until cheese is melted. Serve in buns. Yield: 12 to 14 sandwiches.

NOTE: Do not add any salt till cheese is all melted, as the cheese is salty.

SLOPPY JOES
··· *Mrs. Ammon (Esta) Brenneman*

2 lb. hamburger
2 eggs
$1/2$ cup milk
$1/2$ cup onion, chopped (optional)
$1/2$ cup cracker crumbs
1 cup or 1 can tomato soup
salt and pepper to taste

Mix and bake for 1 hour at 350°. Then rake up and stir to blend. Add half bottle (small size) catsup. Heat through.

NOTE: With 5 lb. meat, double the recipe. Can be made in a crock pot.

BARBECUED HAMBURGERS
··· *Mrs. Lloyd (Bena) Miller*

4 lb. ground beef
2 tsp. salt
dash of pepper

SAUCE
1 can tomato soup
$1/4$ cup chopped onions
1 Tbsp. brown sugar
1 Tbsp. vinegar
1 Tbsp. Worcestershire sauce

Mix beef, salt, and pepper. Make into patties and brown on both sides. Remove from frying pan and pour off grease. Bring the sauce to boiling and pour over burgers. Keep warm until ready to use. These are good to serve on buns.

BARBEQUED HAMBURGER
··· *Mrs. Mary Esta Yoder*

2 lb. hamburger
2 slightly beaten eggs
2 cups soft bread crumbs
2 tsp. salt
$1/4$ tsp. black pepper
$1/4$ cup milk
$1/4$ cup minced onion

Combine all ingredients and mix well. Shape into ten $1/2$-cup burgers. Broil over hot coals, brushing top with barbeque sauce.

GROUND CHICKEN PATTIES
··· *Mrs. Mary Esta Yoder*

5 lb. ground chicken
1 stack Ritz crackers
1 Tbsp. salt
1 tsp. Lawry's seasoning salt
1 tsp. black pepper

Soak crackers in a small amount of water. Add to rest of ingredients and mix well. Make into patties; roll in chicken breading and fry in butter.

"BIG MAC" SAUCE   ⋯ Mrs. Mary Esta Yoder

1¹/₂ cups Miracle Whip   ¹/₂ cup Heinz chili sauce
²/₃ cup Hellmann's mayonnaise   ¹/₃ cup sweet relish
2 tsp. seasoned salt
   Mix together and keep refrigerated. Makes 3 cups.

RANCHO BEANS   ⋯ Mrs. Emanuel (Mary) Nisley

1 can pork and beans   1 cup chopped onions
1 can Great Northern beans   1 cup ketchup
1 can kidney beans   ¹/₂ Tbsp. mustard
1¹/₂ lb. hamburger   ¹/₂ Tbsp. salt
   Bake at 350° for 1¹/₂ hours.

BOSTON BAKED BEANS   ⋯ Mrs. Paul (Linda) Schlabach

4 cups Michigan navy beans   ¹/₂ cup chopped onion
8 cups water   ¹/₂ lb. salt pork, cut into 1" cubes,
3 tsp. salt   or medium ham hock
   SAUCE
¹/₂ cup molasses   ¹/₂ cup catsup
¹/₄ cup (or more) brown sugar   2 cups reserved hot bean liquid
2 tsp. dry mustard
   Wash and pick over beans. Put beans in crock pot. Add water, salt, onion, and pork. Mix well so that pork is covered by beans.
   Cover and cook on low overnight, 10 to 12 hours, or until beans are tender. If you presoak beans, cooking time can be reduced.
   When beans are tender, drain bean liquid and reserve 2 cups of liquid. To beans, add molasses, brown sugar, dry mustard, and catsup; stir. Add bean liquid and stir.
   Simmer beans, covered, another 2 to 3 hours. Makes 3¹/₂ quarts.

The Lord is pleased with your little,
if it is the best you have.

BAKED CHICKEN WITH BARBEQUE SAUCE

··· Leona Sue Miller

³/₄ cup catsup
¹/₂ tsp. black pepper
¹/₂ tsp. red pepper
2 Tbsp. Worcestershire sauce
³/₄ cup water

1 tsp. paprika
2 Tbsp. vinegar
1 tsp. chili powder
1 Tbsp. salt

Lay chicken pieces in baking dish or cake pan and pour the barbeque sauce over the chicken. Baste several times. Bake at 350° for 1 hour or until done. Very good and simple to make.

BAKED CHICKEN BREASTS ··· *Mrs. Larry (Cindy) Schlabach*

6 boneless, skinless chicken breasts
1 to 2 Tbsp. butter
1 can cream of mushroom soup
¹/₂ cup cooking wine
¹/₄ cup shredded cheddar cheese

3 Tbsp. finely diced onion
2 Tbsp. Worcestershire sauce
¹/₃ cup water
pepper to taste

Sear chicken breasts in hot butter for several seconds on each side to seal in juices. Place chicken in bottom of covered casserole. Combine soup, wine, cheese, onion, Worcestershire sauce, water, and pepper together and pour over chicken. Cover dish and bake at 350° for 1 hour.

Sauce makes wonderful gravy.

OVEN BBQ CHICKEN   ··· *Mrs. Marvin (Martha) Mast*

8 to 10 chicken legs or mixture
¹/₃ cup sugar
4 Tbsp. flour
1 tsp. salt
¹/₂ tsp. chili powder

¹/₄ tsp. pepper
¹/₂ cup melted oleo (optional)
4 Tbsp. vinegar
4 Tbsp. catsup
6 Tbsp. hot water

Dip chicken in flour and fry till brown. Place pieces in pan. Mix sugar, flour, salt, chili powder, and pepper. Add oleo or frying drippings from chicken. Mix well: vinegar, catsup, and hot water. Add to other mixture. I also add some Bull's-Eye BBQ sauce to the mixture. Pour over chicken. Bake at 350° for 1¹/₂ hours.

CHICKEN BREAST RECIPE   ··· *Jonas and Katie Raber*
GRAVY

2 sticks butter
1 cup flour
2 qt. water

1 small can College Inn chicken broth
1 tsp. salt
$^1/_2$ tsp. Kitchen Bouquet

Have gravy on the thin side.

Cut chicken into small pieces and salt lightly. Roll in Runion mix and fry in butter. Fill roaster half full of chicken and pour some gravy over it, and again on top. Cover roaster and bake at 350° for 1$^1/_2$ hours. The gravy keeps chicken moist.

GRILLED CHICKEN BREAST   ··· *Mrs. Alton (Nora) Nisley*

chicken breasts, skinless and
    boneless

Wishbone Italian dressing

Take any amount of chicken breasts you want and soak them in Italian dressing for 2 to 3 days before ready to grill them. The longer they marinate, the more flavor they'll have. Pour dressing in the bottom of container, then a layer of breasts; repeat. Make sure breasts are covered well with dressing. Grill until done. Use your own judgment on grilling time. Enjoy!

CHICKEN BREASTS   ··· *Roy M. Schlabach*

6 boneless, skinless chicken breasts
1 pkg. Ritz crackers
1 tsp. seasoned salt

$^1/_2$ tsp. salt
$^1/_2$ tsp. pepper
2 to 3 eggs or $^1/_2$ cup milk

Mix crushed Ritz crackers, seasoned salt, salt, and pepper. Beat eggs or use milk to dip chicken in before frying in oleo, and dip into cracker mixture before frying. You may adjust amount of salt and seasoned salt if you'd like.

BARBEQUE CHICKEN   ··· *Mrs. Linda Mae Troyer*

4 Tbsp. ketchup
4 Tbsp. brown sugar
2 Tbsp. Worcestershire sauce
5 Tbsp. water

1 Tbsp. lemon juice
$^1/_2$ tsp. prepared mustard
$^1/_2$ tsp. chili powder
$^1/_2$ tsp. paprika

Heat and blend these ingredients. Soak chicken pieces in salt or Tender Quick overnight. Dip in sauce and place in roaster. Pour remainder of sauce on meat. Cover with foil. Bake in a 350° oven for 1$^1/_2$ hours or until done.

STUFFED CHICKEN BREASTS   *··· Rhonda Rittenhouse*

10 oz. cheddar or Swiss cheese,
   diced
2 eggs, lightly beaten
3 Tbsp. seasoned bread crumbs
3 Tbsp. chopped fresh parsley
2 Tbsp. olive or vegetable oil
2 cups spaghetti sauce
$^1/_8$ tsp. pepper
pinch of nutmeg
6 large chicken breasts, pounded thin
$^1/_4$ tsp. salt

In a medium bowl, thoroughly combine cheese, eggs, bread crumbs, parsley, salt, pepper, and nutmeg. Place $^1/_4$ cup cheese mixture in the center of each chicken breast. Roll and secure each breast with toothpicks. In a large skillet, thoroughly brown chicken on all sides in hot oil, starting with toothpick side down; drain fat. Pour spaghetti sauce over chicken; simmer, covered, 45 minutes or until chicken is done. Serve with baked potato and broccoli spears. Serves 6.

MOM'S HAWAIIAN CHICKEN

··· Mrs. Jason (Fern) Schlabach

12 to 15 skinned, boned chicken
   breasts
1 cup soy sauce
1 cup water
1 cup lemon juice
1 cup oil
garlic salt and pepper to taste

Mix sauce, water, lemon juice, oil, and seasonings together and marinate chicken breasts from 1 to 4 hours before grilling. Do not overcook.

TURKEY BREAST SUPREME *··· Mrs. Freeman (Naomi) Miller*

1 Tbsp. butter
$1^1/_2$ lb. turkey or chicken breast or
   tenderloins
$^1/_4$ cup chopped green onions
1 can cream of chicken soup
$^1/_2$ cup water
1 cup shredded Swiss cheese

Cut turkey breasts into $^1/_2$" strips. Brown in melted butter. Add onions and sauté 1 to 2 minutes. Stir in soup diluted with water. Cover and simmer 20 minutes or until turkey breasts are tender. Remove turkey to heated serving dish. Add cheese to gravy remaining in skillet. Add melted cheese and gravy to turkey and serve over rice or noodles.

CHICKEN TURNOVERS
··· *Leona Sue Miller*

DOUGH

2 cups flour

3 tsp. baking powder

$^1/_2$ tsp. salt

$^1/_4$ cup shortening

$^3/_4$ cup milk

Mix all ingredients together, then roll out.

FILLING

1 cup chicken, cooked, diced, and drained

1 cup cheese, grated

$^1/_4$ cup celery, chopped

1 Tbsp. chopped onion

salt and pepper to taste

mayonnaise

Mix the first 4 ingredients together. Add salt and pepper to taste and enough mayonnaise to moisten mixture. Put filling inside dough and press together, forming half-moon pies. Bake on greased pan at 400° for 15 minutes. Serve with chicken gravy.

CHICKEN CACCIATORE
··· *Mrs. Jarey (Ruth Davis) Schlabach*

3 whole chicken breasts and 3 chicken legs, or one whole chicken, cut up

$^1/_2$ cup chopped onion

$^1/_2$ cup chopped green pepper

$2^1/_2$ oz. sliced mushrooms

2 cloves garlic

1 or 2 bay leaves

$^1/_2$ tsp. dried rosemary

16 oz. stewed tomatoes

2 tsp. dried oregano

8 oz. tomato sauce

$1^1/_2$ cups mozzarella cheese

Sauté onion, mushrooms, and garlic till tender. Add green pepper, rosemary, oregano, bay leaves, stewed tomatoes, and tomato sauce. Cook until well mixed. Arrange chicken in baking dish. Pour sauce over chicken and bake at 350° for 1 hour and 5 minutes. Before done, top with mozzarella cheese. Serve with pasta (I use angel-hair). Enjoy!

In the morning when you find it difficult to get up, think of all the people who can't.

CHICKEN GRAVY
··· *Leona Sue Miller*

4 1/2 cups chicken broth
(may be part water)
1 1/2 Tbsp. chicken flavored
seasoning
1/8 tsp. garlic salt

5 Tbsp. clear jel
2 Tbsp. flour
1 egg yolk
1/2 cup milk

In a medium saucepan, combine broth, seasoning, and garlic salt. Bring to a boil; remove from heat. Mix clear jel and flour; add a little milk and stir. Add egg yolk and remaining milk. Gradually stir into hot broth. Return to low heat and continue stirring until thickened. Makes 5 cups.

BBQ MEATBALLS
··· *Mrs. Firman (Deborah) Miller*
··· *Melissa Mast* ··· *Mrs. Linda Mae Troyer*

3 lb. ground beef
1 can (12 oz.) evaporated milk
1 cup oatmeal
1 cup cracker crumbs
2 eggs

1/2 cup chopped onion
1/2 tsp. garlic powder
2 tsp. chili powder
2 tsp. salt
1/2 tsp. pepper

SAUCE

2 cups catsup
1 cup brown sugar
1 Tbsp. Worcestershire sauce

1/2 tsp. garlic powder
1/4 cup chopped onion

Combine all ingredients. Mixture will be soft. Shape into walnut size balls. Place meatballs in a single layer on waxed paper-lined cookie sheets and freeze until solid. Store frozen meatballs in freezer bags until ready to cook. To make sauce, combine all ingredients and stir until sugar is dissolved. Place frozen meatballs in a 9" x 13" x 2" baking pan and pour on the sauce. Bake, uncovered, at 350° for one hour or a little longer. Makes 80 meatballs.

PORCUPINE MEATBALLS
··· *Monica Mast*

1 lb. ground beef
1/2 cup bread or cracker crumbs
1/4 cup chopped onions
1 tsp. salt

1 tsp. paprika
1/2 cup uncooked rice
1 - 10 oz. can tomato soup
2 cups boiling water

Mix all but tomato soup and water and shape into balls. Place meatballs into pan with tomato soup and water. Cover and simmer about 45 minutes.

POOR MAN'S STEAK

··· *Mrs. Marvin (Martha) Mast*
··· *Mrs. Jr. (Ruth) Miller*

1 lb. hamburg	1 cup cracker crumbs
1 cup milk	1 small onion, chopped fine
$1/4$ tsp. pepper	some brown sugar
1 tsp. salt	

Mix well and shape into a narrow loaf. Let it set for at least 8 hours, or overnight. Slice in pieces and fry till brown. Put slices in roaster and cover with 1 can mushroom soup mixed with 1 can water. Bake 1 hour at 325°.

MOCK STEAK

··· *Ruth Ann Schlabach*

For each 1 pound hamburger, use:

1 cup white bread cubes (scant)	onion
1 cup milk (scant)	pepper
salt	

Mix:

1 can ($10^1/2$ oz.) cream of mushroom soup	1 can milk

Mix first 5 ingredients. Put in a pan, $1/2$" thick. Refrigerate overnight, 8 to 10 hours. Cut in squares; roll in flour and brown slowly in skillet. Put in roaster. Pour cream of mushroom soup mixture over meat; bake.

HAM LOAF

··· *Mrs. Lloyd (Bena) Miller*

5 lb. ham loaf (equal amount of ham, pork, and beef	$1^1/2$ cups milk
	1 cup graham cracker crumbs
3 eggs, beaten	1 cup soda cracker crumbs

Mix and put in pans. Cover with glaze.

GLAZE

$3/4$ cup brown sugar	$1/4$ cup water
$1/2$ Tbsp. mustard	$1/4$ cup vinegar

Bake for 1 hour at 350°. Baste a few times. Then put the following sauce on top and bake another hour or until done.

PINEAPPLE SAUCE

$1^1/2$ cups pineapple juice	$1/2$ cup brown sugar
2 Tbsp. clear jel	1 tsp. dry mustard
$1/3$ cup dark Karo	2 Tbsp. vinegar

Heat slowly until thickened. Spread on top of ham loaf.

PEPPER STEAK
··· Leona Sue Miller

1 lb. round steak
1 Tbsp. paprika
2 Tbsp. butter
2 cloves garlic
1 1/2 cups beef broth
1 cup onions, sliced

2 green peppers, cut in strips
2 Tbsp. cornstarch
1/4 cup water
1/4 cup soy sauce
1/4 cup tomato sauce

Cut steak into 1/4" wide strips. Sprinkle with paprika and let stand. Brown meat and add garlic and beef broth; simmer 1 hour. Stir in onions and peppers. Blend cornstarch, water, soy sauce, and tomato sauce. Stir into meat mixture and cook until clear and thickened, 2 minutes. Serve over rice.

MOCK HAM LOAF
··· Mrs. Wayne (Emma) Yoder

1 lb. hamburger
1/2 lb. hot dogs, ground
1 cup cracker crumbs

1 egg, beaten
1 tsp. salt
1/4 tsp. pepper

GLAZE

3/4 cup brown sugar
1/2 cup water

1/2 tsp. dry mustard
1 Tbsp. vinegar

Mix all together and add half of the glaze with the meat and put in loaf pan. Pour remaining glaze over top of meat. Bake at 350° for 1 hour.

SAUSAGE LOAF
··· Mrs. Ammon (Esta) Brenneman

2 lb. sausage
2 lb. hamburger

2 eggs
1 can cream of mushroom soup

Mix all together. Press into 9" x 13" loaf pan. Bake at 375° for 1 hour and 15 minutes.

RIB BARBECUE
··· Mrs. Linda Mae Troyer

2 - 14 oz. bottles catsup
6 Tbsp. brown sugar
1 small onion

1 tsp. celery salt
1 clove garlic
4 Tbsp. Worcestershire sauce

Bake Country Style ribs at 400° for 1 hour. Drain off fat. Simmer sauce 15 minutes. Pour sauce over ribs, cover, and bake 3 more hours at 375°. Turn ribs over the last hour of baking. Delicious!

COUNTRY PORK RIBS   ⋯ *Leona Sue Miller*

Cook pork ribs until almost tender. Drain and trim off extra fat. Put in large casserole.

SAUCE

1 cup catsup

4 Tbsp. vinegar

2 Tbsp. brown sugar

3 Tbsp. Worcestershire sauce

$^1/_2$ cup water

2 Tbsp. prepared mustard

1 tsp. dried onion

(may use chopped onion)

Mix together. Heat and pour over Country Pork Ribs. Bake 1 hour, covered. Delicious!

OVEN BAKED PORK CHOPS

⋯ *Mrs. Robert (Audrey) Schlabach*

1 cup sliced onions

1 cup catsup

1 cup water

1 Tbsp. Worcestershire sauce

$^1/_2$ cup brown sugar

1 tsp. dry mustard

$^1/_2$ cup vinegar

Put meat in 9" x 13" pan or roaster. Pour sauce over meat. Bake covered at 350° for 2 hours. Baste with sauce 3 or more times. Remove cover and bake 15 minutes longer.

SMOKED TURKEY   ⋯ *Mrs. Mary Esta Yoder*

1 cup Morton's Tender Quick

12 cups water

1 tsp. liquid smoke

6 to 7 lb. turkey

No salt needed. Adjust recipe so it covers the bird. Refrigerate for 3 to 4 days. Drain. Bake until done.

BARBEQUED STEAK   ⋯ *Jonas and Katie Raber*

1 cup soy sauce

1 tsp. ginger

1 tsp. dry mustard

1 tsp. Accent

3 to 6 whole cloves

3 cloves of garlic

(scant $^1/_2$ tsp. if using powder)

$^1/_2$ cup salad oil

Mix and pour over steak. Soak overnight or at least a few hours.

OHIO STYLE CORN DOGS   ··· Mrs. Linda Mae Troyer

$^1/_2$ cup yellow cornmeal

1 cup flour

1 Tbsp. baking powder

1 tsp. salt

1 Tbsp. sugar

1 cup evaporated milk

1 egg, beaten

$^1/_4$ tsp. paprika

$^1/_2$ tsp. dry mustard

dash of pepper

10 to 16 hot dogs

wooden skewers

vegetable oil for deep-frying

In a bowl, mix first 10 ingredients. Pour mixture into tall glass. Skewer hot dogs with wooden skewers; dip in mixture. Deep-fry at 375° until golden brown (about 2 minutes). Drain on paper towel.

BARBECUE SAUCE   ··· Mrs. Firman (Deborah) Miller

1 onion, chopped

2 Tbsp. oil

2 Tbsp. vinegar

2 Tbsp. brown sugar

$^1/_2$ cup water

$^1/_2$ cup diced celery

$^1/_4$ cup lemon juice

1 cup catsup

3 Tbsp. Worcestershire sauce

$^1/_2$ tsp. mustard

pinch of salt

cayenne

Yields approximately 2 cups.

BARBECUE SAUCE   ··· Mrs. Wayne (Emma) Yoder

2 pt. vinegar

1 cup butter

8 Tbsp. salt

2 tsp. pepper

$^1/_2$ tsp. garlic salt

4 Tbsp. Worcestershire sauce

Put all ingredients in 1 qt. kettle and bring to a boil. Dip chicken into sauce while grilling. This is enough for 3 chickens.

SHAKE AND BAKE CHICKEN

··· Mrs. Paul (Linda) Schlabach

$^1/_2$ cup flour

3 tsp. salt

2 tsp. paprika

$1^1/_4$ tsp. dry mustard

$^3/_4$ tsp. black pepper

1 stick oleo or butter

Mix dry ingredients in small bowl; set aside. Melt butter in saucepan. Roll chicken in butter, then in dry mixture. Put aluminum foil on cookie sheet. Place single layer of meat in pan, then bake at 350° for $1^1/_2$ hours.

REFRIGERATOR MASHED POTATOES

··· Mrs. Andy (Elsie) Schlabach

9 large potatoes (5 lb.)
2 - 3 oz. pkg. cream cheese
1 cup dairy sour cream
2 tsp. onion salt
1 tsp. salt
2 Tbsp. butter or oleo

Cook peeled potatoes in boiling water until tender. Drain; mash until smooth (no lumps). Add remaining ingredients and beat until light and fluffy. Cool. Cover and place in refrigerator. To use, place in greased casserole. Dot with butter and bake in 300° to 350° oven until heated through, about 30 minutes. This is great for Sunday dinner.

CHEESY SCALLOPED POTATOES

··· Mrs. Robert (Audrey) Schlabach

10 medium potatoes
$3/4$ cup sour cream
1 can cream of potato soup
1 cup grated Velveeta cheese
$1/2$ cup chopped onion
$1/4$ cup butter
salt and pepper to taste

Cube and cook the potatoes. Mix sour cream, cream of potato soup, cheese, onion, butter, salt, and pepper. Add to the drained potatoes. Bake 1 hour at 350°.

POTLUCK POTATOES   ··· Owen Schlabach, Jr.

··· Mervin and Rhoda Hilty ··· Mrs. James (Ruth) Schlabach

2 lb. cooked, shredded potatoes
$1/2$ cup butter
1 can cream of mushroom,
   cream of celery, or
   cream of chicken soup
1 tsp. onion salt
1 tsp. Lawry's seasoning salt
$1/4$ tsp. pepper
1 pt. sour cream
2 cups Velveeta cheese
2 cups crushed corn flakes or
   Club crackers
$1/2$ cup melted butter

Mix all except corn flakes or Club crackers and butter and put into a greased 5 qt. casserole dish. Bake at 350° for 45 minutes or until heated. Stir while baking. When almost done, spread corn flakes and butter mixture over top.

GOLDEN PARMESAN POTATOES

··· Mrs. Robert (Audrey) Schlabach

6 large potatoes
$^1/_4$ cup flour
$^1/_4$ cup Parmesan cheese

garlic salt
$^1/_2$ stick butter

Peel potatoes and cut into quarters. Put dry ingredients in a paper bag. Melt butter in a 9" x 13" pan. Take wet potatoes a few at a time and shake them in the bag. Then arrange the potatoes in the pan. Bake 35 minutes at 375°; turn the potatoes over and bake another 35 minutes.

CHICKEN NOODLE DRESSING CASSEROLE

··· Mrs. Lloyd (Bena) Miller

dressing
deboned chicken, cut up
noodles, cooked

cream of chicken soup
chicken gravy
Velveeta cheese

First layer: Make dressing your way and fry a little, then put in roaster or casserole.

Second layer: Chicken, cut up.

Third layer: Noodles cooked in water with chicken base added. Drain and add 1 can cream of chicken soup.

Fourth layer: Chicken gravy.

Fifth layer: Velveeta cheese slices.

Bake 1 hour or till heated through.

CHICKEN YUM YUM
DRESSING

··· Mrs. James (Ruth) Schlabach

1 loaf bread
$^1/_2$ stick butter
1 qt. chicken in broth
1 cup carrots
1 cup potatoes

6 eggs
1 qt. milk
$^1/_2$ tsp. salt
1 tsp. Lawry's seasoning salt
1 Tbsp. chicken base

Fry in skillet with lots of butter till about $^3/_4$ done. Cook fine noodles in 1 box Mrs. Grass noodle soup mix till half done. Put dressing in bottom, and noodles on top of dressing. Put cooked, diced chicken on top of noodles. Take chicken broth and make gravy and put on top of diced chicken. This fills small roaster or casserole dish. Bake at 350° for 30 to 40 minutes. You can fix the day before and refrigerate.

GERMAN PIZZA

··· Mrs. Mark (Ruth) Miller
··· Mrs. Firman (Deborah) Miller

1 lb. hamburger
1/2 medium onion
1/2 green pepper
3 eggs, beaten

1/2 cup milk
2 cups shredded cheese
2 Tbsp. butter
6 medium potatoes, shredded

In a 12" skillet over medium heat, brown hamburger with onion, green pepper, 1/2 tsp. salt, and 1/2 tsp. pepper. Remove meat mixture from skillet and drain fat. Reduce heat to low. Melt butter; spread on potatoes and sprinkle with salt. Top with beef mixture. Combine eggs and milk; pour over all. Cook on low. Keep covered until potatoes are tender, about 30 minutes. Do not stir. Top with cheese; cover and heat until melted. Cut into wedges or squares to serve.

GERMAN PIZZA

··· Mrs. Emanuel (Mary) Nisley

2 cups or more sliced or shredded raw potatoes
bologna
8 eggs or less

cheese slices
1 Tbsp. butter
salt and pepper

Melt butter in saucepan and add potatoes and salt and pepper to taste. Cover and simmer till done. Put potatoes on partly baked crust. Slice bologna on top of potatoes. Beat eggs and pour over top of bologna, then cheese. Bake until done.

PIZZA DOUGH

1/2 cup milk, scalded
1/4 cup shortening
1 Tbsp. sugar
1 1/2 tsp. salt

1 pkt. (scant 1 Tbsp.) yeast dissolved in 1/2 cup lukewarm water
3 cups flour

Beat together milk, shortening, sugar, and salt. Add to yeast and flour. Let rise about 10 minutes before placing into pizza pan.

NOTE: Any meat may be used in this quick and easy dish.

A smile is the prettiest thing you'll ever wear.

CHICKEN RICE CASSEROLE ··· Mrs. Reuben (Betty) Yoder

1 cup seasoned yellow rice   2¹/₂ cups chicken broth
   Cook rice in broth for 20 minutes. Add:
1 can mushroom soup   2 cups cut-up chicken
2 Tbsp. onion (optional)   2 cups diced celery or celery soup
   Top with Velveeta cheese and bake for 30 minutes at 350°. Add crushed corn flakes or cracker crumbs mixed with butter. Bake uncovered for 15 minutes at 350°.

FRENCH CHICKEN AND BROCCOLI CASSEROLE

··· Mrs. Jason (Fern) Schlabach

1 lb. fresh broccoli (or 3 - 10 oz.   3 to 4 cups cooked chicken
   pkgs. frozen)
   SAUCE
¹/₃ cup margarine, melted   ¹/₄ tsp. each salt and pepper
¹/₄ cup cornstarch   2 cups milk
¹/₂ cup water   8 oz. grated cheddar cheese
¹/₃ cup chicken broth
   Slice broccoli into spears and steam 2 minutes. If using frozen broccoli, thaw completely. In greased 13" x 9" deep baking dish, layer broccoli and chicken pieces, skinned, deboned, and torn into large pieces, alternately. Set aside. In saucepan over medium heat, combine margarine, cornstarch (in water), broth, seasonings, and milk. Cook until thickened. Add cheese; stir until melted. Pour warm sauce over top of chicken and broccoli. Bake at 350° for 35 minutes or until bubbly. Makes 6 servings.

CHICKEN SOUFFLÉ ··· Mrs. Freeman (Marie) Schlabach

3 cups cooked chicken, diced   4 eggs, beaten
3 cups grated cheddar or   1 can cream of chicken soup
   American cheese   1 can cream of mushroom soup
2 cups bread crumbs   1 cup milk
   Mix all ingredients well and put in greased 8" x 12" or 9" x 13" pan. Save 1 cup cheese to put on top. Bake 1 hour at 350°. I like to have this in the oven when we come back from Sunday School. Two hours at 325° is just right.

POTATO AND CHICKEN CASSEROLE

... *Mrs. Reuben (Betty) Yoder*

4 cups sliced potatoes, slightly cooked
1 1/2 cups cooked chicken, diced
2/3 cup milk
1 can cream of chicken soup
1/2 tsp. black pepper
1 tsp. salt
2 Tbsp. butter
toasted buttered bread crumbs

Arrange potatoes and chicken in layers. Melt butter; add milk, soup, salt, and pepper. Pour over potatoes and chicken. Bake at 350° for 30 minutes, covered. Put bread crumbs on top and bake another 10 minutes, uncovered.

SHEPHERD'S PIE

... *Mrs. Ralph (Sarah) Schlabach*

Line a greased casserole with mashed potatoes. Fill with fried ground beef, then top with your favorite vegetable. Add bread crumbs, gravy, and seasonings. Bake at 350° till done, about 40 minutes.

MASHED POTATO CASSEROLE

... *Mrs. Alton (Nora) Nisley*

3 lb. potatoes, peeled, cooked, mashed hot
1/4 cup butter
2 beaten eggs
1/2 cup milk
8 oz. cream cheese
1/2 cup sour cream
salt and pepper to taste
2 lb. hamburger
1/4 cup onion
1/2 cup flour
1 can cream of mushroom soup
1 pt. frozen peas

Mash potatoes. Cut cream cheese in small pieces and add to potatoes along with butter. Beat well until melted. Add sour cream. Mix eggs and milk, then add to potato mixture. Add salt to taste. Pour into greased casserole.

Brown hamburger and onion. Season with salt and pepper. Sprinkle with about 1/2 cup flour and brown. Add enough milk to make a creamed hamburger gravy. Stir in 1 can mushroom soup and 1 pt. frozen peas. Pour on top of potato mixture. Bake at 350° for 1 hour or until hot.

HASH BROWN CASSEROLE

··· Mrs. Atlee (Dorothy) Schlabach ··· Mrs. Ralph (Sarah) Schlabach

2 - 10³/₄ oz. cans cream of
  chicken or cream of potato
  soup, undiluted
1 cup sour cream
¹/₂ tsp. garlic salt
1 pkg. frozen hash brown
  potatoes or Tater Tots

2 cups shredded cheddar cheese
¹/₂ cup grated Parmesan cheese
¹/₂ soup can of milk
salt and pepper to taste
3 soda crackers, crumbled
1 Tbsp. butter

Mix thoroughly in large bowl: soup, sour cream, garlic salt, onion (if desired), and milk. Add potatoes and cheddar cheese; mix well. Pour in a greased 13" x 9" x 2" baking dish. Top with Parmesan cheese and mixture of cracker crumbs and butter. Bake at 350° 1¹/₂ hours. Remove lid for final 15 minutes so top will brown. Yield: 12–16 servings.

POTATO HAMBURG CASSEROLE

··· Mrs. Mark (Ruth) Miller

Mix together:

3 lb. potatoes, peeled, cooked,
  and mashed
¹/₄ cup butter
2 beaten eggs
¹/₂ cup milk

¹/₄ cup chopped onion
8 oz. cream cheese, soft (add first)
¹/₂ cup sour cream
salt to taste

Make gravy with:

2 lb. hamburger, browned
3 Tbsp. flour

2 cups milk
salt and pepper

Pour potato mixture into casserole dish and top with gravy. Bake at 350° till hot. I like to put Velveeta cheese slices on top. Can be made ahead.

OVEN MEAL

··· Michelle Schlabach

1 lb. hamburg, fried
1 onion
layer of carrots

layer of potatoes
1 can mushroom soup
1 can water

Top with Velveeta cheese. Bake in a casserole till carrots and potatoes are soft.

FIVE LAYER CASSEROLE *... Mrs. Philip (Denise) Schlabach*

First layer: $1^1/_2$ lb. ground beef, browned and drained

Second layer: slices of raw potatoes

Third layer: slices of raw carrots

Fourth layer: slices of raw onion

Fifth layer: slices of Velveeta cheese

Top with one can cream of mushroom soup (condensed). Cover and bake for 1 hour at 350°.

COMPANY STEW *... Mrs. Steve (Ruth) Schlabach*

1 lb. stewing meat

4 large potatoes, cut in chunks

4 medium carrots, cut in chunks

1 cup celery, cut in small pieces

1 small onion

Put meat (raw) in bottom of casserole and add raw potatoes, carrots, celery, and onion. Sprinkle on top:

1 tsp. salt

$^1/_8$ tsp. pepper

2 Tbsp. minute tapioca

Pour on top:

1 - 10 oz. can tomato soup or tomato juice (if using juice, add 1 tsp. sugar)

1 - 10 oz. can of water

Cover and bake 5 hours at 275° or 30 minutes at 375° and $2^1/_2$ hours at 300°. Vegetables, meat, and gravy should all be a rich brown when done. The trick is "do not peek" or lift that lid—unless you don't trust your oven. Very easy, fast, and tasty!

PORK CHOP-N-POTATO BAKE

... Mrs. Firman (Deborah) Miller

6 pork chops

$^1/_2$ tsp. salt

1 can cream of celery soup

$^1/_2$ cup milk

$^1/_2$ cup sour cream

$^1/_4$ tsp. pepper

1 - 24 oz. pkg. frozen hash brown potatoes, thawed

1 cup shredded cheddar cheese

1 - 2.8 oz. can French fried onions

Brown pork chops in lightly greased skillet. Sprinkle with salt and set aside. Combine soup, milk, sour cream, pepper, and salt. Stir in potatoes, $^1/_2$ cup cheese, and $^1/_2$ cup onions. Spoon mixture into a 9" x 13" baking dish. Arrange pork chops over top. Bake covered at 350° for 40 minutes. Top with remaining cheese and onions. Bake uncovered 5 minutes longer.

UNDERGROUND HAM CASSEROLE

··· Mrs. Reuben (Sara Etta) Schlabach

4 Tbsp. butter
1 tsp. Worcestershire sauce
2 cups Velveeta cheese
1 cup milk
$^1/_2$ cup onions

4 cups ham, chipped or diced
2 cans mushroom soup
4 qt. mashed potatoes
1 pt. sour cream
bacon

Sauté onions and ham in butter. Add Worcestershire sauce, cheese, mushroom soup, and milk till cheese melts. Stir till fairly smooth. Put ham mixture in bottom of roaster. Mash the potatoes till smooth and add sour cream. (I always add some milk to the potatoes.) Spread them over ham and cheese mixture. Sprinkle crumbled bacon over top. Bake in 250° oven. Do not boil.

SAUSAGE SAUERKRAUT CASSEROLE

··· Mrs. Firman (Deborah) Miller

1$^1/_2$ lb. raw sausage
1$^1/_2$ cup sauerkraut
6 medium potatoes

8 oz. sour cream
layer shredded mozzarella cheese

Put sausage in bottom of 3 qt. casserole; add sauerkraut. Bake at 350° for 1 hour, covered. Make mashed potatoes and cover sauerkraut. Top with sour cream. Bake 30 minutes longer. Add cheese 5 minutes before it's done.

CARROT CASSEROLE

··· Mrs. Floyd (Marlene) Yoder

8 cups sliced carrots
2 medium onions, sliced
5 Tbsp. butter
1 can cream of celery soup,
    undiluted

$^1/_2$ tsp. salt
$^1/_4$ tsp. pepper
1 cup shredded cheddar cheese
1 cup seasoned croutons

Place carrots in a saucepan and cover with water; bring to a boil. Cook until crisp–tender. Meanwhile, in a skillet, sauté onions in 3 Tbsp. butter until tender. Stir in the soup, salt, pepper, and cheese. Drain carrots; add to the onion mixture. Pour into a greased 13" x 9" baking dish. Sprinkle with croutons. Melt remaining butter; drizzle over croutons. Bake uncovered at 350° for 20–25 minutes. Yield: 10–12 servings.

SIMPLE ZUCCHINI CASSEROLE

··· *Mrs. Reuben (Betty) Yoder*

4 eggs, slightly beaten
$^1/_2$ cup vegetable oil
1 cup Bisquick
$^1/_2$ tsp. salt
$^1/_2$ tsp. seasoned salt

$^1/_2$ tsp. oregano
dash of pepper
$^1/_2$ cup grated Parmesan cheese
3 cups shredded zucchini
$^1/_2$ cup finely diced onion

Mix all ingredients; put in greased 9" x 13" pan. Bake at 350° for 40 minutes or until golden brown.

VEGETABLE MEDLEY

··· *Mrs. Jason (Fern) Schlabach*

3 - 16 oz. bags mixed vegetables
1 small jar Cheez Whiz
$^1/_3$ cup sour cream

1 can mushroom soup
$^1/_2$ can French fried onions

Cook vegetables a bit and put in pan. Mix cheese, sour cream, and soup. Spread over vegetables. Do not stir. Top with onion rings. Bake for $^1/_2$ hour at 350°.

RAILROAD PIE

··· *favorite of James Schlabach*

PART 1

1 lb. ground beef
1 large chopped onion
1 - 10$^3/_4$ oz. can tomato soup, undiluted
1$^1/_4$ cups water

1 - 12 oz. can whole kernel corn
$^1/_2$ cup chopped green pepper
1 Tbsp. chili powder
1 tsp. salt
dash of pepper

PART 2

$^3/_4$ cup cornmeal
1 Tbsp. flour
1 tsp. salt
$^1/_4$ tsp. soda

1 egg, beaten
$^1/_2$ cup buttermilk
1 Tbsp. melted bacon fat

Cook beef and onion till browned. Stir to crumble. Stir in next 7 ingredients. Simmer 15 minutes. Pour into 2$^1/_2$ qt. casserole. Combine cornmeal, flour, 1 tsp. salt, and soda; mix well. Add egg, buttermilk, and bacon drippings to cornmeal mixture; mix well. Spoon evenly over meat mixture. Bake at 350° for 30–40 minutes. Yield: 6 servings.

SWEET POTATO AND APPLE CASSEROLE

··· *Mrs. Emanuel (Mary) Nisley*

6 to 8 sweet potatoes, peeled
 and sliced
6 to 8 apples, peeled and sliced
$^1/_2$ cup honey or maple syrup

$^1/_2$ cup butter
$^3/_4$ tsp. salt
4 Tbsp. cornstarch

Mix 2 cups water with honey, salt, and cornstarch, and bring to a boil. Add butter and cook until mixture is thick. Grease casserole dish lightly with shortening and alternately layer with apples, potatoes, and sauce. Bake in 350° oven for 1 hour. Complements turkey and dressing.

HOT DOG PIE

··· *Mrs. Paul (Linda) Schlabach*

4 medium potatoes
3 carrots
3 small onions
6 wieners, cut up

3 cups water
$^2/_3$ cup catsup
2 tsp. salt

DOUGH

1 cup flour
1 tsp. baking powder
$^1/_2$ tsp. salt

$1^1/_2$ Tbsp. oleo or lard
$^1/_2$ cup milk

Place veggies, sliced thinly, in 3 qt. saucepan and add water, catsup, and salt. Cover and cook slowly for 25 minutes. Thicken with $^1/_2$ cup flour and water. Add wieners. Pour into well greased pan. Make dough and cover veggies with dough. Bake at 350° for 30 minutes. Serves 6.

CORN DOG CASSEROLE

··· *Mrs. Reuben (Betty) Yoder*

1 pkg. hot dogs, cooked and sliced
2 - 16 oz. cans pork and beans
1 cup pizza sauce
1 cup yellow cornmeal
1 cup flour
$^1/_4$ cup white sugar

$^1/_2$ tsp. salt
4 tsp. baking powder
1 egg
1 cup milk
$^1/_4$ cup margarine, melted
1 cup shredded cheddar cheese

Cook hot dogs. Drain and slice into the bottom of a 9" x 13" pan. Spread pork and beans on top of the hot dogs, then 1 cup pizza sauce. Mix all the remaining ingredients, except the cheese, and pour batter on top. Sprinkle cheese on top before baking. Bake at 400° for 35–40 minutes.

GERMAN POTATO SALAD (WARM)

... Naomi and Willard Schlabach; Zak and Jordan

$^1/_2$ lb. bacon, fried and diced
5 lb. potatoes, diced and
    steamed until tender

1 onion
6 eggs, hard-boiled
2 cups sauce (below)

SAUCE

$^1/_4$ cup flour
1$^1/_4$ cups sugar
1 to 2 tsp. salt (to taste)

1$^1/_4$ cups water
1$^1/_4$ cups vinegar

To make sauce: Stir flour until smooth and browned. Add sugar, salt, and water to flour and boil for 1 minute. Add vinegar. Can cook in a double boiler or skillet.

Mix potato salad with sauce just before serving.

POTATO AND EGG DISH

... Mrs. Mary Esta Yoder

Slice and cook:
3 medium potatoes   3 hard-boiled eggs

Make a white sauce. Sauté $^1/_2$ cup chopped onions in 4 Tbsp. oleo. Add 2 Tbsp. flour, $^1/_2$ tsp. salt, and $^1/_2$ tsp. pepper. Stir till light brown; add 3 cups milk and bring to a boil.

Layer potatoes and sliced eggs in casserole and pour sauce over all. Top with toasted bread cubes and heat till hot through.

Can easily be adapted to your size family.

FARMER TROYER'S SKILLET SUPPER

... Mrs. Linda Mae Troyer

1 lb. hamburger
1 medium onion
2 Tbsp. soy sauce
4 Tbsp. butter
1$^1/_2$ cups mixed vegetables

1 cup Uncle Ben's wild rice
    (with Original Recipe)
3 eggs, beaten
salt and pepper to taste

Brown hamburger and onion. Add butter and soy sauce. Mix in vegetables and cook until soft. Add cooked rice. Beat eggs and pour over mixture. Stir-fry until eggs are well done. Serves 4–6.

GROUND BEEF CASSEROLE   ··· Mrs. David (Susan) Nisley

1 can oven ready biscuits
1 1/2 lb. ground beef
1/2 cup onions, chopped
1 - 8 oz. pkg. Philadelphia
  cream cheese
1 can cream of mushroom or cream
  of chicken soup
1/4 cup milk
1 tsp. salt
1/4 cup catsup

Brown ground beef and onions; drain. Combine softened cream cheese, milk, and soup. Add salt, catsup, and ground beef. Pour into 2 qt. casserole. Bake at 375° for 10 minutes. Place biscuits on top and bake for 15–20 minutes longer or until brown.

GROUND BEEF CASSEROLE   ··· Marlene Schlabach

1 1/2 lb. ground beef
1/4 cup chopped onions
1 - 12 oz. can corn
1 can cream of cheddar cheese
  soup
1 cup sour cream
1/4 cup chopped pimento
1/2 tsp. salt
1/2 tsp. pepper
3 cups noodles, cooked
1 cup cracker crumbs
1/2 cup cheddar cheese
3 Tbsp. butter

Brown beef and onions. Add next six ingredients. Stir in noodles. Sprinkle with crackers and cheese; dot with butter.

QUICK BEEF BAKE   ··· Mrs. Reuben (Sara Etta) Schlabach

1 lb. ground beef
1/2 cup chopped onion
2 cans cream of mushroom soup
2 1/2 cups milk
1 tsp. garlic salt
2 cups frozen mixed vegetables
2 cups Bisquick

Heat oven to 450°. Cook ground beef and onion until browned; drain. Stir in soup, 1 cup milk, garlic salt, and vegetables. Spoon into ungreased 13" x 9" x 2" baking dish. Stir baking mix and remaining milk until blended. Pour over beef mixture. Bake 27–30 minutes. Quick and easy. Delicious with a salad.

Habits are cobwebs at first; cables at last.

STEAMED DUMPLINGS   *... Mrs. Paul (Rebecca) Nisley*

1 1/2 cups sifted flour   1/2 cup milk
3 tsp. baking powder   pinch of salt
1 egg

The secret of good, light dumplings is to go easy with milk. Add only enough to moisten the other ingredients. Drop by spoonfuls into chicken or beef broth. Cover pot lightly for 10 minutes.

CHICKEN AND DUMPLINGS

... Mrs. Freeman (Marie) Schlabach

1 qt. chicken and broth, cooked   1 cup self-rising flour
1 stick butter   1 can cream of mushroom soup

Bring chicken, broth, and butter to a simmer. Remove 1 cup of the broth from pan; mix it with 1 cup or more flour. Add cream of mushroom soup to pan. When it simmers again, turn heat to low and drop biscuits, made of the flour and broth, on top. Heat covered for 20 minutes on low heat. Test with fork. My boys love this!

CHICKEN AND BISCUITS   *... Iva D. Nisley*
DOUGH

2 cups flour   1 1/2 tsp. baking powder
1/2 cup milk   salt to taste
2 Tbsp. lard

Put 1 Tbsp. butter into baking dish. Melt and mix with 3 Tbsp. flour. Cook until creamy. Add 1 qt. chicken broth, then add 1 cup cooked chicken, 1 cup cooked potatoes, 1 cup cooked celery, and 1 1/2 cups cooked carrots. Cover top with dough. Bake in moderate oven.

SUMMER VEGETABLE STEW   *... Mrs. Owen (Elsie) Nisley*

4 cups carrots, sliced   8 cups zucchini, sliced
3 cups celery, chopped   parsley
3 cups onions, chopped   celery leaves
3 cups lima beans (fresh)   salt
3 cups okra (optional)

Put all vegetables (cut up), except zucchini and okra, into an 8 qt. kettle. Cook until half done. Add zucchini, okra, and seasonings and cook until done.

MIDGET POT ROAST

··· Mrs. Atlee (Dorothy) Schlabach

2 beef shanks (about 1 1/2 lb.)
3 Tbsp. all-purpose flour
1 1/2 cups cold water
1/2 cup beef broth
1 Tbsp. dry onion soup mix
1 garlic clove, minced
1 tsp. Worcestershire sauce
1/4 tsp. dried thyme
1 large potato, peeled and cut in eighths
2 carrots, cut in 2" lengths
6 boiling onions
salt and pepper to taste

Sprinkle meat with 1 Tbsp. flour and place in shallow 2 qt. baking dish. Add vegetables on top of meat. Mix 1 cup water, broth, soup mix, garlic, Worcestershire sauce, and thyme; pour over meat and vegetables. Cover and bake at 325° for 1 1/2 hours. Turn meat, potatoes, carrots, and onions. Cover and return to the oven for 30–45 minutes or until meat and vegetables are tender. Remove meat and vegetables and keep warm.

Prepare gravy. Skim fat from pan juices. Place juice in small saucepan. Combine remaining flour and cold water. Stir into juices; cook and stir until thickened and bubbly. Cook and stir 1 minute longer. Season with salt and pepper. Serve with meat and vegetables. Yield: 2 servings.

PERFECT BROWN RICE

··· Mrs. Owen (Elsie) Nisley

1 cup brown rice (long, medium, or short grain)
2 1/2 cups water
1 tsp. sea salt
1 Tbsp. unrefined safflower oil

Place all the ingredients in a saucepan with a tight-fitting lid in the order given. Bring to a boil and stir gently with fork. Cover and simmer over low heat for 10 minutes. Do not lift lid while rice is cooking. Remove from heat and allow to stand 10–20 minutes with lid on before serving. Serves 2 or more.

ZUCCHINI FRITTERS

··· Mrs. Wayne (Emma) Yoder

1/2 cup flour
1 egg
2 Tbsp. onion
1 shredded carrot
1 cup grated zucchini
1/8 tsp. Accent
1/4 tsp. seasoning salt
1/2 lb. meat – hamburger, bologna, or sausage
salt and pepper to taste

Fry in butter. Top with a slice of cheese.

POTATO PATCHES ··· *Mrs. Marion (Rachel) Mullet*

$^1/_4$ cup milk
2 eggs, beaten
1 onion, diced
1$^1/_2$ cups uncooked potatoes
$^1/_4$ cup flour
$^1/_4$ tsp. baking powder
parsley flakes

Peel potatoes and put through fine grater. Beat remaining ingredients together; add potatoes. Bake on greased hot griddle. Yield: 12 - 3" cakes.

CHILI POTATOES ··· *Mrs. Floyd (Marlene) Yoder*

6 medium potatoes, baked
1 lb. hamburger
1 small onion
2 - 11 oz. cans pork and beans
$^1/_3$ cup brown sugar
1$^1/_2$ Tbsp. chili powder
$^1/_2$ tsp. garlic powder
1 pt. tomato juice
sour cream
shredded cheddar cheese

Brown hamburger and onion. Add beans, chili powder, garlic powder, sugar, and tomato juice. Simmer 15 minutes. Serve over baked potato and top with sour cream and cheddar cheese.

HAMBURGER TOPPING FOR
BAKED POTATOES ··· *Mrs. Paul (Linda) Schlabach*

1 lb. hamburger, fried
   (optional: add onions while
   frying)
1 can tomato soup
1 can mushroom soup
1 lb. Velveeta cheese (or to taste)
1 tsp. chili powder
1 tsp. Worcestershire sauce
1 tsp. onion salt
1 tsp. garlic salt

MUSH TACO ··· *favorite of Regina Sue Schlabach ··· Ruth Raber*

mashed potatoes
browned hamburger (with salt,
   pepper, and taco seasoning)
lettuce, cut up
shredded cheddar cheese
cheese sauce
Dorito chips, crushed
taco sauce
onions and peppers if desired

Put on a stack as given. Very good!

FOIL DINNERS ··· *Mrs. Reuben (Betty) Yoder*

Mix hamburger and form into patties—enough for the amount of people you will have. Place each one in the middle of a square piece of foil. Top with the following:

sliced potatoes	onions, diced
peas	green peppers, diced
carrots	shredded cabbage

You may add or omit any vegetable. Season with salt if you wish. Close the foil by folding together at top and sides. Bake at 350° for 1 hour. When ready, put a slice of Velveeta cheese on top of your dinner. A simple but good dinner! Vegetables can be frozen when you put them on.

HAYSTACK ··· *Mrs. Linda Mae Troyer*

Town House crackers, crushed	tomatoes, diced
lettuce, shredded	cheese or nacho cheese soup
rice	sour cream
hamburger – brown and add taco seasoning mix	taco chips, crushed
peppers, diced	taco sauce
onions, diced	Tabasco sauce (optional)

Stack on plate and enjoy.

HAWAIIAN MEAL ··· *Leona Sue Miller*

shredded lettuce	chopped celery
chow mein noodles	chopped onions
chicken pieces, cut up	more gravy
cooked rice	crushed pineapples
chicken gravy	coconut (optional)
chopped tomatoes	slivered almonds (optional)
shredded cheese	

Stew chicken and cut in pieces. Place each ingredient in separate dish or on lazy Susan. Pass in this order: lettuce, noodles, chicken, rice, gravy, tomatoes, cheese, celery, onions, gravy, pineapples, coconut, almonds. Your company should stack it on their plates in this order. (It takes quite an amount of gravy.) Very easy meal.

STRAW HATS   ⋯ *Leona Sue Miller (from German Baptist friends)*

Brown together:

1 lb. hamburger onion

Add:

2 small cans pork and beans $^1/_3$ cup sugar

1 small can chili beans $^3/_4$ small bottle catsup

1 Tbsp. Worcestershire sauce add tomato juice for more liquid

Peel and slice cucumbers. Add:

1$^1/_4$ cup water $^3/_4$ cup vinegar

1 cup sugar

Let set overnight.

Stack on plate in this order:

1. corn chips, crushed
2. bean mixture
3. chopped lettuce
4. tomatoes, diced
5. cucumbers
6. cheddar cheese, grated
7. mustard
8. catsup
9. hot sauce

YUM-E-SETTI   ⋯ *Mrs. Linda Beachy*

1 lb. hamburger

1 pack noodles

1 can cream of tomato soup

1 can cream of chicken soup

1 cup celery, diced and cooked tender

1 lb. Velveeta cheese

salt to taste

Fry hamburger. Cook noodles until tender, not too soft. Mix tomato soup with hamburger and chicken soup with noodles. Add celery to noodles. Put in layers in casserole dish. Cover with Velveeta and bake in slow oven (250° to 300°) for 1 hour.

MACARONI AND CHEESE   ⋯ *Mrs. Freeman (Marie) Schlabach*

3 Tbsp. butter

2$^1/_2$ cups uncooked macaroni

1 tsp. salt

$^1/_4$ tsp. pepper

$^1/_2$ lb. Velveeta cheese, cut in pieces

1 qt. cold milk

Melt butter and stir in macaroni to coat. Add salt, pepper, cheese, and milk. Bake uncovered at 325° for 1$^1/_2$ hours. Don't stir while baking. Comes out golden brown and creamy.

SCALLOPED CHICKEN AND MACARONI

··· Mrs. Paul (Rebecca) Nisley

6 Tbsp. butter
6 Tbsp. flour
$^1/_4$ tsp. pepper
1 tsp. salt
3 cups chicken broth

3 cups cooked chicken, chopped
3 cups cooked macaroni
2 cups navy beans
$^1/_2$ cup buttered bread crumbs

Melt butter; blend in flour, salt, and pepper. Gradually add chicken broth and cook. Stir constantly till mixture thickens. Mix gravy with chicken, macaroni, and beans. Put in casserole. Sprinkle with bread crumbs and bake 30 minutes in oven at 375°.

SISTER SHARON'S MACARONI AND CHEESE

··· Mrs. Jarey (Ruth Davis) Schlabach

$^1/_4$ cup melted margarine or butter
$^1/_4$ cup flour
1 tsp. salt
$^1/_4$ tsp. pepper

2 cups sharp cheddar cheese
8 oz. cooked elbow macaroni
12 oz. evaporated milk
1 cup milk

In medium saucepan, melt butter; add flour, salt, and pepper and mix until smooth. Pour in evaporated milk and regular milk. Stir until slightly thickened. Add $^1/_2$ cup cheese and stir until cheese is melted. Add cooked macaroni; mix until macaroni is coated. Pour into a casserole dish. Sprinkle remaining cheese on top and put under the broiler until cheese is melted.

HUNTINGTON CHICKEN

··· Mrs. Henry (Emma) Troyer

2 lb. chicken
2 cups macaroni
2 cups chicken broth

$^1/_4$ cup flour
$^1/_4$ cup cheese
2 cups buttered bread crumbs

Stew chicken; remove from bones and cut in cubes. Cook macaroni in salt water and drain. Thicken broth with flour mixed with $^1/_2$ cup cold water.

Combine chicken, broth, macaroni, and cheese. Pour into buttered baking dish. Sprinkle with bread crumbs. Bake in 350° oven for 30 minutes.

Fat is the penalty for exceeding the feed limit.

PIZZA CUPS   ··· Julia Yoder

1 lb. sausage or ground beef   2 cans refrigerated biscuits
1 jar (14 oz.) pizza sauce   shredded mozzarella cheese
2 Tbsp. ketchup   grated Parmesan cheese
1/4 tsp. garlic powder (optional)

In a skillet, cook sausage over medium heat; drain. Stir in pizza sauce, ketchup, and garlic powder; set aside. Press biscuits into 20 well greased muffin cups. Spoon 1 or 2 Tbsp. of meat sauce into each biscuit; top with mozzarella cheese. Sprinkle with Parmesan cheese. Bake at 350° for 10–15 minutes or until golden brown.

MANDIE'S PIZZA   ··· Mrs. Freeman (Marie) Schlabach

1 Tbsp. dry yeast   2 1/2 cups flour
1 cup warm water   1 pt. pizza sauce
1 tsp. sugar   hamburger
1 tsp. salt   assorted toppings
2 Tbsp. vegetable oil

Dissolve yeast in water; add sugar, salt, oil, and flour. Mix well. Cover and let rise. Grease sheet cake pan and spread crust till it comes up to the edges of the pan. Pour on pizza sauce and mushrooms, pepperoni, onion, pepper, banana pepper rings, olives (sliced), and browned hamburger, in any order you wish. Let set 15–20 minutes. Bake at 425° for 15 minutes. Top with plenty of cheese.

BUBBLE-UP PIZZA   ··· Jonas and Katie Raber
                                      ··· Lori Ann Schlabach

1 lb. hamburger or sausage,   1/2 green pepper, diced
  browned   1 small can mushroom pieces
2 cans buttermilk biscuits, cut in   1 pkg. pepperoni
  fourths   ham or other pizza toppings as desired
20 oz. pizza sauce
1 pkg. (16 oz.) shredded mozzarella cheese

Reserve some cheese and pepperoni to put on top. Stir everything else together. Put in 13" x 9" pan and bake at 350° for 1 hour.

RHONDA'S BUBBLE-UP PIZZA ··· Rhonda Rittenhouse

3 cans (7.5 oz. each) buttermilk
biscuits
1 1/2 cups (14 oz.) spaghetti sauce

3 cups (12 oz.) shredded mozzarella
cheese
1 clove garlic

OPTIONAL TOPPINGS

onion
olives
mushrooms

bacon
ham
peppers

Preheat oven to 375°. In bowl, quarter biscuits and stir in 1 cup sauce and 2 cups cheese. Press garlic clove and add to biscuit mixture. If desired, add optional toppings and mix to combine. Spread mixture into 9" x 13" dish. Pour remaining sauce and cheese over top. Bake for 30 minutes or until sides are golden brown.

CHILI BEAN CASSEROLE ··· Mrs. Linda Mae Troyer

1 tube biscuits
1 1/2 lb. hamburger
1 can Manwich Sandwich,
Mexican style

1 can chili beans
Colby cheese
shredded lettuce

Bake biscuits at 400° for 8–10 minutes. Brown hamburger; add Manwich and beans. Simmer 20 minutes. Serve in layers: cut-up biscuits, hamburger mixture, cheese, and shredded lettuce.

SPAGHETTI PIZZA ··· Mrs. Mary Esta Yoder

1 lb. thin spaghetti
3 eggs
1 tsp. salt
1 cup milk

15 oz. spaghetti sauce
1 1/2 cups pepperoni slices
2 cups shredded mozzarella cheese

Cook spaghetti until tender; drain. Beat eggs, milk, and salt together; toss with spaghetti. Spread mixture in a greased jelly roll pan or 11" x 18" roasting pan. Pour spaghetti sauce on top. Arrange pepperoni in rows over sauce; sprinkle with cheese. Bake at 350° for 30 minutes. Let stand 5 minutes before cutting into squares.

NOTE: I add 1 lb. hamburger to spaghetti sauce.

SPAGHETTI PIE
··· *Mrs. Floyd (Marlene) Yoder*
··· *Mrs. Marion (Rachel) Mullet*

6 oz. spaghetti, cooked
2 Tbsp. butter, melted
$^1/_3$ cup Parmesan cheese

2 eggs, beaten
1 cup cottage cheese

SAUCE

1 lb. ground beef
$^1/_2$ cup chopped onion
1 cup tomatoes
6 oz. tomato paste

1 Tbsp. sugar
$^1/_2$ tsp. salt
1 tsp. oregano
$^1/_2$ tsp. garlic salt

(instead of tomatoes and tomato paste, I usually just use my own spaghetti sauce)

Cook spaghetti according to package directions; drain. (Yields about 3 cups spaghetti.) Mix together spaghetti, butter, Parmesan cheese, and eggs. Spread in a buttered 10" pie plate, arranging up sides to form a crust. Spread cottage cheese over bottom of spaghetti crust. Fry ground beef with onions. Drain; stir in remaining ingredients and heat thoroughly. Pour mixture into spaghetti crust. Bake uncovered 20 minutes at 350°. Sprinkle $^1/_2$ cup mozzarella cheese on top and bake 5 minutes longer.

LASAGNA (COOK ONCE, EAT TWICE)
··· *Mrs. Steve (Ruth) Schlabach*

2 lb. ground beef
3 - 15$^1/_2$ oz. jars Prego spaghetti
   sauce
2 lb. ricotta cheese
1$^1/_2$ lb. mozzarella cheese

1 egg, beaten
1 Tbsp. parsley flakes
1 lb. lasagna noodles, cooked
1 cup grated Parmesan cheese
salt and pepper to taste

Brown ground beef in large skillet; drain fat. Add spaghetti sauce; heat to boiling. Cut 12 thin slices mozzarella cheese for topping. Shred remainder and mix with ricotta, beaten egg, parsley, salt, and pepper. Ladle 1 cup meat sauce into bottom of each of 2 baking dishes (12" x 8"). Layer cooked noodles, then add about 1 cup cheese mixture, and 1 cup meat sauce in each pan. Repeat twice. Sprinkle $^1/_2$ cup Parmesan cheese onto each. Top with mozzarella cheese slices. Bake 1 pan at 350° for 30 minutes until bubbly. Wrap and freeze other pan.

To serve frozen lasagna, preheat oven to 400°. Heat frozen lasagna 1 hour and 15 minutes; uncover and bake 15 minutes more. Each pan serves 6–8 people.

MACARONI PIZZA
··· *Leona Sue Miller*

1 pkg. (7 oz.) elbow macaroni
2 eggs
1 1/4 cups milk
1/8 tsp. pepper
1 cup pizza sauce
1 1/2 cups shredded mozzarella
cheese

Cook macaroni in salted water according to package directions; drain. In large bowl, beat together eggs, milk, and pepper. Add macaroni. Pour into 9" square baking dish. Bake in preheated 400° oven 10 minutes or until set. Remove from oven. Spread pizza sauce over baked macaroni. Top with cheese and bake for 10 more minutes. Cut into serving portions. Yield: 6 servings.

LASAGNA
··· *Mrs. Linda Mae Troyer*

1 lb. ground beef
1/2 cup chopped onion
1 - 16 oz. can tomato sauce
1 - 6 oz. can tomato paste
1/3 cup water
1/2 tsp. garlic, minced
1 tsp. oregano
1/4 tsp. pepper
8 oz. lasagna noodles, cooked and
drained
2 - 6 oz. pkg. mozzarella cheese
1/2 lb. Colby cheese
1/2 lb. grated Parmesan cheese

Brown meat; drain. Add onions and cook until tender. Add tomato sauce, tomato paste, water, and seasonings. Cover and simmer 30 minutes. In baking dish, layer half of noodles, meat sauce, and cheeses; repeat layers. Bake at 350° for 30 minutes. Let stand 10 minutes before serving. Serves 6–8.

SOFT TACOS
··· *Mrs. Linda Beachy*

4 cups flour
1 1/2 tsp. salt
4 tsp. baking powder
1/2 cup shortening
2 cups water

Sift flour, salt, and baking powder together; add shortening. Add 1 3/4 cups water. Mix dough with hands until it holds together. Knead until dough is smooth and form it into 2" balls. Roll out each ball paper thin! Fry over medium heat, about 1 minute on each side. Works best on a non-stick skillet—you won't need any oil. Makes approximately 15–20, depending on size.

BEEF ENCHILADAS
··· *Julia Yoder*

2 lb. ground beef, fried
1 can cream of chicken soup
4 oz. green chilies (optional)
1 cup sour cream

2 to 3 cups mozzarella cheese
8 to 10 small flour tortillas
2 cups pizza sauce

Fry beef; add soup, sour cream, and green chilies. Spread 1 cup pizza sauce on bottom of cake pan. Spoon beef mixture down the center of each tortilla. Roll up and place in pan, seam down. Spread 1 cup pizza sauce over top of enchiladas and cover with cheese. Bake at 350° for 20 minutes. Serve with sour cream and lettuce.

EASY ENCHILADAS
··· *Mrs. Linda Mae Troyer*

$2^1/_2$ lb. ground beef
1 - 6 oz. can tomato paste
onion salt to taste

12 flour tortillas
2 batches enchilada sauce
2 lb. grated Colby cheese

ENCHILADA SAUCE

Combine all and simmer 20 minutes:

1 - 15 oz. can tomato sauce
$^1/_2$ cup water
$2^1/_2$ tsp. chili powder
1 tsp. salt

$^1/_2$ tsp. garlic powder
$^1/_4$ tsp. ground cumin
dash of Tabasco

Brown beef and drain; season to taste (small amount of salt and pepper). Add onion salt and tomato paste. Add enchilada sauce (if it gets too soupy, save and put on top). Fill tortillas with about $^1/_2$ cup meat mixture and some cheese. Roll and put in baking dish. Mix another batch of enchilada sauce for the top. Cover with remaining cheese. Bake at 350° for 15 minutes. Serve with sour cream, lettuce, and taco sauce.

TURKEY OR CHICKEN ENCHILADAS ··· *Mrs. Kris Miller*

3 cups turkey or chicken, chopped
$^1/_2$ cup salsa

$^1/_2$ cup sour cream
flour tortillas

TOPPING

1 can cream of chicken soup
$^1/_2$ can milk

cheese

Combine meat, salsa, and sour cream. Wrap in flour tortillas and put into baking pan, seam side down. Mix cream of chicken soup and milk; pour over tortillas. Top with shredded cheese. Bake at 350° for 20–30 minutes.

CHEESY ENCHILADAS
··· Mrs. Reuben (Betty) Yoder

CHEESE SAUCE

1 stick oleo	8 oz. Velveeta cheese
4 Tbsp. flour	8 oz. sour cream
3 cups milk	I like to add 1 can nacho cheese soup

MEAT MIXTURE

2 lb. hamburger, browned	1 cup pizza sauce
1 medium onion	$1/2$ tsp. oregano
2 Tbsp. flour	10 to 12 flour tortillas
1 tsp. salt	2 cups grated cheese

Mix together hamburger, onion, flour, salt, pizza sauce, and oregano. Place meat mixture and grated cheese in tortillas. Roll up and place in 9" x 13" greased pan and pour cheese sauce over tortillas. Bake at 350° for 20–30 minutes.

CHICKEN ENCHILADAS
··· Mrs. Linda Mae Troyer

2 Tbsp. butter	6 flour tortillas
1 - 3 oz. pkg. cream cheese, softened	1 can cream of chicken soup
	8 oz. sour cream
1 Tbsp. milk	1 cup milk
$1/2$ tsp. salt	$1/3$ cup jalapeño peppers (optional)
$1/4$ tsp. ground cumin	1 cup cheddar cheese
2 cups cubed cooked chicken	

Combine softened cream cheese, milk, salt, cumin, and chicken. Stir well. Spoon $1/3$ cup chicken mixture onto each tortilla; roll up. Place filled tortillas, seam side down, in a baking dish. In a bowl, combine cream of chicken soup, sour cream, milk, and peppers. Pour the soup mixture evenly over the tortillas. Cover; bake in a 350° oven for about 35 minutes or till heated through. Remove; sprinkle with cheese. Return to oven till cheese is melted.

CHICKEN TORTILLAS
··· Mrs. Steve (Ruth) Schlabach

Mix together:

1 pt. sour cream	1 onion, chopped fine
1 can cream of chicken soup	$2/3$ cup diced chicken
1 - 4 oz. can chopped green chilies	$1/2$ cup cheddar cheese

Cover bottom of 9" x 13" pan with some of the sour cream mixture. Take 9 flour tortillas and fill each with 1 Tbsp. of mixture. Roll up and put in pan; put remaining mixture on top of tortillas. Sprinkle with some more cheddar cheese. Bake at 325° for 1 hour.

EASY BURRITO CASSEROLE ··· Mrs. Wayne (Emma) Yoder
·· favorite of Rita Renae Schlabach, age 8

2 lb. hamburger, browned
1 can refried beans
Mix and set aside.

2 cans cream of chicken soup
2 cups sour cream

1 pkg. taco seasoning

1 pkg. soft tortillas (10 per pkg.)
1 large pkg. cheddar cheese

Mix together soup and sour cream. Put half of soup mixture in the bottom of a 9" x 13" baking dish. Layer half the tortillas on top of soup mixture. Use all of hamburger on top of tortillas. Put remaining tortillas on top. Spread the rest of the soup mixture over it. Bake 1 hour at 325°. Top with cheddar cheese; return to oven till melted. Serve with lettuce, tomatoes, sour cream, and salsa.

STIR-FRIED CHICKEN FAJITAS ··· Mrs. Linda Mae Troyer

4 boneless, skinless chicken breasts, cut in thin strips
soy sauce
1 small onion, sliced – separate rings
1 small pepper, sliced in strips

salt and pepper to taste
flour tortillas
taco sauce
sour cream
Colby cheese

Stir-fry chicken strips in soy sauce until done. Add onions and peppers; continue to stir-fry until crisp and tender. Season with salt and pepper and some garlic salt. Wrap in tortillas and top with cheese. Arrange in pan and bake in 325° oven until cheese is melted. You can put cheese inside your wrapped tortillas instead of on top. Serve with taco sauce and sour cream. I like to use green, red, and yellow peppers to make it colorful.

Some people who say "Our Father" on Sunday go around the rest of the week acting like orphans.

MEXI TACO PIE

··· Mrs. Daniel (Lisa) Schlabach

1 lb. ground beef
1 envelope (1 1/4 oz.) taco
   seasoning mix
1 jar (16 oz.) picante sauce
1 1/2 cups shredded mozzarella
   and cheddar cheese
1/3 cup chopped green pepper
1/3 cup broken tortilla chips
shredded lettuce
dairy sour cream
1 egg
1 deep-dish frozen pie crust

In skillet, brown ground beef; drain. Add taco seasoning mix and 1 cup picante. Simmer 5–8 minutes; remove from heat. Stir in egg.

Sprinkle frozen pie crust with 1/2 cup cheese; top with green peppers. Pour ground beef mixture over peppers. Top with remaining 1 cup cheese; sprinkle tortilla chips over top.

Bake in preheated 350° oven on preheated baking sheet 20–25 minutes. Garnish with shredded lettuce, sour cream, and remaining picante. Makes 6 servings.

When Noah sailed the waters blue,
He had his troubles, same as you~
For forty days he drove the ark
Before he found a place to park!

Life is like a sandwich~
The more you put in it, the better it is!

Cookies

Happiness adds and multiplies as we divide it with others.

Send Them to Bed with a Kiss

O, mothers, so weary, discouraged,
    Worn out with the cares of the day,
You often grow cross and impatient,
    Complain of the noise and the play;
For the day brings so many vexations,
    So many things going amiss;
But, mothers, whatever may vex you,
    Send the children to bed with a kiss.
For someday their noise will not vex you,
    The silence will hurt you far more.
You will long for their sweet, childish voices,
    For a sweet, childish face at the door.
And to press a child's face to your bosom,
    You'd give all the world just for this!
For the comfort 'twill bring you sorrow...
    Send the children to bed with a kiss.

CREAM CHEESE PASTRIES

··· *favorite of Justin Eric Miller, age 6*

$^1/_2$ lb. butter, softened
1 pkg. cream cheese, softened
2 cups flour
$^1/_2$ tsp. salt

approximately 1 qt. pie filling of your
    choice
glaze (powdered sugar and water)

Mix together butter, cream cheese, flour, and salt. Chill 1 hour. Roll out $^1/_4$" thick; cut into 4" squares (I use a freezer container). Spoon 1 tsp. filling in center; bring together 2 corners. Use toothpicks to keep corners together while baking. Bake at 375° for 30 minutes or until light brown. Spoon glaze on top. Keep in loosely covered container to keep from getting soggy.

BUTTER CREAM DROPS (COOKIES)

··· *favorite of Norman Nisley*

$2^1/_2$ cups brown sugar,
    firmly packed
$^1/_2$ cup butter
$^1/_2$ cup soft shortening (lard),
    not melted
4 eggs
$4^2/_3$ cups flour

2 tsp. soda
1 tsp. baking powder
1 tsp. salt
2 cups sour cream
2 tsp. vanilla
1 cup chocolate chips

Cream sugar, butter, and lard thoroughly. Add eggs; mix well. Spoon flour into dry cup; level off and pour flour on waxed paper. Add soda, baking powder, and salt to flour. Stir to blend. Add blended dry ingredients to creamed mixture alternately with sour cream. Stir in vanilla and chips. Drop by teaspoonfuls onto greased cookie sheet. Bake at 350° for 10–12 minutes. Frost while warm.

FROSTING

12 Tbsp. butter or oleo
3 cups powdered sugar

2 tsp. vanilla
8 Tbsp. hot water

Melt oleo in saucepan over medium heat. Brown lightly. Remove from heat and stir in sugar and vanilla. Add water. Beat with spoon until icing reaches spreading consistency.

STRAWBERRY CREAM COOKIES ··· *Mrs. Mary Esta Yoder*

1 cup butter, softened
1 cup white sugar
1 - 3 oz. pkg. cream cheese
1 egg
2¹/₂ cups flour

1 Tbsp. vanilla
¹/₄ tsp. salt
¹/₂ tsp. baking powder
strawberry jam, room temperature

Cream butter, sugar, and cream cheese. Add vanilla and egg. Mix well. Add dry ingredients. Chill dough. Shape into 1" balls and place on ungreased cookie sheet. Using a floured thimble, press a dent in center of each ball; fill with ¹/₂ tsp. jam. Bake at 350° for 10–12 minutes. Frost with white icing, leaving jam exposed.

SOFT SUGAR COOKIES ··· *Mrs. Freeman (Marie) Schlabach*

1 cup brown sugar
1 cup white sugar
1 cup oleo or butter
2 eggs, small
1¹/₂ cups buttermilk

2 Tbsp. baking powder
1 Tbsp. soda
1 tsp. vanilla
flour to make a soft dough

Cream sugar and butter; add remaining ingredients (flour last). Drop on greased cookie sheet and bake at 350° till golden brown.

This is an old recipe and perfect for dunking in milk or coffee.

DROP SUGAR COOKIES ··· *Mrs. Mike (Ruby) Sommers*

2 cups brown sugar
1 cup Crisco
3 beaten eggs
1 cup milk
2 tsp. vanilla

1 tsp. soda
3¹/₂ cups flour
3 tsp. baking powder
dash of salt

ICING

6 Tbsp. brown sugar
6 Tbsp. butter

6 Tbsp. milk
powdered sugar

Cookies: Beat together sugar and Crisco. Add beaten eggs; beat well. Add remaining ingredients. Ice immediately.

Icing: Mix sugar, butter, and milk in saucepan. Cook 4 minutes. Add powdered sugar till right consistency.

Delicious, soft cookies.

WORLD'S BEST SUGAR COOKIES
··· *Mrs. Ammon (Esta) Brenneman*

1 cup powdered sugar	2 tsp. vanilla
1 cup white sugar	1 tsp. salt
1 cup oleo or butter	1 tsp. soda
1 cup cooking oil	1 tsp. cream of tartar
2 eggs	5 cups flour

Cream sugars, oleo, and oil until light and fluffy. Add eggs and vanilla. Sift dry ingredients together. Add and mix well. Roll in balls, or drop from spoon. Flatten slightly with bottom of glass dipped in sugar. Bake at 350° for 15–20 minutes.

GRANDMA'S OLD-FASHIONED SUGAR COOKIES
··· *Edward Raber*

2 cups brown sugar	1 cup milk
1 cup lard or butter	2 tsp. soda
2 eggs	2 tsp. baking powder
2 tsp. vanilla	5 to 5 1/2 cups flour
1 tsp. salt	

Cream sugar and butter well; add eggs and milk. Dissolve soda in a little hot water, then add to first mixture. Sift flour, baking powder, and salt. Add to first mixture.

Roll out and sprinkle with sugar. Bake at 375° until nice and golden brown. Do not overbake.

AUNT ESTHER'S BESTEST COOKIES
··· *Ruth Ann Schlabach*

2/3 cup butter or lard	3 cups flour
1 1/2 cups brown sugar	1 tsp. soda
2 eggs	1/2 tsp. baking powder
1 Tbsp. vinegar	1/2 tsp. salt
1 tsp. vanilla	1 cup chopped nuts
1 cup evaporated milk	

Cream together butter, sugar, and eggs. Sift together dry ingredients. Add to creamed mixture, alternating with milk, vanilla, and vinegar. Last, add nuts. Drop and bake. Frost and eat.

DROP CARAMEL COOKIES   ··· *Mrs. Henry (Emma) Troyer*

2 cups brown sugar	$1/2$ tsp. salt
$1/2$ cup butter or lard	1 tsp. cream of tartar
2 well-beaten eggs	1 tsp. soda
3 Tbsp. water	1 tsp. vanilla
3 to 4 cups flour	$1/2$ cup nuts

This is the kind of cookies that were often found in Grandma Schlabach's cookie jar.

BUTTERMILK COOKIES   ··· *Mrs. Daniel (Lisa) Schlabach*

1 cup white sugar	$1 1/2$ cups buttermilk
1 cup brown sugar	2 tsp. baking soda
$1 1/2$ cups shortening	4 cups flour
2 eggs	1 tsp. cream of tartar
1 Tbsp. vanilla	1 Tbsp. vinegar

Cream together sugars and shortening. Add eggs, vanilla, baking soda, buttermilk, and 2 cups flour. Mix well and add 2 cups flour, cream of tartar, and vinegar. Mix well. Drop onto sheet and bake at 350°.

FROSTING

$1/3$ cup butter	3 cups powdered sugar
$1 1/2$ tsp. vanilla	2 Tbsp. milk

Blend butter and sugar. Stir in vanilla and milk. Beat until smooth.

BUTTERMILK COOKIES   ··· *Leona Sue Miller*

1 cup shortening	2 tsp. soda
2 cups brown sugar	2 tsp. baking powder
2 eggs	$1/3$ tsp. salt
1 cup buttermilk	4 cups flour
2 tsp. vanilla	

Cream shortening and brown sugar. Add eggs and vanilla. Beat well. Add remaining ingredients, alternating buttermilk and flour. Drop on greased cookie sheet. Bake at 325°.

For variation: Add chocolate chips, M&Ms, or nuts. Ice with caramel icing. The bakery's best seller.

ORANGE COOKIES
··· *Mrs. Emanuel (Mary) Nisley*

2 cups white sugar

2 eggs

1 cup shortening

1 cup sour milk or buttermilk

rind and juice of 1 orange

1 tsp. soda

2 tsp. baking powder

6 cups flour (drop cookies)

ICING

2 Tbsp. melted butter

juice of 1 orange and grated rind

powdered sugar to thicken

CUT-OUT COOKIES
··· *Mrs. Mary Kaufman*

2 eggs

1 1/2 cups sugar

1 cup shortening

1 cup sweet milk

1 tsp. vanilla

4 cups flour (rounded)

2 tsp. baking powder

2 tsp. cream of tartar

2 tsp. soda

Cream sugar and shortening and add eggs; mix well. Add baking powder, cream of tartar, and flour alternately with milk (with soda in it) and vanilla. Chill. Keep dough chilled when rolling out. We like cream cheese icing with these.

SOFT CUT-OUT COOKIES
··· *Julia Yoder*

1 cup butter, softened

2 cups white sugar

3 eggs

1 cup whipping cream or
evaporated milk

1 tsp. salt

1 tsp. baking soda

5 tsp. baking powder

1 tsp. vanilla

5 cups flour

CREAM CHEESE FROSTING

8 oz. cream cheese

1/2 cup butter, softened

5 cups powdered sugar

thin with vanilla or milk

Chill dough. Bake at 350°. We sometimes use 1/2 cup less flour and drop them so they're easier to make all through the year.

*Housework is something you do
that nobody notices...unless you don't do it.*

COOKIE PRESS BARS   ··· favorite of Norman Schlabach

1/2 cup shortening
1 cup brown sugar
2 eggs
1 tsp. vanilla
   FILLING
4 Tbsp. melted butter
1 Tbsp. hot cream

2 Tbsp. cream
1 1/2 tsp. soda
1/2 tsp. salt
2 3/4 cups flour

2 cups powdered sugar
1 tsp. vanilla

Cookies: Cream shortening and sugar; add and beat eggs. Add vanilla, cream, soda, and salt. Add flour.

Filling: Beat all together till smooth.

ANGEL FOOD COOKIES   ··· Mrs. Albert (Verna) Yoder

1 cup shortening
1/2 cup white sugar
1/4 tsp. salt
1 tsp. soda
1 tsp. vanilla

1/2 cup brown sugar
1 egg, beaten
2 cups flour
1 tsp. cream of tartar
1 cup coconut

Mix shortening and sugars till creamy. Add egg. Sift dry ingredients together and add. Stir in coconut. Roll dough into small balls and dip top into water, then sugar. Bake at 375° for 15 minutes. Makes 4 dozen.

COFFEE CAKE COOKIES   ··· Mrs. Marion (Rachel) Mullet

1 pkg. dry yeast
1/4 cup lukewarm water
1 tsp. salt
1/4 cup sugar
1 cup shortening (Crisco)

4 cups flour
1 cup milk
2 eggs, beaten
1 tsp. cinnamon
1 cup white sugar

Put flour, salt, and sugar in bowl. Cut in shortening. Dissolve yeast in water. Scald milk and cool. Combine eggs with milk; add yeast. Add the liquid to flour; mix lightly until flour is moist. Do not knead. Refrigerate dough overnight. Divide dough in half. Roll out like cinnamon rolls. Mix 1 tsp. cinnamon and 1 cup sugar. Sprinkle on rolled out dough. Roll up and cut in 5/8" slices. Place on cookie sheets. Do not let rise. Bake at 350° for 10 minutes. When cool, ice with caramel icing.

HONEY DELIGHTS
··· Mrs. Emanuel (Mary) Nisley

1 cup butter (scant)
2 cups honey
2 eggs
$^1/_2$ tsp. cinnamon
$^1/_2$ tsp. cloves
$^1/_2$ tsp. allspice
4 tsp. soda
2 tsp. vanilla
at least 9 cups flour

Boil honey and butter together 1 minute, then cool. Sift and measure flour 3 times with spices. Add beaten eggs to butter mixture, then add flour. Roll about $^3/_8"$ thick. Frost with powdered sugar frosting or Seven-Minute frosting.

CHOCOLATE PRETZEL COOKIES
··· Mrs. Ralph (Sarah) Schlabach

$^1/_2$ cup butter or margarine,
  softened
$^2/_3$ cup sugar
1 egg
2 squares unsweetened chocolate, melted and cooled
2 tsp. vanilla
1$^3/_4$ cups flour
$^1/_2$ tsp. salt

GLAZE
1 cup unsweetened chocolate
  chips
1 tsp. light corn syrup
1 tsp. shortening
1 cup confectioner's sugar
4 to 5 Tbsp. hot coffee

Cookies: In bowl, cream butter and sugar. Add egg, chocolate, and vanilla; mix well. Combine flour and salt. Gradually add to creamed mixture and mix well. Chill 1 hour until firm. Divide dough into fourths; form each portion into a 6" log. Divide each log into 12 pieces. Roll each piece into a 9" rope; form each rope into a pretzel shape on baking sheet. Bake at 400° for 5–7 minutes.

Glaze: Heat chocolate chips, corn syrup, and shortening in saucepan until melted. Stir in sugar and enough coffee to make smooth glaze.

Dip pretzels and place on waxed paper to harden. Drizzle with white chocolate. Let stand till chocolate is set. Store in tight can. Yield: 4 dozen.

Optimism ~ Even when the teakettle is
up to its neck in hot water, it keeps on singing.

PEANUT BUTTER SOFT COOKIES

··· *Mrs. Atlee (Dorothy) Schlabach*

1/2 cup raisins
1/2 cup dates
1 medium banana
1/3 cup peanut butter
1/2 cup whole wheat flour

1/4 cup water
1 egg
1 tsp. vanilla
1 cup oatmeal
1 tsp. baking soda

Combine raisins, dates, banana, peanut butter, water, egg, and vanilla. Beat until blended. Add oatmeal, flour, and baking soda. Mix and blend thoroughly. Place on cookie sheet; flatten with spoon. Bake at 350° for about 10 minutes.

OUTRAGEOUS CHOCOLATE CHIP COOKIES

··· *Marita Mast*

2 cups sugar
1 1/3 cups brown sugar
3 sticks margarine
2 cups peanut butter
2 tsp. vanilla
4 eggs

4 cups flour
2 cups quick oats
4 tsp. soda
1/2 tsp. salt
2 bags chocolate chips

Cream margarine and sugar. Add peanut butter. Beat in eggs and vanilla. Add dry ingredients and chocolate chips. Drop by tsp. on ungreased cookie sheet. Bake at 350°. Cool 1 minute before removing from pan. Can also be made into bars.

CHOCOLATE CHIP OATMEAL COOKIES

··· *favorite of Mary Esther Yoder (10), Verna (9) and Sara (8) Troyer*

1 1/2 cups brown sugar
1 1/2 cups white sugar
1 1/2 cups shortening
2 tsp. vanilla
4 eggs
1 tsp. water

3 cups flour
2 tsp. soda
1 tsp. salt
4 cups rolled oats
1 large package chocolate chips

Drop. Bake at 350°.

CHOC-OAT-CHIP COOKIES   *... Mrs. Linda Beachy*

1 cup butter flavored Crisco
1 1/4 cups brown sugar
1/2 cup white sugar
2 eggs
2 Tbsp. milk
2 tsp. vanilla

1 3/4 cups flour
1 tsp. baking soda
1/2 tsp. salt
2 1/2 cups Quaker oatmeal (instant)
2 cups chocolate chips
1 cup chopped nuts (optional)

Beat Crisco and sugars until creamy. Add eggs, milk, and vanilla. Beat well. Add flour, baking soda, and salt; mix well. Add oatmeal, chocolate chips, and nuts. Bake 10–12 minutes at 375°. Yield: about 5 dozen cookies.

OATMEAL PEANUT BUTTER COOKIES

... Mrs. Mike (Ruby) Sommers

1 cup peanut butter
1 cup shortening or oleo
1 cup brown sugar
1 cup white sugar
3 eggs, beaten
1 tsp. vanilla

1 1/2 cups flour
1 tsp. salt
1 tsp. soda
3 cups quick oatmeal
1 cup chocolate chips (mini)

Cream shortening, sugar, and peanut butter; add eggs and vanilla. Beat well. Add dry ingredients; mix well. Add oatmeal and chips. Bake at 350° on ungreased cookie sheet for 9–11 minutes.

COCONUT OATMEAL COOKIES

... Mrs. Floyd (Marlene) Yoder

2 cups shortening
2 cups brown sugar
2 cups sugar
4 eggs
5 cups oatmeal
2 cups coconut

3 1/2 cups flour
2 tsp. soda
2 tsp. baking powder
2 tsp. vanilla
1 cup nuts
1 pkg. chocolate chips

Mix together. Chill dough for several hours. Bake at 350°. Do not overbake!

MONSTERS ··· *Mrs. Reuben (Betty) Yoder* ··· *Mrs. Jr. (Ruth) Miller*

1 1/2 cups white sugar
1 1/2 cups brown sugar
3/4 cup oleo
4 eggs
1 1/2 cups peanut butter
1 1/2 tsp. vanilla

1 1/2 tsp. soda
1 1/2 tsp. baking powder
7 1/2 cups oatmeal
chocolate chips (amount desired)
M&Ms (amount desired)

Mix everything together and bake at 350°. Do not overbake.

MONSTER COOKIES ··· *Owen Schlabach, Jr.* ··· *Linda Schlabach*

12 eggs
4 cups brown sugar
4 cups sugar
1 Tbsp. vanilla
1 Tbsp. Karo (light)

8 tsp. soda
1 lb. butter or oleo
3 lb. peanut butter
18 cups oatmeal
1 lb. choc. chips, M&Ms, or raisins

Mix in a large bowl in order given. Drop by large tsp. and flatten. Bake at 350° for 12 minutes or so. Do not overbake! Need no flour. Lots of cookies.

BUTTERSCOTCH CRUNCH COOKIES

··· *Mrs. Freeman (Naomi) Miller*

2 cups oleo
2 cups white sugar
2 cups brown sugar
4 eggs
2 tsp. vanilla

2 tsp. soda
1 tsp. salt
4 1/2 cups flour
6 cups oatmeal

Cream oleo and sugars. Add eggs and vanilla. Stir in dry ingredients, leaving oatmeal till last. Drop on greased cookie sheets and bake at 350°. Do not overbake. Ice with caramel icing while still slightly warm.

EASY PEANUT BUTTER COOKIES

··· *favorite of Aaron (10) and Cody (7) Albritton*

1 cup peanut butter, crunchy
1 cup sugar

2 eggs

Mix ingredients with a spoon. Drop by tsp. size on cookie sheet. Bake at 350° for 10–15 minutes or till lightly brown on top. Best when eaten warm.

$400 COOKIES   ··· Julia Yoder ··· Mrs. Floyd (Marlene) Yoder

2 cups oleo

2 cups white sugar

2 cups brown sugar

4 eggs

2 tsp. soda

$^1/_2$ tsp. salt

5 cups oatmeal

4 cups flour

1 - 8 oz. chocolate candy bar, cut up

4 cups chocolate chips

Mix together. Bake at 350° for 10–12 minutes. Do not overbake.

SIMPLE COOKIES   ··· Mose A. Schlabach

2 cups oleo

1 cup brown sugar

1 tsp. soda

2 boxes vanilla instant pudding

chocolate chips to suit your taste

1 cup white sugar

4 eggs

5 cups flour

Mix as listed. These were Freda's favorite to make.

HEAVENLY CHOCOLATE CHIP COOKIES

··· Mrs. Linda Mae Troyer

$^1/_2$ cup margarine, softened

$^2/_3$ cup Crisco shortening

1 cup white sugar

1 cup brown sugar

2 eggs

1 tsp. vanilla

$3^1/_2$ cups flour

1 tsp. salt

1 tsp. soda

1 pkg. chocolate chips

Mix in order given. Bake 10 minutes at 350°.

CHOCOLATE CHIP COOKIES

··· Mrs. Albert (Verna) Yoder (from Mose Freda)

3 cups butter or oleo

3 cups brown sugar

6 beaten eggs

3 tsp. vanilla

$4^1/_2$ tsp. soda

6 Tbsp. cream

9 cups flour

salt

1 bag chocolate chips

Mix ingredients together one by one, beating well after each addition. Let stand overnight in cold place. Roll in balls and bake in 375°–400° oven. For a soft cookie, use $1^1/_2$ cups less flour.

CHOCOLATE CHIP COOKIES ... *Mrs. Paul (Linda) Schlabach*

Combine:

3 cups oil	3 cups brown sugar
3 cups white sugar	

Add:

8 beaten eggs

Add:

10 1/2 cups flour	4 tsp. water
4 tsp. salt	4 tsp. vanilla
4 tsp. soda	6 cups chocolate chips

Bake at 350° until light brown. Yield: 12 dozen cookies.

CHOCOLATE CHIP PUDDING COOKIES

... *favorite of Regina Sue Schlabach*
... *Mrs. Steve (Bena) Yoder* ... *Edward Raber*

2 cups oleo	2 - 3 oz. boxes vanilla instant pudding
1 cup brown sugar	2 tsp. soda
1 cup white sugar	5 cups flour
4 eggs	

Mix ingredients in order given. Drop by tsp. on baking sheet. Bake in 350° oven.

Grandma Schlabach used to make these. They are one of our favorites.

ORIGINAL TOLL HOUSE COOKIES   ... *Hannah Yoder*

2 3/4 cups flour	3/4 cup brown sugar
1 tsp. salt	3/4 cup white sugar
1 tsp. baking soda	1 tsp. vanilla
1 cup softened shortening	1/2 tsp. water
2 eggs	12 oz. mini chocolate chips

Sift together dry ingredients; set aside. Beat butter, sugars, water, and vanilla until creamy. Add eggs and beat well. Add dry ingredients. Mix well; add chocolate chips. Chill dough. On a floured surface, roll dough into 1/2" ropes. Slice off 1/4" slices and bake at 350°, 45–50 per cookie sheet. These bite-size cookies are an excellent after-school treat!

CHOCOLATE CHIP COOKIES ··· *Mrs. Steve (Ruth) Schlabach*

2 1/4 cups flour   1 tsp. vanilla
1 tsp. soda   2 eggs
1 cup margarine   1 - 4 oz. pkg. instant vanilla pudding
1/4 cup white sugar   12 oz. chocolate chips
3/4 cup brown sugar   nuts (optional)

   Melt margarine and mix with sugar, vanilla, and instant pudding. Beat
and add eggs, then add remaining ingredients. Bake on ungreased cookie
sheet at 350°.

FARMER BOY FAVORITE COOKIES   ··· *Julia Yoder*
                                   ··· *Mrs. Lloyd (Bena) Miller*

4 cups butter   4 tsp. soda
3 cups brown sugar   4 tsp. salt
3 cups white sugar   2 cups chocolate chips
4 tsp. vanilla   3 cups M&Ms
8 eggs   4 cups chopped nuts
9 to 13 cups cake flour

   Cream butter and sugar. Add vanilla and eggs, beating well. Set aside.
Sift dry ingredients. Slowly stir dry mixture into creamed mixture. When
well blended, stir in nuts, chocolate chips, and candy. Bake at 375° for
10 minutes. This is a large recipe, but they usually disappear very quickly.
Yield: 13 1/2 dozen cookies.

KONG'S BIG COOKIE   ··· *Mrs. Freeman (Marie) Schlabach*

2 1/4 cups flour   3/4 cup brown sugar
1 tsp. soda   1 tsp. vanilla
1 tsp. salt   2 eggs
1 cup butter, softened   2 cups chocolate chips
3/4 cup sugar   1 cup chopped nuts

   Beat butter, sugars, and vanilla till creamy. Beat in eggs. Gradually add
flour, soda, and salt. Stir in chips and nuts. Spread on greased 15" round
pizza pan. Bake in 375° oven for 20–25 minutes.

MOUNTAIN COOKIES   *... Melissa Mast*

1 cup butter, softened   2 tsp. vanilla extract
  (no substitutes)   2 cups all-purpose flour
1 cup confectioner's sugar $^1/_2$ tsp. salt

FILLING

1 - 3 oz. pkg. cream cheese,   1 tsp. vanilla extract
  softened $^1/_2$ cup finely chopped pecans
1 cup confectioner's sugar $^1/_2$ cup flaked coconut
2 Tbsp. all-purpose flour

TOPPING

$^1/_2$ cup semisweet chocolate chips   2 Tbsp. water
2 Tbsp. butter or margarine $^1/_2$ cup confectioner's sugar

In a mixing bowl, cream butter, sugar, and vanilla. Combine flour and salt; gradually add to creamed mixture and mix well. Shape into 1" balls; place 2" apart on ungreased baking sheets. Make a deep indentation in the center of each cookie. Bake at 350° for 10–12 minutes or until edges start to brown. Remove to wire racks to cool completely.

For the filling, beat cream cheese, sugar, flour, and vanilla in a mixing bowl. Add pecans and coconut; mix well. Spoon $^1/_2$ tsp. into each cookie.

For topping, heat chocolate chips, butter, and water in a small saucepan until melted. Stir in sugar. Drizzle over cookies.

Yield: 4 dozen.

SADIE DOUGLAS COOKIES   *... Leroy and Betty Schlabach*

1 cup brown sugar   3 tsp. soda
1 cup lard   2 tsp. ginger
2 eggs   2 tsp. cinnamon
1 cup molasses $4^1/_2$ cups flour
1 cup hot water

MOLASSES COOKIES   *... Mrs. Paul (Rebecca) Nisley*

$4^1/_2$ cups Robin Hood flour   1 tsp. cloves
4 tsp. soda   2 cups brown sugar
$^1/_2$ tsp. salt $1^1/_2$ cups shortening
2 tsp. cinnamon $^2/_3$ cup molasses
2 tsp. ginger   2 eggs

Form into little balls and roll in white sugar. Bake at 375°.

GINGER COOKIES   ··· *Michelle Schlabach*

1 1/2 cups shortening   1/2 tsp. salt
2 cups white sugar   4 tsp. baking soda
2 eggs   2 Tbsp. cinnamon
1/3 cup molasses   2 tsp. cloves
4 cups flour   2 tsp. ginger

Cream together shortening and sugar. Add eggs and molasses; mix well. Sift together and add remaining ingredients. Roll into 1" balls and roll in sugar. Bake on greased cookie sheet. Do not overbake. Bake at 350° for 12 minutes.

RAISIN-FILLED COOKIES   ··· *Mrs. Leroy (Betty) Schlabach*
                                   ··· *Mrs. Lloyd (Bena) Miller*

1 cup shortening   1 cup sweet milk
2 cups sugar, white or brown   7 cups flour
2 eggs   2 tsp. soda
2 tsp. vanilla   4 tsp. baking powder

FILLING

2 cups raisins soaked in water,   2 cups water
  then ground   2 Tbsp. clear jel
1 1/2 cups sugar   1 Tbsp. lemon juice

Cook together filling ingredients until thick and clear; cool. Mix cookie dough. Roll out and cut in a circle. Put 1 tsp. filling on center; fold over and seal edges. Bake at 350° for 20 minutes. Frost when cool.

A good angle to approach any problem
is the try~angle.

PINEAPPLE-FILLED COOKIES ··· *Mrs. Linda Mae Troyer*

5 cups flour	2 cups sugar
2 tsp. baking powder	2 eggs
1 tsp. soda	1 tsp. vanilla
$^1/_2$ tsp. salt	1 cup sour cream
1 cup shortening	1 recipe pineapple filling

Sift together first 4 ingredients. Mix shortening, sugar, eggs, and vanilla until creamy. Gradually mix in sour cream and the flour mixture. Chill until easy to handle. Heat oven to 425°. Roll dough to $^1/_8$" thickness. Cut with 3" round. Place half of rounds on ungreased cookie sheet; place rounded tsp. of pineapple filling on center of each. Top with remaining rounds, with center cut out. Press edges together with floured fork. Bake for 8–10 minutes or until golden.

PINEAPPLE FILLING

1 cup white sugar	$^1/_4$ cup (4 Tbsp.) lemon juice
$^1/_4$ cup flour	3 Tbsp. butter
No. 2 can ($1^1/_2$ cups) well-drained crushed pineapple (save juice)	$^3/_4$ cup pineapple juice

Mix sugar and flour in saucepan. Stir in remaining ingredients. (If necessary, add water to reserved pineapple juice to make required amount.) Cook slowly, stirring constantly, until thickened (5–10 minutes). Cool.

PEANUT BUTTER COOKIES ··· *Mrs. Henry (Emma) Troyer*

1 cup brown sugar	2 Tbsp. soda
1 cup white sugar	1 Tbsp. salt
1 scant cup peanut butter	1 Tbsp. vanilla
2 eggs	1 cup lard or butter
3 cups flour	

Cream shortening with sugar; add eggs, peanut butter, and vanilla. Work in flour with soda and salt; mix well. Roll in 3 rolls; let stand overnight. Slice and bake. Make sandwich cookies.

FILLING

$^1/_2$ cup peanut butter	4 Tbsp. milk
1 tsp. vanilla	3 cups powdered sugar

TRIPLE TREAT COOKIES   ··· *Mrs. Mary Esta Yoder*

1 cup margarine

1 cup white sugar

2 eggs

1 tsp. vanilla

3 cups flour

1 cup brown sugar

1 cup peanut butter

2 tsp. soda

1 tsp. salt

1 1/2 cups mini chocolate chips

FILLING

1/3 cup peanut butter

1/3 cup milk

1 tsp. vanilla

3 cups powdered sugar

Combine ingredients and shape into balls; roll in white sugar. Bake on ungreased baking sheet at 350° for 8–10 minutes. When cooled, spread filling between 2 cookies to form a sandwich.

BUTTERSCOTCH CRUNCH SANDWICH COOKIES

··· *favorite of Kimberly Miller, age 3*

2 cups shortening

2 cups brown sugar

2 cups white sugar

2 tsp. vanilla

4 eggs

3 cups flour

2 tsp. salt

2 tsp. soda

6 cups oatmeal

FILLING

1/2 cup butter, softened

1/2 pkg. cream cheese

maple flavoring

2 1/2 cups powdered sugar

Mix well and bake at 400° for 10 minutes. Do not overbake.

CHOCOLATE MINT COOKIES   ··· *Mrs. Mary Esta Yoder*

2/3 cup oleo

1 cup sugar

1 egg

1/2 tsp. salt

1 1/2 cups flour

1/2 cup cocoa

1/2 tsp. soda

1 cup chopped nuts (optional)

Cream oleo and sugar; add egg; beat smooth. Add remaining ingredients. Form into a roll; wrap in waxed paper and chill overnight. Slice thin and bake at 375° for 8–10 minutes. When cool, put 2 cookies together with mint flavored frosting, tinted green.

MOLASSES SANDWICH COOKIES

··· Mrs. Alton (Nora) Nisley

3 cups brown sugar

2 cups white sugar

3 cups butter

4 eggs

8 tsp. baking soda dissolved in
    1 cup buttermilk

1 cup Brer Rabbit molasses

2 tsp. baking powder

4 tsp. cinnamon

1 tsp. salt

10 cups cake flour (9 cups other flour;
    more may be used)

I use cake flour and it doesn't make a stiff dough like some flours do. Roll in balls, then in white sugar. Bake at 350° for 10–12 minutes. Do not overbake. Put together sandwich style.

FILLING

2 egg whites, beaten well

2 tsp. vanilla

2 cups (or more) powdered sugar

1^1/$_2$ cups Crisco

DOUBLE CHOCOLATE JUMBO CRISPS

··· Mrs. Marion (Rachel) Mullet

Cream:

1^1/$_4$ cups butter

Beat in:

1 egg

1 tsp. vanilla

6 Tbsp. cocoa

Blend in:

1^1/$_4$ to 1^3/$_4$ cups flour

Stir in:

3 cups quick oats

1^1/$_2$ cups sugar

^{1}/$_2$ tsp. baking soda

^{1}/$_2$ tsp. salt

^{1}/$_4$ cup hot water

1 cup chocolate chips

Drop by tsp. onto ungreased cookie sheet. Bake at 350° for 15 minutes. When cool, place filling between 2 cookies.

FILLING

2 egg whites, beaten

1 Tbsp. vanilla

1^1/$_2$ cups Crisco

2 cups powdered sugar

Combine all ingredients and beat till smooth. I prefer to add some marshmallow topping. The more you beat, the better it is.

CREAM WAFER COOKIES   ⋯ Leona Sue Miller

(A DAINTY BUTTER COOKIE)

2 cups butter	1 cup cream
1 cup oleo	white sugar
6 cups flour	

Mix butter, oleo, cream, and flour. Chill 1 hour. Roll dough $1/8$" thick on floured surface. Cut into $1 1/2$" rounds. Prick each cookie 4 times with fork and coat both sides with white sugar. Bake 7–9 minutes at 375° or until lightly browned. Put together with filling.

FILLING

1 cup soft butter	4 tsp. vanilla
6 Tbsp. milk	8 cups powdered sugar

Tint as desired. Look nice with pink, green, and yellow. A specialty on our Christmas cookie plate!

OREO COOKIES   ⋯ Iva Nisley

1 - 18 oz. cake mix, white or yellow	2 Tbsp. cooking oil
	$1/2$ cup cocoa
2 eggs plus 2 Tbsp. water	

FILLING

1 envelope Knox gelatin	1 tsp. vanilla
$1/4$ cup cold water	$1/2$ cup Crisco
1 cup plus 1 Tbsp. powdered sugar	

Let stand 20 minutes. Do not refrigerate. Shape into balls. Flatten with bottom of glass greased once and dipped into Nestlé Quik for each cookie. Bake about 8 minutes at 300°.

PEANUT BUTTER–CHOCOLATE CHIP BARS

⋯ Mrs. Freeman (Naomi) Miller

$1 1/2$ cups sugar	1 tsp. baking powder
$1/2$ cup shortening	$1/2$ tsp. salt
$1/2$ cup peanut butter	$1 1/2$ cups flour
3 eggs	1 cup chocolate chips
1 tsp. vanilla	

Cream together sugar, peanut butter, and shortening. Add eggs and vanilla, stirring thoroughly. Stir in flour, baking powder, and salt. Add chocolate chips. Spread in a greased 9" x 13" pan. Bake at 350° for 35–40 minutes.

PEANUT BUTTER OATMEAL BARS

··· Mrs. Firman (Deborah) Miller

$^1/_2$ cup butter	$^1/_2$ cup brown sugar
$^1/_2$ cup white sugar	

Cream well and add:

1 egg	$^1/_2$ tsp. vanilla
$^1/_2$ cup peanut butter	1 cup flour
$^1/_2$ tsp. soda	1 cup quick oats
$^1/_4$ tsp. salt	

Bake in a greased 13" x 9" pan at 350° for 20–25 minutes. After removed from oven, immediately sprinkle with 1 cup chocolate chips.

Mix together until creamy:

$^1/_2$ cup powdered sugar	2 to 4 Tbsp. milk
$^1/_2$ cup peanut butter	

When chocolate chips are melted, spread them and drizzle peanut butter mixture on top and swirl. Let cool for a while, then cut in bars.

PEANUT BUTTER PIZZA BARS

··· Mrs. Marion (Rachel) Mullet

1 cup oleo	1 tsp. vanilla
1 cup peanut butter	2 cups flour
1 cup brown sugar	2 cups chocolate chips
$^2/_3$ cup white sugar	$^1/_2$ cup peanut butter
2 eggs	

TOPPINGS

1 cup mini baking milk chocolate M&Ms	$^1/_2$ cup crushed peanuts
	4 cups miniature marshmallows

Mix together oleo and sugars till creamy. Add peanut butter, eggs, and vanilla; mix well. Add flour. Spread dough evenly in a cookie sheet. Bake 15–20 minutes at 350°. Melt together chocolate chips and $^1/_2$ cup peanut butter. Spread over baked cookie crust while hot. Sprinkle M&Ms, peanuts, and marshmallows on top. Put back in oven for about 5 minutes, or until marshmallows become puffy.

Reputation is precious, but character is priceless.

PEANUT BUTTER FINGERS   *··· Mervin and Rhoda Hilty*

$1/2$ cup butter	$1/2$ tsp. vanilla
$1/3$ cup peanut butter	1 cup flour
$1/2$ cup sugar	1 cup oatmeal
$1/2$ cup brown sugar	1 cup chocolate chips
1 egg	$1/2$ cup powdered sugar
$1/2$ tsp. soda	$1/4$ cup peanut butter
$1/4$ tsp. salt	2 to 4 Tbsp. milk

Cream butter, $1/3$ cup peanut butter, and sugars; add egg, soda, salt, and vanilla. Beat well; add flour and oatmeal. Spread into a 9" x 13" pan. Bake at 350° for 20–25 minutes. Sprinkle immediately with chocolate chips. Combine powdered sugar, $1/4$ cup peanut butter, and milk till proper consistency to drizzle. Drizzle frosting on top of warm bars and use a knife to swirl frosting and chocolate chips together.

PEANUT BUTTER FINGERS   *··· Mrs. Mary Esta Yoder*

1 cup white sugar	2 tsp. salt
1 cup brown sugar	1 tsp. vanilla
1 cup shortening	1 tsp. soda
2 cups flour	$3/4$ cup peanut butter
2 cups oatmeal	mini marshmallows
3 eggs	

Mix together everything except marshmallows; put on large cookie sheet and bake at 350° for 35 minutes. When done, cover with small marshmallows. Return to oven for 5 minutes.

In top of double boiler, melt:

1 cup chocolate chips	$1/2$ cup peanut butter

Add:

$1/3$ cup milk	2 cups powdered sugar

Spread over marshmallows while still warm. Cool. Cut in finger size bars.

Gossip is like a snowball~
the longer it rolls, the bigger it gets.

REESE'S M&M BARS

··· Mrs. Linda Mae Troyer
··· favorite of Christina Sue Miller, age 9

2 cups soft butter
2 cups brown sugar
2 tsp. soda
1 1/2 tsp. salt
3 cups flour

4 cups oatmeal
1 cup nuts
1 can Eagle Brand milk
1/3 cup peanut butter
1 cup M&Ms

Mix. Reserve 2 cups of mixture. Press remaining mixture in cookie sheet with sides. Bake at 350° for 12 minutes. Combine 1 can Eagle Brand milk and 1/3 cup peanut butter and spread over crust. Sprinkle 1 cup M&Ms and rest of dough over peanut butter mixture. Continue baking for 20 minutes.

BUTTERSCOTCH BARS

··· Mrs. Reuben (Betty) Yoder

1/2 cup oleo
3/4 cup white sugar
2 eggs
3/4 cup flour
1/4 tsp. baking powder
pinch of salt

1 tsp. vanilla
3 cups mini marshmallows
6 oz. butterscotch chips
1 cup peanut butter
1 1/2 cups Rice Krispies

Mix first 7 ingredients and bake 20 minutes in a 9" x 13" cake pan. Remove from oven and sprinkle with marshmallows. Bake till they are melted. Cool. In a saucepan, melt butterscotch chips and peanut butter; add Rice Krispies. Spread on top of bars once they are cooled. Yummy!

DOUBLE CHOCOLATE CRUMBLE BARS

··· Mrs. Paul (Linda) Schlabach

1/2 cup oleo
3/4 cup sugar
2 eggs
1 tsp. vanilla
3/4 cup flour
2 Tbsp. cocoa

1/4 tsp. baking powder
1/2 cup nuts (optional)
2 cups small marshmallows
6 to 8 oz. chocolate chips
1 1/2 cups Rice Krispies
1 cup peanut butter

Cream together sugar and oleo; add eggs and vanilla. Mix well, then add flour, cocoa, baking powder, and nuts. Spread on greased pan (9" x 13") and bake at 350° for 15 minutes. Remove from oven and sprinkle marshmallows over top. Return to oven for 3 minutes. In saucepan, melt chocolate chips with peanut butter and stir in Rice Krispies. Then spread on baked mixture. Cool and cut.

CHOCOLATE MALLOW BARS   ··· Mrs. Linda Mae Troyer

1 cup margarine	1 tsp. soda
3/4 cup white sugar	1 tsp. salt
3/4 cup brown sugar	1 cup nuts
2 eggs	2 cups chocolate chips
1 tsp. vanilla	2 cups mini marshmallows
2 1/4 cups flour	

Combine sugar with margarine and beat until creamy. Beat in eggs and vanilla. Gradually add flour, soda, and salt. Stir in nuts, chips, and marshmallows. Spread on a greased 10" x 15" cookie sheet. Bake 20 minutes at 375°.

HIP-PADDER BARS   ··· Mrs. Mark (Ruth) Miller

1 - 14 oz. can sweetened condensed milk	2 Tbsp. butter
	1 - 6 oz. pkg. chocolate chips

Combine milk, butter, and chocolate chips in top of double boiler. Cook, stirring, until melted and smooth. Cool.

1/2 cup butter	1/2 cup quick oats
1 cup brown sugar	1 tsp. vanilla
1 egg, beaten	1/2 cup nuts (optional)
1 1/4 cups flour	

Cream together butter and sugar. Add egg, mixing well. Blend in flour, oats, and vanilla. Stir in nuts. Pat into greased 9" square pan. Pour chocolate mixture over top, spreading evenly. Bake at 350° for 25–30 minutes. Do not overbake.

SPICY CHOCOLATE BARS   ··· Ruth Ann Schlabach

1 1/2 cups shortening	2 tsp. soda
1 1/2 cups sugar	4 tsp. cinnamon
1 1/2 cups brown sugar	1 tsp. cloves
4 eggs	1 tsp. nutmeg
2 tsp. vanilla	2 cups chocolate chips
4 cups sifted flour	

Cream shortening and sugar till fluffy. Beat in eggs one at a time. Add vanilla. Blend in dry ingredients. Spread into two ungreased 15 1/2" x 10 1/2" x 1" sheets. Sprinkle chips over dough before baking. Bake at 350° for 20 minutes. Cut into bars while warm. Cool.

Less sugar can be used for a softer cookie.

CHOCOLATE STREUSEL BARS   ··· Leona Sue Miller

1 3/4 cups unsifted flour
1 1/2 cups powdered sugar
1/2 cup cocoa
1 cup cold butter or margarine
1 - 8 oz. pkg. cream cheese, softened

1 - 14 oz. can Eagle Brand sweetened condensed milk
1 egg
2 tsp. vanilla extract
1/2 cup chopped nuts

Preheat oven to 350°. In large bowl, combine flour, sugar, and cocoa. Cut in margarine until crumbly (mixture will be dry). Reserving 2 cups crumb mixture, press remainder firmly on bottom of 9" x 13" pan. Bake 15 minutes. In bowl, beat cheese until fluffy. Gradually beat in sweetened condensed milk until smooth. Add egg and vanilla; mix well. Pour over prepared crust. Combine nuts with reserved crumbs. Sprinkle over cheese mixture. Bake 25 minutes or until bubbly. Cool. Cut into bars. Yield: 24–36 bars.

CHOCOLATE CARAMELITA BARS

··· Mrs. Linda Mae Troyer

1 3/4 cups oatmeal
1 1/2 cups flour
3/4 cup brown sugar, packed
3/4 cup Crisco, melted
1 Tbsp. water
1/2 tsp. soda

1/4 tsp. salt
1 cup chopped nuts
1 cup (6 oz.) chocolate chips
1 - 12 1/2 oz. jar or 1 cup caramel ice cream topping
1/4 cup flour

Heat oven to 350°. Grease 13" x 9" pan. Combine first seven ingredients; mix well. Reserve 1 cup. Press remaining mixture into bottom of pan. Bake 10–12 minutes or until light brown. Cool 10 minutes. Top with nuts and chocolate chips. Mix caramel topping and 1/4 cup flour until smooth; drizzle over chocolate chips. Sprinkle with reserved oat mixture. Bake additional 18–22 minutes. Cool completely.

*A young child, a fresh, uncluttered mind,
a world before him...
to what treasures will you lead him?*

MOIST BROWNIES   *··· Leona Sue Miller*

2 cups flour	2 cups sugar

Place into mixing bowl.

4 Tbsp. cocoa	$^1/_2$ cup oleo
$^1/_2$ cup vegetable oil	1 cup water

Boil together and pour over sugar and flour mixture. Stir.

2 eggs, beaten	1 tsp. soda
$^1/_4$ tsp. salt	1 tsp. vanilla
$^1/_2$ cup buttermilk	

Add to above mixture. Bake at 300° on cookie sheet until done.

FROSTING

$^1/_2$ cup oleo	6 Tbsp. milk
4 Tbsp. cocoa	powdered sugar to spread easily

Boil for 1 minute.

HINT: We like to melt small marshmallows on top of baked brownies before icing them.

PEANUT BUTTER BROWNIES

··· Mrs. Reuben (Sara Etta) Schlabach

3 eggs	1$^1/_2$ tsp. vanilla
1 cup white sugar	2 cups flour
$^3/_4$ cup brown sugar	$^3/_4$ tsp. baking powder
$^1/_2$ cup peanut butter	$^3/_4$ tsp. salt
$^1/_4$ cup shortening	$^1/_4$ cup nuts

Cream together sugar, shortening, and peanut butter. Add eggs and vanilla, then dry ingredients. Press on 1 cookie sheet. Bake at 350° for 30 minutes. When done, sprinkle with powdered sugar.

SURPRISE BARS   *··· Mrs. Albert (Verna) Yoder*

1$^1/_2$ cups cooking oil	2 tsp. baking soda
2 cups white sugar	2 tsp. cinnamon
4 eggs	3 heaping cups grated carrots
2 cups sifted flour	1 cup nuts

Cream sugar and oil; add eggs, beating well. Add dry ingredients to egg mixture. Fold in carrots and nuts. Pour in greased 10" x 15" cookie sheet. Bake at 350°. Frost with cream cheese frosting.

MARBLE SQUARES
··· Mrs. Mary Esta Yoder
··· Mrs. Ammon (Esta) Brenneman

2½ cups oleo
2¼ cups white sugar
2¼ cups brown sugar
1½ tsp. salt
6 eggs
3 tsp. vanilla

7¾ cups flour
1 tsp. soda
2 tsp. baking powder
1½ cups chocolate chips
1 cup chopped nuts

Cream oleo, sugars, eggs, and vanilla. Add flour, soda, baking powder, and salt. Spread in 2 greased jelly roll pans. Sprinkle chips on top. Put in preheated oven for 2 minutes. Take out and marbleize with knife. Sprinkle nuts on top. Bake 20 minutes. When cooled, drizzle glaze over top.

FRUIT SQUARES
··· Mrs. Mary Esta Yoder

1 cup butter or oleo
1¾ cups white sugar
4 eggs
1 tsp. vanilla
1 tsp. almond extract

3 cups flour
1½ tsp. baking powder
½ tsp. salt
1 can (2¼ cups) pie filling

GLAZE

1½ cups powdered sugar
½ tsp. vanilla

warm water to spreading consistency

Cream butter and sugar; add eggs and flavorings. Add dry ingredients. Spread ⅔ of batter on a greased 15" x 10" baking sheet. Cover with pie filling. Drop spoonfuls of batter over fruit filling. Bake at 350° for 40–45 minutes. Drizzle with glaze when cool.

BEST ZUCCHINI BARS
··· Mrs. Roy (Freda) Miller

2 cups sugar
3 eggs
1 tsp. cinnamon
1 tsp. salt
1 tsp. vanilla
1 cup vegetable oil

2 cups flour
2 tsp. soda
¼ tsp. baking powder
3 cups shredded zucchini
nuts

Bake at 350° for 15–20 minutes. Very moist. Frost with cream cheese frosting.

ALMOND COOKIE STRIPS   ··· Mrs. Lloyd (Bena) Miller

1 cup butter	2 cups sifted cake flour
1 cup sugar	1 egg white
1 egg yolk	$^1/_2$ cup finely chopped almonds
$^1/_8$ tsp. salt	3 Tbsp. sugar
1 tsp. vanilla	$^1/_2$ tsp. cinnamon

Cream butter and 1 cup sugar till light and fluffy. Add egg yolk, salt, and vanilla. Stir till blended. Add flour; mix well. Pat mixture into a $15^1/_2$" x $10^1/_2$" baking sheet. Beat egg white till stiff and spread over cookie layer. Sprinkle with mixture of 3 Tbsp. sugar, cinnamon, and almonds. Bake at 350°–375° for 15–20 minutes. Cut into strips while warm. We use chopped walnuts instead of almonds.

PAUL'S PUMPKIN BARS   ··· Mrs. Paul (Rebecca) Nisley
··· Joyce (Schlabach) Albritton

4 eggs, beaten	2 tsp. baking powder
1 cup pumpkin	1 tsp. soda
$1^2/_3$ cups sugar	$1^1/_2$ tsp. cinnamon
1 cup vegetable oil	1 tsp. vanilla
2 cups flour	

Cream oil, sugar, and eggs. Add pumpkin, then dry ingredients. Bake in greased 11" x 17" cookie sheet at 350° for 25–30 minutes. Cool.

FROSTING

3 oz. cream cheese	2 cups powdered sugar
1 tsp. vanilla	chopped nuts (optional)
$^1/_4$ cup butter, softened	

CONGO SQUARES   ··· Mrs. Henry (Emma) Troyer

$^2/_3$ cup butter	$2^1/_2$ tsp. baking powder
1 lb. brown sugar	$^1/_2$ tsp. salt
1 tsp. vanilla	2 cups chopped dates or chocolate
3 eggs	chips
$2^3/_4$ cups flour	1 cup pecans

Cream together sugar and butter until well blended. Add vanilla. Add the eggs one at a time, beating thoroughly after each addition. Sift together flour, baking powder, and salt and add to the mixture. Mix in dates and nuts. Bake at 350° for 20–30 minutes in an 8" x 12" pan. Cut in squares while warm.

LEMON-FROSTED COCONUT BARS

··· *Leona Sue Miller*

1 1/2 cups flour   1/2 cup butter, softened
1/2 cup brown sugar

Stir together flour and sugar, then cut in butter. Pat into a buttered pan. Bake at 275° for 10 minutes. Beat together:

2 eggs, beaten   1/2 tsp. salt
1 cup brown sugar   1/2 tsp. vanilla
2 Tbsp. flour   1 1/2 cups coconut
1/2 tsp. baking powder   1 cup chopped nuts

Spread coconut mixture on baked crust; bake at 375° for 20 minutes. Frost while hot with Lemon Frosting. Cool before cutting into squares.

LEMON FROSTING

Beat until smooth:

1 cup powdered sugar   1 Tbsp. lemon juice
1 Tbsp. butter, melted   1 Tbsp. lemon rind

LEMON SQUARES

··· *Mrs. Emanuel (Mary) Nisley*

1 cup quick-cooking rolled oats   4 egg yolks
1/3 cup sifted flour   1/2 cup sugar
1/2 cup brown sugar   1 tsp. grated lemon rind
1/2 tsp. salt   1/2 cup lemon juice
1/3 cup butter, melted   4 egg whites
1 envelope unflavored gelatin   1/2 cup sugar
1/2 cup water

Combine rolled oats, flour, brown sugar, and salt. Stir in butter. Turn into 8" x 8" x 2" baking pan. Bake in moderate oven (350°) about 10 minutes, stirring once; cool. Remove 1/2 cup of crumbs; pat remaining crumbs evenly on bottom of pan. Soften gelatin in water. In a small saucepan, combine egg yolks, 1/2 cup sugar, lemon rind, and lemon juice. Cook and stir till mixture thickens and bubbles. Remove from heat; stir in gelatin. Cool. Beat egg whites to soft peaks; gradually beat in 1/2 cup sugar. Continue beating till stiff peaks form. Fold gelatin mixture into egg whites. Pour into crumb-lined pan; sprinkle with reserved crumbs. Chill till firm. Cut into squares.

SOUR CREAM RAISIN BARS
··· Mrs. Jr. (Ruth) Miller
··· Mrs. David (Susan) Nisley

2³/₄ cups quick oatmeal
2³/₄ cups flour
1¹/₂ cups brown sugar
1¹/₂ tsp. baking soda
1 cup and 5 Tbsp. oleo

4 egg yolks
1¹/₄ cups white sugar
1 Tbsp. cornstarch
2 cups sour cream
2 cups raisins

Combine oatmeal, flour, brown sugar, soda, and oleo. Pat ²/₃ of crumbs into bottom of greased cookie sheet with sides. Bake 15–20 minutes at 350°. Cool. In saucepan, combine egg yolks, white sugar, cornstarch, sour cream, and raisins. Boil 5–10 minutes, stirring constantly. Pour over baked crumb layer; cover with remaining crumbs and bake 20 minutes at 350°.

ANGEL FOOD BARS
··· Mrs. Marion (Rachel) Mullet

1 cup sugar
¹/₂ cup butter
3 eggs
1 tsp. vanilla

1 - 12 oz. box vanilla wafers, finely
    crushed
1¹/₂ cups angel flake coconut

TOPPING

¹/₂ cup butter
5 Tbsp. cream

1 cup brown sugar
¹/₂ cup chopped pecans or walnuts

Cream sugar and butter; add eggs one at a time, beating after each addition. Add vanilla; beat until batter is light and fluffy. Stir in cookie crumbs and coconut. Drop by large spoonfuls evenly over lightly greased 15" x 10" x 1" cookie sheet. Wet fingertips slightly, then pat dough evenly over bottom of pan. Bake at 325° for 20–25 minutes, until lightly browned. Do not overbake.

For topping: Combine ingredients in saucepan. Bring to a boil over medium heat; boil gently for 3 minutes. Pour and spread over hot bars. Broil until topping bubbles. This takes only about 2–3 minutes. Cool. Cut into bars.

Living without faith is like driving in the fog.

NAPOLEON CREME BARS   ··· Hannah Yoder

$^1/_2$ cup butter, softened
$^1/_4$ cup sugar
$^1/_4$ cup cocoa
1 tsp. vanilla
1 egg, slightly beaten
2 cups graham cracker crumbs
1 cup coconut

$^1/_2$ cup butter
3 Tbsp. milk
1 - 3$^3/_4$ oz. box instant vanilla
    pudding
2 cups powdered sugar
6 oz. chocolate chips
2 Tbsp. butter

Combine first 4 ingredients in saucepan; cook slowly till butter melts. Stir in egg and cook until mixture thickens. Blend in crumbs and coconut. Press into buttered 9" x 9" pan. Cream $^1/_2$ cup butter; stir in pudding mix, milk, and powdered sugar. Beat until fluffy; spread evenly on cooled crust. Chill until firm. Melt chocolate chips and 2 Tbsp. butter; cool, then spread onto pudding layer. Chill; cut into bars.

BROWNIE CHEESECAKE BARS

··· Mrs. Atlee (Dorothy) Schlabach

1$^1/_2$ cups all-purpose flour
1$^1/_2$ cups sugar
$^2/_3$ cup butter or margarine, melted
$^2/_3$ cup Hershey's cocoa
3 eggs, divided
$^1/_2$ cup milk
3 tsp. vanilla extract, divided
$^1/_2$ tsp. baking powder

1 cup chopped nuts
1 - 8 oz. pkg. cream cheese, softened
2 Tbsp. butter or margarine
1 Tbsp. cornstarch
1 - 14 oz. can Eagle Brand
    sweetened condensed milk
    (not evaporated milk)

Heat oven to 350°. Grease baking pan. In mixing bowl, beat flour, sugar, melted butter, cocoa, 2 eggs, milk, 2 tsp. vanilla, and baking powder until well blended. Stir in nuts. Spread into pan. In small mixing bowl, beat cream cheese, 2 Tbsp. butter, and cornstarch until fluffy. Gradually add sweetened condensed milk, then remaining egg and 1 tsp. vanilla, beating until smooth. Pour over brownie batter. Bake 35–40 minutes or until top is lightly browned. Cool. Refrigerate. Cut into bars. Store covered in fridge.

*The mighty oak was once a little nut
that stood its ground.*

CARA-CHOCOLATE SQUARES ··· Mrs. Linda Mae Troyer

1 - 14 oz. pkg. caramels

1 - 5 oz. can evaporated milk

1 pkg. chocolate cake mix

$^2/_3$ cup butter, melted

$^3/_4$ cup chopped nuts

1 pkg. chocolate chips

1 cup coconut

Heat caramels and $^1/_4$ cup of milk in saucepan over medium heat, stirring constantly, until caramels are melted and mixture is smooth. Keep warm; mix cake mix (dry), butter, remaining milk, and nuts. Spread half of dough (1$^1/_2$ cups) in ungreased 13" x 9" x 2" pan. Bake at 350° for 6 minutes. Remove; sprinkle chocolate chips and coconut over baked layer. Drizzle caramel mixture over chocolate chips and coconut. Drop remaining dough onto caramel layer. Bake 15–20 minutes longer.

MALLOW GRANOLA BARS ··· Mrs. Marion (Rachel) Mullet

Melt $^1/_2$ cup butter in a large pan. Add 4 cups mini marshmallows and stir. Turn the burner off before the marshmallows are completely melted. (This keeps bars softer.) Add 5 to 5$^1/_2$ cups of your favorite granola cereal. Stir. Pour into greased loaf pan and press down with waxed paper. Sprinkle chocolate or butterscotch chips on top and press down. I like to use warm granola so the marshmallow is easier to work with. Cut into bars when cool.

For variation, try melting chocolate chips and peanut butter together and spreading on top. Add raisins to the granola. Delicious as a snack!

GRANOLA BARS ··· Mrs. Mike (Ruby) Sommers

1$^1/_2$ lb. marshmallows

$^1/_4$ cup butter

$^1/_4$ cup vegetable oil

$^1/_4$ cup honey

$^1/_4$ cup peanut butter

4$^1/_2$ cups Rice Krispies

1 cup graham cracker crumbs

5 cups oatmeal

1 cup crushed peanuts

1$^1/_2$ cups raisins

1 cup coconut

1 cup chocolate chips

Heat butter and oil on low heat until butter melts. Add marshmallows and stir till melted; remove from heat and add honey and peanut butter. In a large bowl, mix remaining ingredients. Make well in center of mixture and pour in marshmallow mixture. Stir immediately. Press into greased cookie sheet; cool and cut into bars. I like to wrap them individually.

GRANOLA BARS   *... favorite of Bryan Mark Miller, age 7*

2 cups brown sugar   7^1/$_2$ cups oatmeal
1 cup white sugar   1^1/$_2$ cups milk chocolate chips
2 cups butter   1^1/$_2$ cups peanut butter

Mix sugars, butter, and oatmeal until crumbly. Press in a large cookie sheet and bake at 350° for 25 minutes. Melt chocolate chips and peanut butter in double boiler. Spread on top of first mixture. Keep in cool place.

Sad fact of life:
Square meals make round people.

Words seldom break bones, but they
do break hearts.

Cakes
& Icings

*A good rule for talking
is one used in measuring flour ... sift first.*

Happiness Cake

1 cup good thoughts

1 cup consideration

2 cups well beaten faults

1 cup kind deeds

2 cups sacrifice

3 cups forgiveness

Mix thoroughly. Add a teaspoon each of joy, sorrow, and sympathy. Flavor with love and kindly service. Fold in 4 cups each of prayer and faith. Blend well; fold into daily life. Bake well with the warmth of human kindness and serve with a smile any time. It will satisfy the hunger of all our souls.

A Love Cake for Mother

1 can of obedience

several lb. of affection

1 pt. neatness

some holiday, birthday, and
   everyday surprises

1 can of running errands (Willing brand)

1 box powdered "get up when I
   should"

1 bottle of "keep sunny all day long"

1 can of pure thoughtfulness

Mix well; bake in a hearty, warm oven. Serve to Mother every day. She ought to have it in big slices.

"Practice makes perfect,"
so be careful what you practice.

AMISH FRIENDSHIP CAKE STARTER

1 cup flour   1 pkg. yeast
$^1/_2$ cup sugar   1 cup warm water

Mix ingredients well and place in a glass bowl. Cover with a dinner plate so it is not tight. Let stand in a warm place (85°) overnight. Follow instructions below for cake of your choice.

AMISH FRIENDSHIP CAKE

*Do not refrigerate. *Do not use metal spoon.

Day 1 – Do nothing.
Days 2, 3, 4, and 5 – Stir batter.
Day 6 – Add:

1 cup flour   1 cup milk
1 cup sugar
  Mix well.

Days 7, 8, and 9 – Stir batter.
Day 10 – Add:

1 cup flour   1 cup milk
1 cup sugar

Stir batter and pour 4 - 1 cup starters into separate containers. Give these to friends with the instructions. Use what is left and in a large bowl add:

1 cup vegetable oil   3 eggs
$^1/_2$ cup milk   1 tsp. vanilla
  Mix well. In separate bowl, mix:
2 cups flour $^1/_2$ tsp. soda
1 large (5 oz.) box vanilla instant   2 tsp. cinnamon
  pudding   1 cup chopped nuts
$1^1/_2$ tsp. baking powder

Add dry ingredients to first mixture and mix thoroughly. Pour into 2 well greased and sugared loaf pans. Mix cinnamon and white sugar and sprinkle over top.

*If you worry, you don't trust...
If you trust, you don't worry!*

STREUSEL FRIENDSHIP CAKE

Days 1, 2, 3, 4, and 5 – Stir batter. Do not refrigerate.

Day 6 – Add:

1 cup flour   1 cup milk
1 cup sugar
  Mix well.

Days 7, 8, and 9 – Stir batter.

Day 10 – Add:

1 cup flour   1 cup milk
1 cup sugar

  Give 1 cup starter and a copy of the instructions to each of 3 friends.
  To the remainder of the starter, add:

^{2}/$_3$ cup vegetable oil   2 cups flour
1 cup sugar   2 tsp. soda
3 eggs ^{1}/$_2$ tsp. salt

STREUSEL

^{1}/$_2$ cup quick oats   1 tsp. cinnamon
^{1}/$_2$ cup brown sugar ^{1}/$_3$ cup melted margarine
^{1}/$_2$ cup white sugar   1 cup nuts (optional)

  Pour half of the batter into a 9" x 13" greased and floured cake pan.
Sprinkle with half of streusel mixture. Spread remaining batter over crumbs
and top with rest of streusel. Bake at 350° for 35–40 minutes.

"HERMAN" STARTER

2 cups flour ^{1}/$_4$ cup sugar
2 cups warm water   1 Tbsp. yeast

  Mix all ingredients and place in a plastic or glass container. Let stand
overnight in a warm place. Cover tightly with lid. Refrigerate covered, but
stir every day for 4 days. The fifth day you have to feed "Herman" with:

1 cup flour ^{1}/$_2$ cup sugar
1 cup milk

  Cover and refrigerate, stirring every day for 5 more days. On the tenth
day, you can bake with Herman one of the following recipes. Before you
bake, make sure you reserve 1 cup "Herman" to start again by feeding and
stirring it like on the fifth day; repeat directions through day 10. You also
have 1 cup to share with a friend to start. Give her the feeding ingredients,
instructions, and the following recipes.

"HERMAN" – THE TEN-DAY CAKE

2 cups Herman

1 cup sugar

2 eggs

2 cups flour

$^3/_4$ cup milk

$^1/_2$ tsp. soda

$^1/_2$ tsp. baking powder

2 tsp. salt

$1^1/_2$ tsp. cinnamon

$^2/_3$ cup vegetable oil

1 cup nuts

1 cup raisins

Mix all ingredients, adding nuts and raisins last. Pour into greased and floured 9" x 13" x 2" pan. Mix 1 cup brown sugar, 1 Tbsp. flour, 1 Tbsp. cinnamon, and $^1/_4$ cup soft margarine. Mix and sprinkle over batter in pan. Bake at 350°.

"HERMAN" CARROT CAKE

2 cups flour

2 cups sugar

1 tsp. salt

1 tsp. baking powder

1 tsp. cinnamon

1 tsp. soda

1 cup vegetable oil

2 cups finely shredded carrots

1 cup "Herman"

4 eggs

$^1/_2$ cup chopped nuts

Sift together dry ingredients. Beat eggs; add "Herman," vegetable oil, and carrots. Blend well. Add nuts. Pour batter into greased and floured 13" x 9" cake pan. Bake at 325° for 55 minutes. Spread with cream cheese icing when cooled.

"HERMAN" COOKIES

$^1/_2$ cup "Herman"

$^1/_2$ cup shortening

$1^1/_2$ cups brown sugar

$1^1/_2$ cups sour milk

2 eggs

2 cups flour

1 tsp. soda

1 tsp. baking powder

1 tsp. salt

1 tsp. cinnamon

3 cups quick oats

$^1/_2$ cup milk

1 cup raisins (optional)

Cream shortening and sugar. Add eggs and "Herman." Mix well. Add remaining ingredients. Drop by spoonfuls on greased cookie sheets. Bake in 375° oven for 10 minutes.

"HERMAN" CINNAMON ROLLS

2 cups "Herman" $^1/_2$ tsp. soda
2 cups flour   4 tsp. baking powder
$^1/_2$ tsp. salt $^1/_2$ cup vegetable oil

Combine "Herman," flour, soda, baking powder, salt, and vegetable oil. Knead lightly on floured board until dough is no longer sticky. Roll to $^1/_4$" thickness and spread with butter, cinnamon, and sugar. Roll up jelly roll fashion; cut in $^1/_2$" slices.

In 9" x 13" pan, combine:

$^1/_2$ cup butter, melted $^1/_2$ cup nuts
1 cup brown sugar

Spread evenly; place rolls on top of mixture and bake at 350° for 30 minutes or till golden brown. Invert pan immediately and remove rolls.

BETTER CAKE MIXES   ··· Mose A. Schlabach
                                    ··· Mrs. Alton (Nora) Nisley

Add to cake mix:
$^3/_4$ cup flour   1 tsp. baking powder
$^1/_2$ cup sugar
Add to batter:
1 egg $^1/_4$ cup water
1 Tbsp. vegetable oil

Follow directions on cake box. The above ingredients would be added extra. A tip for better cake mixes. "This is what Freda used," writes Mose.

TWO-BANANA CAKE – VERY GOOD!
                                    ··· Mrs. Marvin (Martha) Mast

1 cup shortening   1 tsp. soda
2 cups white sugar   1 tsp. baking powder
2 eggs $^1/_4$ tsp. salt
1 cup sour milk   1 tsp. vanilla
3 cups cake flour   2 large or 3 small bananas, mashed

Cream shortening and sugar; beat in eggs. Dissolve soda in sour milk; sift dry ingredients together and add alternately to mixture. Add vanilla and mashed bananas last. Bake at 350° till cake tests done.

EMMA YELLOW CAKE
... *Mrs. Henry (Emma) Troyer*

2 cups white sugar
3 eggs
$1/2$ cup butter
1 cup sweet milk
    Bake at 350°.

3 tsp. baking powder
3 cups flour
vanilla
any flavoring – orange rind is good

GLAZED ORANGE CAKE
... *Mrs. Mary Esta Yoder*

2 cups sifted flour
$2^1/2$ tsp. baking powder
$1/4$ tsp. soda
$1/4$ tsp. salt
$1/2$ cup butter

1 cup sugar
$1/2$ cup nuts
1 Tbsp. grated orange rind
2 eggs, beaten
$3/4$ cup sour cream

GLAZE
1 cup sugar
$1/2$ cup strained orange juice

Mix and sift dry ingredients. Cream butter; add sugar and beat until fluffy. Add beaten eggs, rind, and nuts. Mix well. Add dry ingredients alternately with sour cream. Mix just enough after each addition to keep batter smooth. Put in greased 9" square pan. Bake at 350°.

Combine glaze ingredients and boil 5 minutes. Pour over hot cake.

CHOCAROON CAKE
... *Mrs. Linda Mae Troyer*

2 egg whites
$1/3$ cup sugar
2 Tbsp. flour
$1^3/4$ cups coconut
1 pkg. chocolate cake mix

1 pkg. chocolate instant pudding
2 eggs
2 egg yolks
$1^1/4$ cups water
$1/3$ cup oil

Beat egg whites until foamy. Gradually add sugar and beat until mixture forms stiff, shiny peaks. Blend in flour and coconut; set aside. Combine remaining ingredients in large bowl. Blend, then beat at medium speed for 2 minutes. Pour $1/3$ of batter into a greased and floured 10" bundt pan. Spoon in coconut mixture and top with remaining batter. Bake at 350° for 50–55 minutes or until cake springs back in center. Cool about 15 minutes. Remove from pan and finish cooling on rack. Top with glaze.

GLAZE
Gradually add about 1 Tbsp. milk to 1 cup powdered sugar in a bowl. Makes $1/3$ cup.

EASY LEMON POUND CAKE

··· *Mrs. Richard (Wilma) Schlabach*

2 Tbsp. melted butter
1/2 cup chopped nuts
1/2 cup coconut
1 lemon cake mix
1 cup sour cream

4 eggs
1/4 cup water
2 Tbsp. vegetable oil
1 cup powdered sugar
2 Tbsp. lemon juice

Combine first 3 ingredients and press into greased bundt pan. Beat next 5 ingredients and pour over crumbs. Bake at 350° for 45–50 minutes. Mix last 2 ingredients and drizzle over warm cake.

JIFFY CHOCOLATE CAKE

··· *Mrs. Henry (Emma) Troyer*

1 egg
1 cup sugar
1/2 cup shortening or oleo
2 cups sifted flour
1/2 cup buttermilk

1 tsp. soda
1/2 cup boiling water
1 tsp. vanilla
1/2 tsp. salt
1/2 cup chocolate chips

Combine all ingredients in a bowl in order given, except chocolate chips. Do not beat or mix any ingredients until all are together. Beat until well blended, then add chocolate chips and stir until they are well covered. Bake in well greased 8" x 8" x 2" cake pan, or bake as cupcakes. Bake in 350° oven about 30 minutes for cake; 18 or 20 minutes for cupcakes.

FUDGE CAKE

··· *Mrs. Owen (Ada) Schlabach*

3/4 cup butter or margarine
2 1/4 cups sugar
1 1/2 tsp. vanilla
3 eggs
3 oz. unsweetened chocolate, melted

3 cups cake flour sifted with
   1 1/2 tsp. soda
3/4 tsp. salt
1 1/2 cups ice water

Cream butter, sugar, and vanilla. Add eggs, beating until light and fluffy. Blend in melted chocolate. Add dry ingredients alternately with ice water. Makes large loaf cake or 3 - 8" layers. Bake at 350° for 30–35 minutes.

I made this cake many times while the family was growing up.

DELUXE CHOCOLATE CHERRY CAKE

··· *Mrs. Mary Esta Yoder*

1 box Duncan Hines chocolate
    cake mix

2 eggs
1 can cherry pie filling

CREAM CHEESE ICING

8 oz. cream cheese
$^1/_2$ cup margarine

powdered sugar

Mix cake mix, eggs, and pie filling. Bake in 9" x 13" cake pan at 350° for 25–30 minutes. When cool, frost with Cream Cheese Icing.

AUNT SARAH'S CHOCOLATE CAKE

··· *Mrs. Floyd (Marlene) Yoder* ··· *Rhonda Rittenhouse*

$1^1/_3$ cups white sugar
2 eggs
$1^1/_2$ cups flour
1 tsp. baking powder
1 tsp. soda

$^1/_2$ tsp. salt
$^1/_2$ cup cocoa
1 cup hot water
1 tsp. vanilla
$^1/_2$ cup Wesson oil

Beat oil, eggs, and sugar together. Add remaining ingredients; mix well. Pour into a 13" x 9" greased and floured pan. Bake at 350° for 35 minutes.

CHOCOLATE CAKE

··· *favorite of Marlin A. Yoder*

3 cups brown sugar
1 cup shortening
3 eggs
$^1/_2$ cup cocoa
vanilla

4 cups flour
4 tsp. soda
1 cup sour milk
1 cup boiling water

Cream sugar and shortening together. Beat in eggs. Add flour, cocoa, soda, and sour milk. Beat until smooth. Add boiling water last. Bake at 350°.

Whistle and hoe, sing as you go;
Shorten the row by the songs you know.

TEXAS SHEET CAKE

... Mrs. Albert (Verna) Yoder
... favorite of Jeremy (Jim) Schlabach

1 cup oleo
1 cup water
4 Tbsp. cocoa
2 cups sugar
2 cups flour

1 tsp. vanilla
2 eggs
$^1/_2$ cup sour cream or milk
$^1/_2$ tsp. salt
1 tsp. soda

Melt oleo in saucepan. Add water and cocoa. Bring to a boil and add remaining ingredients, stirring lightly. Pour into greased and floured 10" x 15" cookie sheet. Bake at 375° for 15–20 minutes. While cake is baking, prepare icing.

ICING

$^1/_2$ cup oleo
4 Tbsp. cocoa
1 lb. powdered sugar

6 Tbsp. milk
1 tsp. vanilla
$^1/_2$ cup nuts

Boil together milk, oleo, and cocoa. Add powdered sugar and vanilla. Spread on cake while warm. Sprinkle nuts on top.

PEANUT BUTTER SHEET CAKE

... Mrs. Emanuel (Mary) Nisley

1 stick oleo or butter
$^1/_2$ cup peanut butter

1 cup water
$^1/_2$ cup cooking oil

Bring to a boil; take off heat. Add mixture to following ingredients:

2 eggs, slightly beaten
$^1/_2$ cup milk
2 cups sugar

1 tsp. soda
1 tsp. vanilla
2 cups flour

Stir until well mixed. Pour in greased jelly roll pan. Bake at 350° for 20 minutes or until well done.

PEANUT BUTTER FROSTING

$^1/_2$ cup butter
$^1/_2$ cup peanut butter

$^1/_3$ cup milk

Cook over medium heat until ingredients come to a boil. Remove from heat and add:

1 tsp. vanilla

enough powdered sugar to spread on cake

ALASKA SHEET CAKE
... Mrs. Wayne (Emma) Yoder

2¹/₂ cups flour
2 cups white sugar
1 tsp. soda
1 tsp. salt

1 cup oleo
1 cup water
3 eggs
¹/₂ cup buttermilk

Bring oleo and water to a boil. Add dry ingredients; mix well. Add eggs and buttermilk. Bake in a large cookie sheet at 375° for 20 minutes.

FROSTING

¹/₂ cup oleo
3 Tbsp. milk

Bring to a boil and add:

1 lb. powdered sugar
1 tsp. vanilla

Spread on cake while warm. Spread coconut or nuts on top.

BEST EVER CAKE
... Rosanna Nisley

2 cups granulated sugar
2 cups flour
1 cup chopped nuts
2 tsp. soda

1 tsp. vanilla
2 eggs
1 - #2 (20 oz.) can crushed pineapple

Put in mixer or mix well with spoon. Pour in 9" x 13" pan, well greased and floured. Bake at 350° for 45 minutes. Ice cake while hot.

PHILADELPHIA CREAM CHEESE ICING

1 - 8 oz. pkg. cream cheese
¹/₂ stick butter
2 cups powdered sugar

1 tsp. vanilla or lemon extract
¹/₂ cup nuts

Mix well and spread on cake.

APPLE BUTTER CAKE
... Mrs. Emanuel (Mary) Nisley (from Mother's cookbook)

1 cup sugar
¹/₂ cup butter
4 eggs
4 Tbsp. sour milk

2 cups flour
1 cup apple butter
1 tsp. each of cinnamon, nutmeg,
    cloves, allspice, and soda

Dissolve soda in milk. Don't put apple butter into batter till ready to bake.

TROPICAL CARROT CAKE   ··· Mrs. Linda Mae Troyer

3 eggs, beaten
3/4 cup vegetable oil
2 tsp. vanilla
3/4 cup buttermilk
2 cups white sugar
2 cups all-purpose flour
2 tsp. soda
1/2 tsp. salt

1 tsp. cinnamon
1 - 8 oz. can crushed pineapple, undrained
2 cups finely shredded carrots
1 cup raisins
1 cup nuts
1 cup coconut

Combine eggs, oil, buttermilk, sugar, and vanilla; mix well. Combine dry ingredients; stir into egg mixture. Stir in pineapple, carrots, raisins, nuts, and coconut. Pour into a greased and floured 13" x 9" pan. Bake at 350° for 50–55 minutes. Do not overbake.

CREAM CHEESE ICING

1/2 cup butter
1 tsp. vanilla
2 Tbsp. heavy cream

8 oz. cream cheese
16 oz. powdered sugar

Combine all frosting ingredients and beat until creamy. Spread on cooled cake.

APPLESAUCE WALNUT CAKE

··· Mrs. Freeman (Marie) Schlabach

1 butter recipe Golden Cake mix
1 stick oleo
1 1/3 cups applesauce

3 eggs
1 tsp. cinnamon
2 1/4 cups chopped black walnuts

Beat all ingredients together and bake at 375° till cake tests done. Serve with brown sugar frosting.

CARAMEL APPLE CAKE   ··· Mrs. Jason (Fern) Schlabach

1 1/2 cups vegetable oil
1 1/2 cups white sugar
1/2 cup brown sugar
3 eggs
3 cups flour
2 tsp. vanilla

2 tsp. cinnamon
1/2 tsp. nutmeg
1 tsp. soda
1/2 tsp. salt
3 1/2 cups peeled and shredded apples

Mix in order given. Bake for 1 1/2 hours in bundt cake pan. Ice with favorite caramel icing. Delicious!

FRESH APPLE CAKE ··· *Mrs. Robert (Audrey) Schlabach*

$^1/_2$ cup margarine
1 cup brown sugar
1 egg, beaten
1$^1/_2$ cups flour

1 tsp. cinnamon
1 tsp. soda
$^1/_4$ tsp. salt
2 cups peeled, chopped apples

TOPPING

$^1/_4$ cup brown sugar
1 Tbsp. margarine

$^1/_4$ cup chopped nuts

Cream together margarine and brown sugar. Add egg. Sift together flour, cinnamon, soda, and salt. Add to creamed mixture and fold in apples. Pour into greased 9" x 9" pan. Sprinkle with topping. Bake at 350° for 30–35 minutes.

GERMAN APPLE CAKE ··· *Mrs. Owen (Elsie) Nisley*

2 eggs
2 cups sugar
$^3/_4$ cup oil plus $^1/_4$ cup water
1 tsp. vanilla
1 tsp. soda

$^1/_2$ tsp. salt
2 tsp. cinnamon
2 cups sifted flour
4 cups apples, thickly sliced
$^1/_2$ to 1 cup English walnuts

Mix all ingredients together with a spoon. Do not use mixer. Batter will be stiff. Spread into greased and floured 13" x 9" pan. Bake at 350° for 45–60 minutes. Make a powdered sugar frosting and mix in some peanut butter. Spread on cake while still warm.

KNOBBY APPLE CAKE ··· *Mrs. Owen (Ada) Schlabach*

3 Tbsp. butter
1 cup sugar
1 egg, beaten
$^1/_2$ tsp. cinnamon
$^1/_2$ tsp. salt

1 tsp. soda
1 cup sifted flour
3 cups diced apples
$^1/_4$ cup chopped nuts
1 tsp. vanilla

Cream butter and sugar; add egg and mix well. Sift dry ingredients together; add to creamed mixture. Stir in diced apples, nuts, and vanilla. Pour into greased 8" x 8" x 2" pan. Bake at 350° for 40–45 minutes. Serve hot or cold, with or without whipped cream or ice cream. Makes 8 to 9 servings.

ALMOND JOY CAKE

··· *Mrs. Mary Esta Yoder*

1 box chocolate cake mix with
  pudding
1 cup evaporated milk
1 cup white sugar
24 large marshmallows
14 oz. coconut

$^1/_2$ cup butter or oleo
$^1/_2$ cup evaporated milk
1$^1/_2$ cups white sugar
1$^1/_2$ cups chocolate chips
chopped pecans (optional)

Mix cake mix as directed on box. Bake in a cookie sheet. When done, cool 10 minutes; invert onto tray. Mix together 1 cup milk, 1 cup sugar, and marshmallows. Heat till marshmallows are melted; add coconut. Spread over top of cake while still warm. Heat remaining sugar, milk, and butter; add chocolate chips. Stir until melted. Add nuts if desired. Spread on cake, top and sides.

HO-HO CAKE

··· *Mrs. Wayne (Emma) Yoder*

2 cups white sugar
3 cups flour
$^2/_3$ cup cocoa
$^1/_2$ tsp. salt
1 cup sour milk

1 cup salad oil
3 eggs
2 tsp. soda
1 cup boiling water

FROSTING

$^1/_2$ cup margarine
$^1/_2$ cup shortening
1 cup white sugar
1 tsp. vanilla
$^1/_2$ cup hot milk

$^1/_2$ cup melted margarine
1 cup brown sugar
3 Tbsp. cocoa
$^1/_3$ cup milk
1$^1/_2$ cups powdered sugar

Mix together flour, sugar, cocoa, and salt. Add sour milk and oil, 1 whole egg, and 2 egg yolks. Combine soda with boiling water and add to mixture. Pour into sheet pan and bake at 350° for 25 minutes. Mix together shortening, margarine, sugar, and vanilla until fluffy. Add hot milk 1 Tbsp. at a time, beating with each addition. This is very important. If it gets watery, it is not beaten enough and will not stay on cake. Place filling on cooled cake. Combine brown sugar and cocoa with melted margarine, then add milk. Bring to a boil and cool a little. Add powdered sugar and drizzle over top of cake.

TURTLE CAKE
... favorite of Reuben Miller

1 - 14 oz. pkg. caramels
1 stick oleo
1 can Eagle Brand milk

1 chocolate cake mix
6 oz. semisweet chocolate chips
6 oz. chopped pecans or walnuts

Melt caramels, oleo, and Eagle Brand milk over low heat. Cool before pouring on cake. Mix cake according to directions. Pour half of cake batter into greased pan. Bake at 350° until done. Remove from oven and pour cooled caramel mixture on top. Spoon remaining batter on top. Sprinkle with nuts and chocolate chips. Finish baking at 350° for 20 minutes, then at 250° for 10 minutes. My favorite!

PRALINE CRUNCH CAKE
... Mrs. Linda Mae Troyer

2 cups flour
1 1/4 cups sugar
2 tsp. baking powder
2 tsp. instant coffee crystals
1 tsp. salt

1 cup milk
1/2 cup melted butter
2 eggs, beaten
2 Tbsp. molasses
1 tsp. vanilla

CRUNCH TOPPING
1/4 cup flour
2 Tbsp. brown sugar

2 Tbsp. butter

FROSTING
2 Tbsp. butter
2 Tbsp. milk
1 tsp. instant coffee crystals

1 tsp. vanilla
1 1/2 cups powdered sugar

Stir together flour, sugar, baking powder, coffee, and salt. Beat in milk, butter, eggs, molasses, and vanilla. Pour into greased 13" x 9" pan; bake at 350° for 40–45 minutes. Frost when cool, then sprinkle with Crunch Topping.

For Crunch Topping, mix together and press into a pie pan. Bake 15 minutes; cool and break apart.

For frosting, beat together butter, milk, coffee, and vanilla. Blend in powdered sugar.

*For he satisfieth the thirsty and fills the hungry
with good things. Psalm 107:9*

SNICKER CAKE
··· Julia Yoder

1 chocolate cake mix
1 pkg. caramels
$^1/_3$ cup milk

1 stick oleo
$^3/_4$ cup nuts
$^3/_4$ cup chocolate chips

Prepare cake mix according to package directions. Pour half of batter in pan. Bake at 350° for 20 minutes. Melt caramels with oleo and milk; pour over baked cake. Sprinkle chocolate chips and nuts on top. Dot on remaining batter. Return to oven and bake 7 minutes at 350° and 20 minutes at 250°. Serve with Cool Whip or ice cream.

EARTHQUAKE CAKE
··· Mrs. Linda Mae Troyer

$1^1/_2$ cups pecans, chopped
1 - 3 oz. can coconut
   Mix until smooth:
1 - 8 oz. pkg. cream cheese
1 stick margarine, melted

1 box German chocolate cake mix
   (according to directions)

1 lb. ($3^1/_2$ cups) powdered sugar

Put pecans in bottom of 9" x 13" pan. Spread coconut over pecans. Pour cake mix over coconut and pecans. Spread cream cheese mixture over cake mix. Bake at 350° for 45 minutes to 1 hour.

COCONUT CHIFFON CAKE
··· Mrs. Henry (Emma) Troyer

STEP 1

2 cups sifted flour
$1^1/_2$ cups sugar
   Make a well and add, in order:
$^1/_2$ cup cooking oil
7 unbeaten egg yolks

1 tsp. salt
3 tsp. baking powder

$^3/_4$ cup cold water
1 tsp. vanilla

Beat with spoon until smooth. Do not overbeat.

STEP 2

Measure into large mixing bowl:
1 cup egg whites $^1/_2$ tsp. cream of tartar
Whip until whites form very stiff peaks.

STEP 3

Pour egg yolk mixture over egg whites, gently folding with rubber scraper just until blended. Fold in $^3/_4$ cup coconut. Bake in ungreased 10" tube pan.

CHAMPION SPONGE CAKE ··· *Mrs. Emanuel (Mary) Nisley*

$1^1/_2$ cups sifted flour

1 cup sugar

$^1/_2$ tsp. baking powder

$^1/_2$ tsp. salt

6 egg yolks

$^1/_4$ cup water

6 egg whites

1 tsp. cream of tartar

$^1/_2$ cup sugar

1 tsp. vanilla

Sift together flour, 1 cup sugar, baking powder, and salt. In large mixing bowl, beat egg whites until frothy. Add cream of tartar. Gradually beat in $^1/_2$ cup sugar. Beat until it forms stiff, not dry, peaks. In small bowl, combine egg yolks, water, vanilla, and sifted dry ingredients. Beat until light and fluffy. Fold yolk mixture gently but thoroughly into the beaten egg whites. Turn into an ungreased 10" tube pan. Bake at 350° for about 45 minutes. Invert pan to cool. Frost with Creamy Pineapple Frosting.

CREAMY PINEAPPLE FROSTING

Cream scant $^1/_2$ cup butter; gradually add 3 cups powdered sugar. Beat until light and fluffy. Blend in 1 - $8^1/_2$ oz. can well drained crushed pineapple, $^1/_2$ tsp. salt, $^1/_2$ tsp. vanilla, and $^1/_2$ tsp. grated lemon rind.

DAFFODIL ANGEL CAKE   ··· *Mrs. Mary Esta Yoder*

2 cups egg whites

$1^1/_2$ tsp. cream of tartar

$1^1/_3$ cups white sugar

1 tsp. salt

$^1/_2$ tsp. vanilla

$1^1/_2$ cups cake flour

$^1/_2$ cup sugar

6 to 8 egg yolks

Beat egg whites and cream of tartar until very stiff (egg whites don't slide out of bowl held upside down). Add sugar, salt, and vanilla. Beat well, then fold in flour sifted with $^1/_2$ cup sugar. In separate bowl, beat egg yolks until thick and lemon colored. Fold in half of the egg white mixture. Alternate white and yellow mixtures in 10" tube cake pan. Bake at 350° for 50–55 minutes on low rack.

Honey from the comb is sweet to your taste.
Know also that wisdom is sweet to your soul.
Proverbs 24:13 and 14b

WEST VIRGINIA BLACKBERRY CAKE

··· Mrs. Freeman (Marie) Schlabach

2 cups sugar	1 tsp. cinnamon
1 cup butter	1 tsp. soda
4 eggs	1 tsp. baking powder
3 cups flour	1 cup buttermilk
1 tsp. cloves	1 1/2 cups fresh or frozen drained
1 tsp. nutmeg	blackberries or black raspberries

Cream butter and sugar; add eggs. Mix flour and spices, soda, and baking powder. Beat in alternately with buttermilk. Fold in berries. Bake in 3 layer pans at 350° for 30 minutes.

FROSTING

Beat:

1 cup oleo	1 lb. powdered sugar
3 Tbsp. cold coffee	1 tsp. vanilla

PEACHY SOUR CREAM COFFEE CAKE

··· Mrs. Jim (Ruth) Schlabach

STREUSEL TOPPING

2 cups chopped pecans	1 tsp. ground cinnamon
3 Tbsp. sugar	1/2 cup packed brown sugar

CAKE

1/2 cup butter flavored shortening	1 cup sugar
2 cups all-purpose flour	2 eggs
1 1/2 tsp. baking powder	1/2 tsp. baking soda
1/2 tsp. salt	1 cup sour cream
1 tsp. vanilla extract	2 cups sliced peaches

Combine all streusel ingredients; set aside. In a large mixing bowl, cream shortening and sugar until fluffy. Beat in 2 eggs; combine all dry ingredients. Add alternately with the sour cream and vanilla to the creamed mixture. Beat until smooth. Add peaches. Pour half the batter into a 9" springform pan. Sprinkle with 1 cup of the streusel. Top with remaining batter and 1/2 cup streusel. Bake at 350° for 40 minutes or until done. Cool 10 minutes before removing sides of pan.

GRAHAM STREUSEL COFFEE CAKE

··· *Mrs. Willis (Ruth) Schlabach*

1 yellow cake mix	3 eggs
$^1/_3$ cup oil	1 cup water

Mix together and pour into 13" x 9" cake pan.

CRUMBS

2 cups graham cracker crumbs	$^3/_4$ cup butter
$^3/_4$ cup nuts (optional)	$1^1/_2$ tsp. cinnamon
$^3/_4$ cup brown sugar	

Sprinkle on top of cake mix. Bake at 350° for 30 minutes. Glaze with 1 cup powdered sugar and 1 to 2 Tbsp. water.

GOOD EVENING COFFEE CAKE   ··· *Owen A. Yoder*

$1^1/_2$ cups sifted flour	$^1/_4$ cup lard or oleo
2 tsp. baking powder	1 egg, beaten
$^1/_2$ tsp. salt	$^1/_2$ cup milk
$^1/_2$ cup sugar	1 tsp. vanilla

TOPPING MIXTURE

$^1/_2$ cup brown sugar	3 Tbsp. butter
2 Tbsp. flour	$^1/_2$ cup chocolate chips
1 tsp. cinnamon	$^1/_2$ cup nuts, if desired

Mix first part together like you would a cake; beat well. Spread half of batter in greased pan. Cover with half of topping mixture. Put rest of batter over this and cover with remaining topping mixture. Bake at 375°. Serve warm with milk and fresh or frozen strawberries. Delicious!

COFFEE CAKE   ··· *Mrs. Wayne (Emma) Yoder*

1 box yellow cake mix	1 cup plus 1 Tbsp. vegetable oil
1 box instant vanilla pudding	4 eggs
1 box instant butterscotch pudding	1 cup water

TOPPING

1 cup brown sugar	2 Tbsp. cinnamon
$^1/_2$ cup nuts	

Mix all together well. Pour into 9" x 13" cake pan. Put topping on top and bake at 350° till done.

NEW ENGLAND BLUEBERRY COFFEE CAKE

··· *Mrs. Freeman (Marie) Schlabach*

1 1/2 cups flour
1/2 cup sugar
1 Tbsp. baking powder
1 tsp. cinnamon
1/2 tsp. salt

1 1/2 cups fresh blueberries
1 egg
1/2 cup milk
1/4 cup butter, melted

In a large bowl, combine flour, sugar, baking powder, cinnamon, and salt. Gently fold in berries. In small bowl, whisk together egg, milk, and butter. Add carefully to flour mixture. Spread in 8" x 8" baking pan. Combine and sprinkle over batter:

1/4 cup melted butter
3/4 cup brown sugar

1 Tbsp. flour
1/2 cup chopped nuts

Bake at 425° for 20–25 minutes or till golden brown. Makes 12 servings.

CINNAMON SOUR CREAM COFFEE CAKE

··· *Naomi and Willard Schlabach, Zak and Jordan*

1/2 cup soft margarine
1 cup sugar
2 eggs
1 cup sour cream

2 cups flour
1 tsp. baking powder
1/2 tsp. soda

TOPPING

3/4 cup chopped pecans
1/4 cup brown sugar

2 tsp. cinnamon

Cream margarine and add remaining ingredients, adding sour cream last. In small bowl, mix topping ingredients. Grease pan/bundt pan and spoon in batter, adding topping last. Bake at 350° for 1 hour.

MARY BIG CAKE

··· *Mrs. Emanuel Nisley (from Mother's cookbook)*

1 cup sugar
2 eggs
1/2 cup sweet milk
1/2 cup sweet cream

1 tsp. soda
2 tsp. baking powder
enough flour to make a soft dough

Can be used for shortcake.

COFFEE CAKE   *... Mrs. Mary Kaufman*

1 cup white sugar
1/2 cup shortening
1 egg
1 tsp. soda (mixed in)

1 cup buttermilk or sour milk
1/4 tsp. salt
2 cups flour
1 tsp. baking powder

CRUMBS

1 cup brown sugar
3 Tbsp. butter

2 Tbsp. flour
1 tsp. cinnamon

Cream shortening, sugar, and egg. Add dry ingredients alternately with milk and soda. Pour half of batter into greased pan. Sprinkle half of crumbs. Put remaining batter on top. Sprinkle rest of crumbs. Bake at 350° for approximately 40 minutes.

STRAWBERRY SHORTCAKE   *... Mrs. Albert (Verna) Yoder*

1 cup sour cream
2 eggs
1 tsp. cream of tartar

1 tsp. soda
1 cup white sugar
2 cups flour

If I don't have sour cream, I use 1/2 cup butter or oleo and milk, with the same results. Mix well and bake at 350°. Serve warm with milk and strawberries!

MY OWN HEALTHY SHORTCAKE

... Mrs. Owen (Ada) Schlabach

1 cup whole wheat flour
1/2 cup oat flour
1/2 cup fructose (fruit sugar)
  Sift together and add:
1 Tbsp. vinegar
1 Tbsp. vanilla

1/4 tsp. salt
2 tsp. soda

1/4 cup oil (applesauce is good, too)
1 cup cold water

Mix all together well; no need to beat. Pour in 8" square pan. Bake at 350° for 25–30 minutes. We like this with fruit and milk for supper.

PUMPKIN GEMS   ··· *Mrs. Linda Mae Troyer*

1 pkg. yellow cake mix
3 eggs
$^1/_2$ cup oil

1 tsp. soda
2 tsp. cinnamon
1 - 20 oz. can pumpkin

FROSTING

1 - 8 oz. pkg. cream cheese,
   softened
1 cup butter, softened

$^1/_2$ tsp. vanilla
1 Tbsp. milk
2 cups powdered sugar

Preheat oven to 350°. Blend together all ingredients. Fill paper mini-muffin pans $^2/_3$ full. Bake 15 minutes. Cool, then frost.

Frosting: Cream together butter and cream cheese; beat in vanilla and milk. Gradually add powdered sugar, until frosting is desired consistency. Great to serve at a tea party. Yield: 100 mini cupcakes.

PUMPKIN ROLL   ··· *Mrs. Marion (Rachel) Mullet*

5 eggs, separated
$1^1/_2$ cups sugar
1 cup pumpkin
$1^1/_4$ cups flour

$1^1/_2$ tsp. salt
$1^1/_2$ tsp. soda
$1^1/_2$ tsp. cinnamon
1 cup chopped nuts (optional)

Sift flour, soda, salt, and cinnamon together. Beat egg whites till soft peaks form. Gradually add the sugar, continuing to beat till stiff peaks form. Beat egg yolks at high speed till thick and foamy. Add pumpkin to yolks; fold gently into egg whites. Fold in dry ingredients gently, but thoroughly. Grease a large $12^1/_2$" x $17^1/_4$" cookie sheet. Line with waxed paper. I usually lightly grease and flour the waxed paper. Pour batter in pan and spread evenly. Sprinkle with nuts. Bake at 400° for 12–15 minutes. Loosen edges and turn hot cake onto towel dusted with powdered sugar. Remove waxed paper. Roll up with towel while still warm and let cool. Unroll and fill with the following:

FILLING

2 Tbsp. margarine
8 oz. cream cheese, softened
1 tsp. vanilla

2 cups powdered sugar
whipped topping

Mix ingredients until creamy. Add whipped topping last. Refrigerate.

BLACK BOTTOM CUPCAKES

... Mrs. Firman (Deborah) Miller

1 - 8 oz. pkg. cream cheese
$1/2$ cup sugar
$1/8$ tsp. salt

1 egg
$3/4$ cup chocolate chips

Have cream cheese at room temperature. Combine cheese, egg, sugar, and salt. Stir in chocolate chips. Set aside.

$1 1/2$ cups sifted flour
1 cup sugar
$1/4$ cup cocoa
$1/2$ tsp. salt
1 tsp. soda dissolved in 1 Tbsp. vinegar

1 tsp. vanilla
$1/3$ cup cooking oil
1 cup water

Mix dry ingredients. Add water, oil, vinegar, and vanilla. Mix well. Fill cupcake papers $1/3$ full with chocolate batter. Place a heaping tsp. of cheese mixture in center of batter. Sprinkle tops with sugar and nuts (optional). Bake at 350° for 30–35 minutes. Yields 24. This can also be made into a cake.

EASY CHOCOLATE ROLL-UP

... Mrs. Linda Mae Troyer

$1/4$ cup butter
1 cup chopped pecans

$1 1/3$ cups coconut
1 - $15 1/2$ oz. can Eagle Brand milk

CAKE

3 eggs
1 cup white sugar
$1/3$ cup cocoa
$2/3$ cup all-purpose flour

$1/4$ tsp. salt
$1/4$ tsp. soda
$1/3$ cup water
1 tsp. vanilla

Line 15" x 10" jelly roll pan with waxed paper. Melt butter in pan. Sprinkle nuts and coconut evenly in pan; drizzle with Eagle Brand milk.

Cake: Beat eggs thoroughly 2 minutes, until fluffy. Gradually add sugar. Continue beating 2 minutes. Add remaining ingredients; blend 1 minute. Pour evenly into pan. Bake at 375° for 20–25 minutes, until cake springs back when touched in center. When done, invert onto a towel dusted with powdered sugar. Remove waxed paper. Roll up jelly roll fashion, using towel to roll cake.

They who indulge, bulge!

CHOCOLATE CAKE ROLL
··· *Mrs. Lloyd (Bena) Miller*

$^1/_2$ cup all-purpose flour
$^1/_3$ cup cocoa
$^1/_2$ tsp. baking soda
$^1/_2$ tsp. salt

4 eggs, separated
$^3/_4$ cup sugar
1 tsp. vanilla
vanilla ice cream

Sift flour, cocoa, soda, and salt; set aside. Beat egg whites until soft peaks form. Gradually add sugar, continuing to beat until stiff peaks form. Beat egg yolks at high speed until thick and foamy. Blend in vanilla; fold gently into egg whites. Fold in dry ingredients gently but thoroughly. Put waxed paper in pan. Pour batter into pan; spread evenly. Bake 12 minutes at 400°. Loosen edges and turn hot cake onto towel dusted with powdered sugar. Roll up cake with towel from wide end. Cool completely; unroll and spread with softened ice cream. Reroll; wrap in waxed paper and freeze until ready to serve. For a yellow cake roll, use $^1/_3$ cup flour instead of cocoa.

Variation: Use cream stick filling instead of ice cream.

WAYNE BETTY'S ICING
··· *Mrs. Mary Kaufman*

3 cups Crisco
3 cups white sugar
butter flavoring

vanilla flavoring
9 Tbsp. flour
2 cups milk

Heat flour and milk till thick. Beat Crisco and sugar lightly, then add milk mixture (which has been cooled slightly). Beat at high speed for 5–10 minutes. Add butter flavoring and vanilla flavoring (I use butter flavored Crisco instead of butter flavoring). If you want your icing very white, use regular Crisco. This makes a very good cream filling.

CREAM FILLING
··· *Mrs. Mary Esta Yoder*

2 Tbsp. flour
$^1/_2$ cup milk
$^1/_4$ cup margarine
$^1/_4$ cup Crisco

pinch of salt
$^1/_2$ tsp. vanilla
$^1/_2$ cup white sugar

Mix flour and milk until smooth. Cook over low heat until thick, stirring constantly. Cool completely. In a bowl, blend the flour mixture, margarine, and shortening on low speed. Add salt; beat until smooth and fluffy at high speed. Add vanilla and sugar. Beat one more minute on high. I use this for cream rolls, Twinkies, Ho-Ho Cake, and coffee cakes. Freezes well.

BUTTER ICING   ... *Mrs. Mary Esta Yoder*

Brown $^1/_4$ cup butter. Stir in $^3/_4$ cup powdered sugar. Add $^1/_2$ tsp. vanilla and a dash of salt. Add $^3/_4$ cup powdered sugar alternately with $2^1/_4$ Tbsp. cream, beating smooth after each addition. I use this as a glaze for angel food cake.

NEVER FAIL CARAMEL FROSTING

... *Mrs. Ammon (Esta) Brenneman* ... *Mrs. Jr. (Ruth) Miller*

$^1/_2$ cup butter	$1^1/_2$ to 2 cups powdered sugar
1 cup brown sugar	$^1/_8$ tsp. salt
$^1/_4$ cup milk	

Melt butter. Add brown sugar and milk. Boil 2 minutes. Remove from heat; add powdered sugar. Stir until smooth. If mixture is too thick, add a little milk. It will not crack or be sticky. Enough for 2 - 9" cakes.

CARAMEL ICING   ... *Mrs. Linda Mae Troyer*

$1^1/_2$ cups brown sugar	$^1/_4$ tsp. salt
3 Tbsp. butter	1 tsp. vanilla
$^1/_2$ cup milk	3 cups powdered sugar

In a saucepan, combine sugar, salt, milk, butter, and vanilla; cook 5 minutes. Cool slightly. Add powdered sugar and beat until smooth.

CHOCOLATE ICING   ... *Mrs. Linda Mae Troyer*

$^1/_3$ cup butter	2 Tbsp. cocoa
$^1/_2$ cup brown sugar	$^1/_4$ cup milk

Boil until large bubbles form. Cool and add powdered sugar to thicken. This is very good on a Ho-Ho Cake.

CHOCOLATE GLAZE   ... *Mrs. Mary Esta Yoder*

In double boiler over hot, not boiling, water, melt:

$^1/_2$ cup semisweet chocolate chips	$1^1/_2$ tsp. light corn syrup
1 Tbsp. butter	$1^1/_2$ tsp. milk

Stir until smooth. Drizzle over cakes, cream rolls, and cookies.

COCONUT PECAN FROSTING

... Mrs. Freeman (Naomi) Miller ... Mrs. Mary Kaufman

1 cup evaporated milk

1 cup sugar

3 egg yolks

1/2 cup butter or oleo

1 tsp. vanilla

1/3 cup angel flake coconut

1 cup chopped pecans or walnuts

Combine milk, sugar, egg yolks, butter, and vanilla in saucepan. Cook over medium heat until mixture thickens. When mixture has cooled, add coconut and pecans. This icing is especially good on chocolate or oatmeal cake, and on top and between layers of German chocolate cake.

CHURCH SUCCESS CAKE

... Mrs. Owen Schlabach

10 pkg. happy church members

1 sorehead, well boiled, handled with care

1 pkg. members who don't fizzle out when something does not suit them

1 pkg. members who don't criticize a job they would not think of doing themselves

1 pkg. shut-ins who need our gifts and prayers

1 pkg. future generations

1 cup kindness and love

1 cup oil of peace

1 cup flour of forgiveness

5 cups power of prayer of the Holy Spirit

1 pkg. members who contribute regularly, not just when the notion comes

Season with humor and the spice of life in Christ. Avoid cheap, poisonous substitutes, like idle gossip and petty jealousies. Stir all ingredients together vigorously in the bowl of good fellowship until they form a smooth, rich mixture. Add yeast of patient hope. Let rise until ready. Bake during a warmhearted worship service. Cut into pieces as needed and serve to all to nourish and strengthen.

Come to the table, have a good look~
The first to complain is the next meal's cook!

Desserts

*Sharing is such a simple way
of sweetening someone else's day!*

House Blessing

Dear Lord,
    swing the doors
    of our home
        wide
    so all people
        will feel
    welcome
        and loved~
May the floors
        and walls
be strong enough
        to carry the burdens
            of those who come~
We pray
        no one leaves
        feeling less
    than when he entered~
May Your love
        and peace
cover and protect
        as each one departs.   Amen.

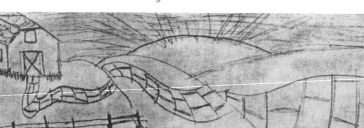

YOGURT
··· *Mrs. Paul M. (Wilma) Schlabach*

1 gal. milk

$^1/_2$ cup cold water

$2^1/_2$ Tbsp. gelatin

1 tsp. vanilla

4 Tbsp. yogurt (vanilla or plain)

$1^3/_4$ cups white sugar

Heat milk to 190°. Cool to 130°. While cooling, soak gelatin in cold water. When milk has cooled to 130°, add gelatin, vanilla, yogurt, and sugar. Strain into jars; put lids on jars and set in oven 8 hours. Makes about $4^1/_2$ qt. Refrigerate and flavor. I use about 2 Tbsp. jello per qt.

JELLO CHEESECAKE
··· *Mrs. Firman (Deborah) Miller*

28 graham crackers, crushed

2 - 3 oz. boxes orange jello

2 - 8 oz. pkg. cream cheese

2 cups Rich's Topping, whipped

$^1/_2$ cup butter, melted

2 cups hot water

$^1/_2$ cup white sugar

Combine graham crackers and butter. Layer bottom of your favorite 9" x 9" pan. Combine jello and hot water; set aside. Cream the cream cheese and white sugar together, then add whipped topping and stir well. Combine this mixture with the jello and let thicken slightly before pouring over the crackers.

OWEN'S FAVORITE BAKED PUDDING
··· *Mrs. Owen (Ada) Schlabach*

Cook together:

$3^1/_2$ cups milk

$^3/_4$ cup sugar

$^1/_3$ cup cornstarch

$^1/_2$ tsp. salt

Beat and add:

2 egg yolks

$^1/_2$ cup milk

Bring to a boil. Take off heat and add:

1 Tbsp. butter

1 tsp. vanilla

You will need 2 egg whites for meringue.

Fix graham cracker crumbs. Save some for top. Put rest in bottom and on sides of pan. Put pudding on crumbs, then meringue; sprinkle remaining crumbs on top. Bake in medium oven until slightly browned on top. Watch carefully so it won't burn.

A note from Mary Esta: I remember Grandma Schlabach made this—she called it "Sweetheart Pudding." Even the name made it delicious!

EASY CUSTARD   ··· *Mrs. Reuben (Betty) Yoder*

1 can Eagle Brand milk   1 tsp. vanilla
4 eggs, beaten   4 cups boiling water
$^1/_2$ tsp. salt

   Mix together and fill greased custard cups. Sprinkle nutmeg on top. Set
cups in a pan of hot water. Bake at 325° for 1 hour and 15 minutes.

CREAM CHEESE SALAD   ··· *Mrs. Linda Mae Troyer*

$1^1/_2$ cups flour   1 - 8 oz. pkg. cream cheese
$^1/_4$ cup brown sugar   1 cup Rich's Topping, whipped
$^1/_2$ cup nuts   1 cup powdered sugar
$^1/_2$ cup oleo   1 cup crushed pineapple (optional)
1 - 3 oz. box orange jello –
    add 1 cup hot water only; jell

   Mix flour, sugar, nuts, and oleo like pie dough. Press in cake pan and
bake 15–20 minutes at 350°. Cool; take a fork and crumble it.

   Beat the topping, softened cream cheese, and powdered sugar together.
Fold in partly jelled jello; add pineapples. Pour this over the crumbs and
chill at least 2 hours. Nuts may be put on top. Fills 1 - 9" x 13" pan.

PINEAPPLE DAPPLE   ··· *Mrs. Mary Esta Yoder*

   Mix:
1 cup graham cracker crumbs $^1/_4$ cup melted butter
2 Tbsp. brown sugar
   Press into an 8" square pan.
1 cup (1 - $8^1/_2$ oz. can)   3 Tbsp. sugar
   pineapple, drained   1 cup Rich's Topping
$1^1/_4$ cups boiling water   1 - 3 oz. pkg. orange jello
$^1/_4$ tsp. orange rind   1 - 3 oz. pkg. cream cheese
$^1/_2$ tsp. vanilla

   Drain pineapple. Dissolve jello in boiling water; add pineapple juice.
Cool. Combine softened cream cheese, sugar, orange rind, and vanilla.
Combine half of the jello and pineapples; set aside. Add rest of jello to
cream cheese mixture. Fold into whipped topping. Pour onto cracker crust;
chill till firm. Spoon pineapple jello mixture on top.

BROKEN GLASS JELLO SALAD

··· *Mrs. Reuben (Betty) Yoder*

3 oz. orange jello   3 oz. cherry jello
3 oz. lime jello
   Prepare each with:
1 cup boiling water $^1/_2$ cup cold water
   Pour each separately in shallow pans. Chill until firm.
   Mix:
1 cup pineapple juice $^1/_4$ cup white sugar
   Cook until dissolved. Add:
3 oz. lemon jello $^1/_2$ cup cold water
   Chill until slightly thickened. Cut the firm jello in $^1/_2$" cubes. Whip 2 cups
whipped topping. Blend in the lemon–pineapple mixture. Fold in jello cubes.
Chill at least 5 hours or overnight.

LAYERED GRAPE JELLO SALAD ··· *Mrs. Mark (Ruth) Miller*
··· *Mrs. Mary Esta Yoder*

3 - 3 oz. boxes grape jello   1 - 8 oz. pkg. cream cheese, softened
$^3/_4$ cup water   1 Tbsp. ReaLemon juice
$^3/_4$ cup sour cream (scant)   1 - 8 oz. pkg. Cool Whip
   Prepare 1 box jello according to package directions. Pour into Tupperware and let set till firm.
   Prepare second box jello with $^3/_4$ cup hot water. When starting to set,
add softened cream cheese, sour cream, lemon juice, and Cool Whip. Mix
well; pour over jello layer.
   Prepare remaining jello according to package directions. When cool and
second layer has set, pour over top and let set.

*Few of us will do great deeds and be remembered by history,
but all of us can do some little things that will
cheer a heart and lighten a day.*

STRAWBERRY JELLO SALAD   ··· Mrs. Lloyd (Bena) Miller
··· Mrs. Marion (Rachel) Mullet ··· Mrs. Reuben (Betty) Yoder

3 - 3 oz. boxes strawberry jello $^1/_2$ cup sugar (omit if strawberries
1 - 8 oz. cream cheese   were sweetened)
1 - 8 oz. container Cool Whip
1 cup crushed strawberries, unsweetened

Prepare 1 box jello as directed on package. Pour into Tupperware square. For second layer: Dissolve 1 box jello in 1 cup hot water; add strawberries and sugar. Mix cream cheese and Cool Whip and fold into jello and strawberries. Pour onto first layer which has been jelled. Prepare last box of jello as directed. When cool, pour onto second layer.

STRAWBERRY PRETZEL DESSERT
··· Mervin and Rhoda Hilty

2 cups finely crushed pretzels   1 - 8 oz. carton Cool Whip
3 Tbsp. sugar   2 cups miniature marshmallows
$^3/_4$ cup melted margarine   6 oz. pkg. strawberry jello
8 oz. cream cheese, softened $2^1/_2$ cups boiling water
$^1/_2$ cup powdered sugar   1 - 10 oz. pkg. strawberries

Mix pretzels, sugar, and margarine. Press into a 9" x 13" pan. Bake at 350° for 15 minutes. Cool. Cream cream cheese and powdered sugar. Fold in Cool Whip. Add marshmallows and spread on cool crust. Dissolve jello in water; stir in strawberries. Chill until slightly thickened. Spread over cream cheese layer; chill overnight.

STRAWBERRY SHORTCAKE   ··· Mrs. Jim (Ruth) Schlabach
··· Mrs. Paul (Rebecca) Nisley

2 eggs $^1/_2$ cup butter
2 cups white sugar   1 cup milk
3 cups flour   3 tsp. baking powder
1 tsp. vanilla

Beat eggs; add melted butter and milk. Stir and add flour, sugar, baking powder, and vanilla. Pour into 2 round cake pans. Bake 25–30 minutes at 350°. Eat with Raw Fruit Dessert (on following page).

RAW FRUIT DESSERT   *... Mrs. Jim (Ruth) Schlabach*

2 pkg. Kool-Aid (any flavor)   7 cups water
3 cups sugar $^1/_3$ cup dry jello

   Boil together. Mix 1 cup clear jel with 1 cup water. Add. Cook till clear
and thick. Cool and use with fresh fruit over Strawberry Shortcake (page
168).

GRAHAM CRACKER FLUFF   *... Mrs. Floyd (Marlene) Yoder*
... Mrs. Wayne (Emma) Yoder

2 eggs, separated   2 tsp. vanilla
$^1/_2$ cup milk   2 cups Rich's Topping
$^3/_4$ cup sugar

GRAHAM CRACKER CRUST

10 graham crackers, crushed fine   3 Tbsp. brown sugar
3 Tbsp. butter

   Dissolve 1 pkg. gelatin in $^1/_3$ cup cold water. Mix milk and sugar; add
beaten egg yolks. Bring to a boil. Remove from heat and add gelatin. Let
mixture cool until slightly thickened. Add beaten egg whites and 2 cups
whipped cream. Pour over graham cracker crust.

   *TIP: Fold whipped topping into beaten egg whites before adding to the
custard mixture.*

GRAPE TAPIOCA   *... Mrs. Mary Esta Yoder*

$2^1/_2$ cups grape juice   pinch of salt
5 Tbsp. seed pearl tapioca   1 cup Rich's Topping
$^1/_2$ cup sugar

   Mix together juice, sugar, tapioca, and salt. Bring to a full boil, stirring
constantly. Remove from heat and chill thoroughly without stirring.

   Mixture will be rather thin. Fold in stiffly beaten topping.

CRANBERRY FLUFF   *... Mrs. Mary Esta Yoder*

2 cups ground, raw cranberries $^1/_2$ cup seedless grapes
$^3/_4$ cup sugar $^1/_4$ tsp. salt
3 cups mini marshmallows $^1/_2$ cup chopped nuts (optional)
2 cups diced, unpared apples   1 cup cream or Rich's Topping

   Combine first 3 ingredients; cover and chill overnight. Add rest of ingredients and fold in whipped cream.

RHUBARB CREAM DELIGHT DESSERT

··· *Mrs. Marion (Rachel) Mullet*

CRUST

1 cup flour

$^1/_4$ cup white sugar

$^1/_2$ cup butter or margarine

RHUBARB LAYER

3 cups fresh rhubarb, cut up

$^1/_2$ cup sugar

1 Tbsp. flour

CREAM LAYER

12 oz. cream cheese, softened

$^1/_2$ cup sugar

2 eggs

TOPPING

8 oz. sour cream

2 Tbsp. sugar

1 tsp. vanilla

For crust, mix flour, sugar, and butter; pat into 10" pie plate. Set aside. Combine rhubarb layer; toss lightly and pour into crust. Bake at 375° for 15 minutes. Meanwhile, prepare cream layer by beating cream cheese and sugar together till fluffy. Beat in eggs, one at a time, then pour over hot rhubarb layer. Bake at 350° for about 30 minutes or until almost set. Combine topping ingredients. Spread over hot layers. Chill. Yield: 12 servings.

RHUBARB CRUNCH

··· *Mrs. Paul (Rebecca) Nisley*

4 cups fresh rhubarb

2 Tbsp. flour

1 cup white sugar

2 Tbsp. butter

1 Tbsp. shortening

1 cup sifted flour

$^1/_4$ tsp. salt

1 cup brown sugar

1 tsp. baking powder

1 large beaten egg

Cut rhubarb in $^1/_2$" lengths. Sift 1 cup white sugar and 2 Tbsp. flour together and mix with the rhubarb. Pour into an 8" or 9" baking pan and dot with butter. Sift remaining sugar and flour together; add shortening, salt, and baking powder. Stir in beaten egg. The mixture will be crumbly. Sprinkle it over the rhubarb and shake the pan a little so the crumbs will settle down in the rhubarb. Bake about 40 minutes at 350° or till the top is nice and brown. Serve with milk. To avoid tartness in rhubarb, soak awhile in water.

APPLE CRISP
... Jeremy Schlabach

$^3/_4$ cup sugar
$^1/_4$ tsp. salt
1 Tbsp. flour
TOPPING
$^3/_4$ cup oatmeal
$^3/_4$ cup flour
$^1/_4$ tsp. soda

$^1/_2$ tsp. cinnamon
4 cups sliced apples

$^1/_2$ cup brown sugar
$^3/_4$ cup butter
$^3/_4$ tsp. baking powder

Mix flour, sugar, salt, and cinnamon with apples. Mix well and place in casserole. Combine dry ingredients and rub in butter to make crumbs. Put crumbs on top of apple mixture. Bake at 350° for 40 minutes. Serve hot or cold. Delicious hot with ice cream.

CHERRY CRUNCH
... Leona Sue Miller

1 can (21 oz.) cherry pie filling
1 tsp. lemon juice
1 box white cake mix

$^1/_2$ cup melted butter or margarine
$^1/_2$ cup nuts (optional)
whipped topping or ice cream

Preheat oven to 350°. Spread pie filling in bottom of pan. Sprinkle with lemon juice. Combine dry cake mix, nuts, and melted butter until crumbly. Sprinkle over pie filling. Bake for 40–45 minutes or until golden brown. Serve with whipped topping or ice cream. This is delicious served warm with ice cream.

STRAWBERRY CREAM ANGEL TORTE
... Mrs. Willis (Ruth) Schlabach

1 angel food cake
FILLING
1 cup powdered sugar
8 oz. cream cheese
TOPPING
$2^1/_2$ cups water
$^3/_4$ cup white sugar
1 box Danish Dessert

1 pt. whipping cream, whipped
1 tsp. vanilla

1 Tbsp. cornstarch
1 qt. fresh strawberries

To make filling, cream together sugar and cream cheese. Add vanilla and fold in whipped cream.

Cut cake into small pieces and layer cake, filling, and topping; repeat.

CHERRY ANGEL DESSERT

··· Mrs. Floyd (Marlene) Yoder
··· Mrs. Marion (Rachel) Mullet

1 - 8 oz. pkg. cream cheese
1 cup powdered sugar
1 1/2 cups Rich's Topping

1 angel food cake
2 - 20 oz. cans cherry pie filling, or
    use your own filling

Combine sugar and cream cheese until well blended. Add whipped topping. Cut cake in cubes. Pour mixture over cake and mix well. Put in 13" x 9" pan; pat down. Gently spread pie filling over cake. Refrigerate overnight. Enjoy.

CHERRY SUPREME

··· Mrs. David (Susan) Nisley

6 egg whites
2 cups white sugar

1/4 tsp. cream of tartar

Beat above ingredients together until stiff, then add 2 cups white cracker crumbs and 3/4 cup nuts. Bake at 350° for 25–30 minutes, till done. Cool.

Whip 2 cups whipped topping; add 1 pkg. cream cheese and 1/2 cup white sugar. Spread on top of crust. Top with cherry pie filling.

FLUFFY PINEAPPLE TORTE ··· Mrs. Atlee (Dorothy) Schlabach

1 1/2 cups graham cracker crumbs
1/4 cup butter or margarine, melted

2 Tbsp. sugar

FILLING

1 - 12 oz. can evaporated milk
1 - 3 oz. pkg. lemon gelatin
1 cup boiling water
1 - 8 oz. pkg. cream cheese,
    softened

1/2 cup sugar
1 - 8 oz. can crushed pineapple,
    drained
1 cup chopped walnuts, divided

Combine crumbs, butter, and sugar; press into bottom of an 11" x 7" x 2" baking dish. Bake at 325° for 10 minutes; cool. Place can of evaporated milk in the refrigerator for 1 1/2 hours. Meanwhile, in a small bowl, dissolve gelatin in water. Chill until syrupy (1 1/2 hours). In small mixing bowl, beat milk until stiff peaks form. In large mixing bowl, beat cream cheese and sugar until smooth. Add gelatin; mix well. Stir in pineapple and 3/4 cup walnuts. Fold in milk. Pour over crust. Chill for at least 3 hours or overnight. Sprinkle remaining walnuts over the top before filling is completely firm. Yield: 12 servings.

JUDY'S CHOCOLATE CHIP TORTE

··· Mrs. Marion (Rachel) Mullet

2¹/₂ cups flour
1 tsp. soda
1 tsp. salt
1 cup butter
1 cup brown sugar
¹/₂ cup white sugar

2 eggs
1 tsp. vanilla
1 - 6 oz. pkg. milk chocolate chips
1 - 3 oz. pkg. instant vanilla pudding

8 oz. Cool Whip

Cream butter and sugars; add eggs and vanilla. Beat till light and fluffy. Add dry ingredients; stir well. Add chocolate chips. Put into a 14" pizza pan. Bake at 350°. Remove from oven and cool. Mix instant pudding according to package directions; let set. When ready to serve, put instant pudding on top of the cookie, then put the Cool Whip on top of the pudding. Garnish with chocolate chips. Great to serve at parties or as a simple snack.

CHOCOLATE ANGEL DESSERT

··· Mrs. Mary Esta Yoder
··· Leona Sue Miller

1 - 10" angel food cake
6 oz. chocolate chips
2 Tbsp. milk
¹/₂ cup white sugar

pinch of salt
2 egg yolks
2 egg whites
2 cups Rich's Topping

Melt chocolate chips over low heat. Beat egg yolks; add milk, sugar, and salt. Add to melted chocolate chips and heat. Cool. Beat egg whites till stiff. Beat topping and fold into egg whites; add to cooled chocolate mixture and stir to blend. Break up angel food cake and layer in a serving dish. Refrigerate 24 hours. To serve, garnish with whipped topping and chopped M&Ms or chocolate crunch candy bar pieces.

Hey, diddle, diddle, I'm watching my middle,
I'm hoping to whittle it soon.
But eating's such fun, I may not get it done
Till my dish runs away with my spoon.

BAVARIAN APPLE TORTE   ··· *Mrs. Emanuel (Mary) Nisley*

1/2 cup butter or margarine	1/4 tsp. vanilla
1/3 cup sugar	1 cup flour

Cream butter, vanilla, and sugar; blend in flour. Spread dough on bottom and sides of pan.

1 - 8 oz. pkg. Philadelphia cream cheese	1 egg
	vanilla
1/4 cup sugar	

Combine sugar and cream cheese and mix well. Add beaten egg and vanilla. Pour into pastry filled pan.

1/3 cup sugar	4 cups sliced apples
1/2 tsp. cinnamon	1/4 cup sliced almonds or other nuts

Combine sugar and cinnamon. Toss apples in sugar; mix. Spoon mixture over cheese layer; sprinkle top with nuts. Bake at 350° till done. Loosen torte from rim of pan. Cool before removing from pan.

BUTTERSCOTCH TORTE   ··· *Mrs. Mary Esta Yoder*
TORTE

6 eggs, separated	2 tsp. vanilla
1 1/2 cups white sugar	2 cups graham cracker crumbs
1 tsp. baking powder	1 cup chopped nuts

Beat egg yolks till thick and lemon colored. Add sugar, vanilla, and baking powder. Mix well. Beat egg whites till very stiff. Fold egg whites, nuts, and crumbs into egg yolk batter. Spread in 2 - 9" layer pans, greased and lined with waxed paper. Bake at 325° for 30–35 minutes. When cool, remove from pan and remove waxed paper.

SYRUP

1/4 cup melted butter	1/4 cup water
1 cup brown sugar	1 egg, well beaten
1/4 cup orange juice	1 1/2 Tbsp. flour

Cook together syrup ingredients till thickened; cool.

2 cups Rich's Topping or whipping cream

Frost cake top and sides with whipped topping. Drizzle syrup over topping. I prefer to cut in cubes and prepare like date pudding.

CREME PUFF RING
... Mrs. Firman (Deborah) Miller

1 cup water

$^1/_2$ cup butter or margarine

$^1/_4$ tsp. salt

1 cup all-purpose flour

4 eggs

Heat water, butter, and salt until butter melts and mixture boils. Vigorously stir in flour all at once until mixture forms a ball and leaves side of saucepan. Add eggs to flour mixture, one at a time, beating after each addition until mixture is smooth. Cool slightly. Preheat oven to 400°. Lightly grease and flour large cookie sheet. Trace a 7" circle in flour and drop batter by heaping Tbsp. into 10 mounds inside circle. Bake ring 40 minutes or until golden. Turn off oven. Let ring remain in oven 15 minutes. When ring is cool, slice horizontally in half. Prepare almond filling; spoon into bottom of ring. Replace top of ring. Prepare chocolate glaze. Spoon over top of ring. Makes 10 servings.

CHOCOLATE GLAZE

Heat $^1/_2$ cup semisweet chocolate pieces with 1 Tbsp. butter or margarine, $1^1/_2$ tsp. milk, and $1^1/_2$ tsp. light corn syrup until smooth, stirring constantly.

ALMOND CREME FILLING

Prepare vanilla instant pudding as label directs, but use only $1^1/_4$ cups milk. Fold in 1 cup whipped cream and 1 tsp. almond extract.

FRUIT PIZZA
... Daniel Raber

1 egg

$^1/_2$ cup brown sugar

$^1/_2$ cup margarine, softened

$1^1/_3$ cups flour

1 tsp. baking powder

Cream together and press into 14" pizza pan. Bake at 350° for 10–12 minutes. Do not overbake.

GLAZE

4 cups water

1 heaping Tbsp. clear jel

$^3/_4$ cup white sugar

1 cup pineapple juice

CREAM CHEESE MIXTURE

$^1/_3$ cup white sugar

1 - 8 oz. pkg. cream cheese

1 Tbsp. lemon juice

Spread cream cheese mixture on cooled crust. Arrange assorted fresh fruits over cream cheese mixture. Spread glaze over fruit. Refrigerate until serving time.

BUTTERSCOTCH SAUCE FOR DATE PUDDING

··· Mrs. Alton (Nora) Nisley

2 Tbsp. butter
1 cup brown sugar

1¹/2 cups cold water

Put 1 cup of the cold water in sugar and save ¹/2 cup cold water. Mix with:

2¹/2 Tbsp. clear jel
³/4 tsp. vanilla

¹/2 tsp. maple flavoring

CARAMEL SAUCE FOR DATE PUDDING

··· Mrs. Jr. (Ruth) Miller ··· Mrs. Henry (Emma) Troyer

1 cup butter (no substitutes)
4 cups brown sugar
1 tsp. salt
4 cups water

³/4 cup clear jel
2 cups cold water
4 tsp. vanilla

Bring butter, brown sugar, salt, and 4 cups water to a boil. Mix clear jel in 2 cups cold water. Add to other mixture and bring to a boil again. Remove from heat and add vanilla. This recipe can also be halved.

DATE PUDDING

··· Mrs. Andy (Elsie) Schlabach

¹/2 cup white sugar
¹/2 cup brown sugar
1¹/2 cups flour
1 tsp. soda
1 tsp. baking powder

¹/4 tsp. salt
1 egg
2 Tbsp. melted butter
1 cup nuts
1 cup dates, chopped

Pour 1 cup boiling water over dates; add soda and set aside to cool. Add this to the remaining ingredients. Pour mixture into large loaf pan, then pour the following sauce over the top:

1¹/2 cups boiling water
1 cup brown sugar

1 Tbsp. butter

Bake at 350° for 35 minutes. Serve with Rich's Topping, bananas, and nuts.

DATE NUT PUDDING   *... Mrs. Jason (Fern) Schlabach*

1 cup cut-up dates   1 cup boiling water
1 tsp. baking soda
  Let set till cold.
1 cup white sugar $^1/_2$ cup English walnuts
1 beaten egg   1 Tbsp. oleo
1 cup Gold Medal flour   1 tsp. vanilla
  Mix all together and bake at 350° for 35–40 minutes.

SAUCE

1 cup brown sugar   3 Tbsp. butter

Melt together and cook 5–10 minutes. Add 1 cup water and cook till dissolved. Add $2^1/_2$ Tbsp. clear jel mixed with $^1/_2$ cup cold water. Simmer 10 minutes. Add 1 tsp. vanilla flavoring and $^1/_2$ tsp. maple flavoring. Cut cake in 1" squares. Put in layers with Rich's Topping (whipped), bananas, and sauce.

RICH PUMPKIN CHEESECAKE   *... Mrs. Linda Mae Troyer*

1 pkg. spice cake mix   4 eggs
$^1/_2$ cup butter, melted   1 Tbsp. pumpkin pie spice
3 - 8 oz. pkg. cream cheese   1 pkg. sliced almonds
1 - 14 oz. can condensed milk   2 cups whipped cream
1 - 16 oz. can pumpkin $^1/_4$ cup powdered sugar

Preheat oven to 375°. For crust: Combine cake mix and $^1/_2$ cup melted butter. Press in bottom of an ungreased 10" springform pan. For filling: Combine cream cheese and milk; beat 2 minutes. Add pumpkin, eggs, and spice. Beat on high speed for 1 minute. Pour over crust. Bake for 65–70 minutes or until set. Cool; remove from pan. For topping: Toast almonds on baking sheet at 300° for 4–5 minutes. Cool. Beat whipping cream; add sugar. Spread over top of chilled cake. Garnish with almonds. To prepare in a 13" x 9" x 2" pan, bake at 350° for 35 minutes.

*Cherished memories shine through the darkest sorrows
with a light that is bright for all times.*

PUMPKIN CAKE DESSERT

... Mrs. Jarey (Ruth Davis) Schlabach

1 pkg. yellow cake mix
  (reserve one cup of cake mix)
$^1/_2$ cup butter, melted
3 eggs

$^2/_3$ cup milk
$^1/_4$ cup sugar
1 tsp. cinnamon
1 tsp. butter

1 large can (1 lb. 14 oz.) pumpkin pie filling

Step one: Mix together yellow cake mix, butter, and 1 egg. Press into 9" x 13" pan.

Step two: Mix together pumpkin pie filling, 2 eggs, and $^2/_3$ cup milk. Pour over cake mix.

Step three: Mix the reserved 1 cup of cake mix, sugar, cinnamon, and 1 tsp. butter and sprinkle onto mixture. Bake at 350° for 45–50 minutes.

CHEESECAKES

... Erica Kaufman

2 eggs
Nilla Wafer cookies
2 - 8 oz. pkg. cream cheese,
  softened

$^3/_4$ cup white sugar
1 Tbsp. lemon juice
1 tsp. vanilla

Put wafer in bottom of cupcake liner. Mix other ingredients and fill liners to $^2/_3$ full. Bake at 375° for 15 minutes. Refrigerate. Top with cherry pie filling just before serving. Makes approximately 2 dozen.

PUMPKIN SWIRL CHEESECAKE *... Mrs. Linda Mae Troyer*

2 cups vanilla wafer crumbs
$^1/_4$ cup butter, melted
2 - 8 oz. pkg. cream cheese,
  softened
$^3/_4$ cup white sugar

1 tsp. vanilla
3 eggs
1 cup canned pumpkin
$^3/_4$ tsp. cinnamon
$^1/_4$ tsp. ground nutmeg

Combine crumbs and butter; press onto bottom and sides of 9" spring-form pan. Combine cream cheese, $^1/_2$ cup sugar, and vanilla. Mix until well blended. Add eggs one at a time, mixing well after each addition. Reserve 1 cup cheese mixture; add pumpkin, remaining sugar, and spices to remaining cheese mixture. Mix well. Layer half of pumpkin mix, then half of plain cheese mix over crust. Repeat layers. Cut through batter with knife several times for marble effect. Bake at 350° for 55 minutes. Loosen cake from rim of pan; cool before removing rim of pan. Chill.

CHOCO CHEESE PUDDING ... *Mrs. Freeman (Naomi) Miller*

2 cups crushed graham crackers
1/3 cup oleo, melted
1/2 cup sugar
1 Tbsp. unflavored gelatin
1 cup milk
1/2 cup sugar

1/2 cup chocolate syrup
1 - 8 oz. pkg. cream cheese
1/3 cup sugar
1 tsp. vanilla
1 cup cream (Rich's Topping)

Combine graham crackers, 1/2 cup sugar, and 1/3 cup melted oleo. Press into a 9" x 9" Tupperware, keeping 1/4 cup for sprinkling on top. Dissolve gelatin in cold milk; add chocolate syrup and 1/2 cup sugar. Heat until sugar and gelatin are dissolved; cool. Cream cream cheese, 1/3 cup sugar, and 1 tsp. vanilla. Slowly add cooked chocolate mixture. Whip 1 cup cream. Alternately spoon chocolate cream cheese mixture and whipped cream into crust. Swirl with spoon or knife for a marble effect. Sprinkle with remaining crumbs.

PEANUT BUTTER CHEESECAKE   ... *Reuben Miller*

1 - 8 oz. pkg. cream cheese
1 cup peanut butter
1 1/2 cups powdered sugar
1 1/2 cups milk
1 large container Cool Whip or
    whipped cream

1 1/2 pkg. graham crackers,
    crushed into crumbs
1/4 cup white sugar
2 Tbsp. butter, melted
dash of cinnamon

Melt butter and add to cracker crumbs, white sugar, and cinnamon. Line 9" x 13" Tupperware (or Rubbermaid) with crumb mixture. Cream together cream cheese and peanut butter. Add powdered sugar; add milk. Stir in whipped cream. Pour over crumbs. Freeze...yummy!

NO BAKE CHEESECAKE   ... *Joyce (Schlabach) Albritton*

1 - 8 oz. pkg. cream cheese,
    softened
1/3 cup sugar
1 cup (1/2 pt.) sour cream
2 tsp. vanilla

1 - 8 oz. container Cool Whip, thawed
1 Ready-Crust graham cracker pie
    shell
fresh strawberries for garnish

Beat cheese with mixer until smooth; gradually beat in sugar. Blend in sour cream and vanilla. Fold in whipped topping (lowest speed), blending well. Spoon into crust. Chill until set (minimum 4 hours). Garnish with fresh strawberries, if desired. Can substitute chocolate pie crust for graham cracker and top with shavings from Hershey bar instead of strawberries.

BANANA SPLIT DESSERT   ··· *Mrs. Linda Beachy*
CRUST
1 1/2 sticks oleo   3 cups graham crackers

Cover bottom and sides of 9" x 13" pan.

FILLING
2 sticks oleo   2 cups powdered sugar

2 eggs   1 Tbsp. vanilla

Beat for 20 minutes. Put into crust.

5 or 6 bananas   maraschino cherries

Cool Whip   nuts

Slice bananas in half lengthwise and dip in lemon juice. Put on the filling. Cover with Cool Whip, nuts, and maraschino cherries. Refrigerate.

APPLE CAKE   ··· *Mrs. Reuben (Betty) Yoder*
2 cups brown sugar   2 cups flour

2 eggs   2 cups diced apples

1/2 cup vegetable oil   1 tsp. cinnamon

1 tsp. vanilla   1/2 cup nuts (optional)

2 tsp. soda   1/2 tsp. salt

SAUCE
3 cups water   pinch of salt

1 1/2 cups brown sugar

Bake at 350° for 55 minutes. Cook sauce ingredients and thicken slightly with clear jel. Cut cake in square pieces and serve with some sauce and a few scoops of ice cream. Cake and sauce can be served either warm or cold. Delicious!

LEMON PUDDING CAKE   ··· *Mrs. Freeman (Naomi) Miller*
4 eggs, separated   1 1/2 cups sugar

1/3 cup lemon juice   1/2 cup flour

1 tsp. lemon peel, grated   1/2 tsp. salt

1 Tbsp. butter or oleo, melted   1 1/2 cups milk

In mixing bowl, beat yolks until thick and lemon colored (3–5 minutes). Blend in lemon juice, peel, and butter. Combine flour, sugar, and salt. Add alternately with milk, beating after each addition. Beat egg whites till stiff; fold into batter. Pour into an ungreased 1 1/2 qt. baking dish; set in a pan of hot water. Bake at 350° for 50 minutes or until lightly browned. Serve warm with whipped topping.

LEMON DELIGHT   ⋯ Mrs. Linda Mae Troyer
CRUST
1 1/2 cups flour

1/4 cup brown sugar

1/2 cup nuts

1/2 cup butter or oleo

FILLING
1 - 8 oz. pkg. cream cheese,
  softened

1 cup powdered sugar

1 1/2 cups Rich's Topping, whipped

1 tsp. vanilla

2 pkg. lemon instant pudding

1 cup whipped topping

Mix crust ingredients; press in pan and bake at 350° for 10–15 minutes. Cool. Take a fork and crumble it. Press in an oblong Tupperware. For filling: Cream cream cheese and powdered sugar; add vanilla. Whip Rich's Topping and fold in cream cheese mixture. Put on top of cool crust; chill. Make lemon pudding with 3 cups milk. Spread on cream cheese filling. Top with whipped topping.

LEMON–LIME REFRIGERATOR SHEET CAKE
⋯ Mrs. Marvin (Martha) Mast

1 box lemon cake mix

1 - 3 oz. pkg. lime-flavored gelatin

TOPPING
1 - 1 1/2 oz. envelope whipped
  topping mix

1 1/2 cups cold milk

1 pkg. (4 serving size) instant pudding mix

Dissolve gelatin in 3/4 cup boiling water. Add 1/2 cup cold water; set aside at room temperature. Mix and bake cake as directed on package in one 9" x 13" pan. Cool cake 20–25 minutes. With cake still in the pan and warm, poke deep holes through top of cake with a meat fork or toothpick; space holes about 1" apart. With a cup, slowly pour gelatin over cake. Refrigerate cake while preparing topping.

For topping, blend topping mix and instant pudding mix. Add cold milk. Beat until stiff (3–8 minutes). Immediately frost cake.

NOTE: Cake must be stored in refrigerator and served chilled. Very cool and refreshing!

APPLE CAKE
··· Mrs. Floyd (Marlene) Yoder

4 cups apples, diced
2 eggs
$^1/_2$ cup salad oil
1 tsp. vanilla
2 cups brown sugar

2 cups flour
2 tsp. soda
$^1/_2$ tsp. cinnamon
$^1/_2$ tsp. salt
1 cup nuts

Dice apples; beat eggs and pour over apples. Mix well. Add oil and mix well. Add remaining ingredients and mix. Bake at 350° for 45–55 minutes.

GLAZE

$^1/_4$ cup oleo
1 Tbsp. flour
1 tsp. vanilla

$^1/_2$ cup brown sugar
$^1/_2$ cup milk

Mix together and cook till thick. Pour over cake when you are ready to eat. This cake is good warm, served with ice cream.

OLD-FASHIONED APPLE DUMPLINGS
··· Mrs. Lloyd (Bena) Miller

6 medium sized apples
2 cups flour
$2^1/_2$ tsp. baking powder

$^1/_2$ tsp. salt
$^2/_3$ cup shortening
$^1/_2$ cup buttermilk

SAUCE

2 cups brown sugar
2 cups water

$^1/_4$ cup butter
$^1/_4$ tsp. cinnamon

Peel apples; cut in halves. Sift flour, baking powder, and salt together. Cut in shortening until particles are the size of peas. Pour milk over mixture and work dough only enough to hold together. Roll dough as for pastry and cut into 6 squares. Place one apple piece on each square. Fill cavity of apple with sugar and cinnamon. Put dough around apple to cover it completely. Place dumplings 1" apart into a greased baking dish. Cook sauce ingredients together 5 minutes and pour over dumplings. Bake at 375° for 30–40 minutes.

*This world was a much better place
when people tried to get to Heaven instead of to the moon.*

COCONUT APPLE COBBLER   *... Mrs. Linda Mae Troyer*

4 apples	2 Tbsp. butter, melted
1/2 cup caramel ice cream topping	3 Tbsp. white sugar
1 Tbsp. flour	3/4 cup coconut
1 - 10 oz. can buttermilk biscuits	

Preheat oven to 375°. Peel, core, and slice apples; cut apples in half. Combine apple slices, caramel topping, and flour. Spoon into a deep dish. Peel apart each biscuit into 2 biscuits and place on top of apples. Drizzle melted butter over biscuits. Combine sugar and coconut. Sprinkle coconut mixture over biscuits. Bake 30 minutes or until light golden brown. Substitute for coconut mixture: Combine 2 Tbsp. melted butter, 1/4 cup brown sugar, and 1/3 cup chopped pecans or walnuts. Spread over biscuits.

PEACH COBBLER   *... Mrs. Daniel (Lisa) Schlabach*

2 cups flour	1 cup milk
1 cup sugar	4 Tbsp. melted oleo
2 eggs	4 tsp. baking powder

Combine above ingredients in mixing bowl. Cover bottom of a 9" x 13" pan well with sliced peaches. Sprinkle some cinnamon over peaches. Pour batter over peaches. Mix together 1 3/4 cup sugar and 3 to 4 Tbsp. cornstarch; sprinkle on top of batter. Pour 1 cup hot water over all. Bake at 350° for 45 minutes.

PEACH UPSIDE-DOWN CAKE   *... Mrs. Mary Esta Yoder*

2 Tbsp. butter	1 cup brown sugar

Melt together in 9" x 13" pan. Arrange peach slices over sugar sauce.

BATTER

3 egg yolks	10 Tbsp. peach syrup
1 1/3 cups white sugar	2 cups sifted flour
4 tsp. baking powder	3 egg whites, beaten stiff

Beat egg yolks till light; add sugar and peach syrup. Blend in dry ingredients; fold in egg whites. Spread over peaches; bake at 350° for 50 minutes or till done. Turn upside down on serving plate. Serve warm with milk. Our wintertime fruit shortcake.

PEACH COBBLER WITH PRALINE BISCUITS

··· Mrs. Larry (Cindy) Schlabach

1 1/2 cups sugar	1/4 cup brown sugar
2 Tbsp. cornstarch	1 cup chopped pecans
1 tsp. cinnamon	2 cups flour
1 cup water	2 tsp. baking powder
8 cups sliced fresh peaches (about 5 1/2 lb.)	2 tsp. sugar
	1/2 cup shortening
3 Tbsp. melted butter	3/4 cup buttermilk

Combine sugar, cornstarch, cinnamon, and water in a saucepan; add peaches. Bring to a boil and cook 1 minute, stirring often. Remove from heat. Pour into a greased 9" x 13" cake pan; set aside. Combine butter, brown sugar, and pecans; set aside. Combine flour, baking powder, and 2 tsp. sugar; cut in shortening with a pastry knife until mixture is crumbly. Add buttermilk, stirring just until combined. Turn dough out onto a floured surface and knead 3 or 4 times. Roll dough to a 12" x 8" rectangle; spread with pecan mixture. Starting with long side, roll up jelly roll fashion. Cut roll into 1/2" slices; arrange slices over peach mixture. Bake at 400° for 25–30 minutes or until slightly browned.

PEACHIE CINNAMON WHIRLIGIGS

··· Mrs. Lloyd (Bena) Miller ··· Mrs. Mary Esta Yoder

1 - 29 oz. can sliced peaches	1/3 cup milk
2 Tbsp. cornstarch	2 Tbsp. oleo, softened
1 1/3 cups Bisquick	1/4 cup sugar
2 Tbsp. sugar	1 tsp. cinnamon
2 Tbsp. oleo, melted	

Heat oven to 425°. Combine peaches with syrup and cornstarch in saucepan. Cook, stirring constantly, over medium heat, until mixture thickens and boils. Boil 1 minute. Keep hot.

Stir Bisquick, 2 Tbsp. sugar, 2 Tbsp. melted oleo, and the milk to a soft dough. Gently smooth into a ball on well-floured board. Knead 8–10 times. Roll dough into 9" square; spread with 2 Tbsp. softened oleo. Mix 1/4 cup sugar and cinnamon; sprinkle over dough. Roll up; seal well by pinching edge of dough into roll.

Pour peach mixture into 8" x 8" x 2" square pan. Cut roll into 1" slices. Place slices, cut side up, on hot peach mixture. Bake 20–25 minutes. Serve warm with cream or ice cream.

GINGERBREAD

··· Ruth Ann Schlabach ··· Mrs. Emanuel (Mary) Nisley

3/4 cup shortening

3/4 cup brown sugar, packed

3/4 cup molasses

2 eggs

2 1/2 cups flour, sifted

2 tsp. baking powder

1/2 tsp. soda

1/2 tsp. salt

2 tsp. ginger

1 tsp. cinnamon

1/2 tsp. nutmeg

1/4 tsp. cloves

1 cup boiling water

Sift together dry ingredients. Melt shortening; beat into sugar, molasses, and eggs. Add sifted ingredients, gradually beating after each addition. Add boiling water all at once; stir until well mixed. Mixture will be quite thin. Bake.

Serve hot with raspberries or strawberries and milk, or cold with whipped cream.

BAKED CHOCOLATE FUDGE PUDDING ··· *Julia Yoder*

Cream together:

3 Tbsp. shortening   3/4 cup white sugar

Sift together:

1 cup flour   1/2 tsp. salt

1 1/2 tsp. baking powder

Add alternately with:

1/2 cup milk

Fold in:

1/2 cup nuts (optional)

Spread batter into ungreased 8" x 8" pan. Mix:

1 cup brown sugar   1/4 tsp. salt

1/4 cup cocoa

Sprinkle over top of batter. Do not stir. Pour 1 1/2 cups boiling water over top. Bake at 350° for 40–45 minutes. Delicious served warm with ice cream!

*Never miss an opportunity
to say a kind word or do a kind deed.*

BROWNIE PUDDING CAKE   ··· Mrs. Jr. (Ruth) Miller

2 cups flour
4 tsp. baking powder
1 tsp. salt
1 1/2 cups white sugar
4 Tbsp. cocoa

1 cup milk
2 tsp. vanilla
4 Tbsp. melted shortening
1 cup chopped walnuts (optional)

TOPPING

3/4 cup brown sugar
1/4 cup cocoa

2 cups hot water

Sift together flour, baking powder, salt, white sugar, and 4 Tbsp. cocoa. Add milk, vanilla, and shortening. Mix until smooth. Add nuts. Pour in greased 9" x 13" cake pan. Mix brown sugar and 1/4 cup cocoa. Sprinkle over batter. Pour hot water over entire batter. Bake at 350°. This has become a family favorite, eaten warm with ice cream.

HOT FUDGE SUNDAE CAKE   ··· Dora Nisley

2 cups flour
1 1/2 cups sugar
2 Tbsp. cocoa
4 tsp. baking powder

1/2 tsp. salt
1 cup milk
4 Tbsp. salad oil
2 tsp. vanilla

Combine first 5 ingredients. Mix in milk, oil, and vanilla until smooth. Spread evenly in ungreased cake pan. Sprinkle on 2 cups brown sugar, then 1/2 cup cocoa. Do not mix! Pour 3 1/2 cups hot water on top of this. Bake 40 minutes at 350°. Let stand 15 minutes. Invert each helping on plate. Top with ice cream and serve.

JOYCE'S DELIGHTFUL DESSERT

··· Joyce (Schlabach) Albritton

1/2 cup butter
1 1/2 cups graham cracker crumbs
1 - 14 oz. can Eagle Brand milk

16 oz. semisweet chocolate chips
1 - 3 oz. can coconut
1 cup chopped nuts

Preheat oven to 350° (325° for glass pan). Melt butter, then spread in bottom of pan. Spread graham crackers. Pour milk and spread on. Spread chocolate chips, then coconut and nuts. Bake 25–30 minutes. Let cool. Cut into squares. Enjoy!

ICE CREAM PUDDING
··· Mrs. Mary Kaufman

30 Ritz crackers, crushed
1 stick oleo or butter
1 box instant vanilla pudding
1 box instant butter pecan pudding
1 1/2 cups milk
1 1/2 qt. vanilla ice cream

Melt butter and add crackers. Press in bottom of cake pan. Mix remaining ingredients (all but ice cream) and beat 2 minutes. After thickened, add ice cream and pour over crackers. Before serving, you may add whipped cream and crushed Heath bars on top.

FROZEN CHEESECAKE
··· favorite of Jessica Ruth Yoder, age 10

CRUST

2 pkg. graham crackers, crushed
3/4 cup melted butter
6 Tbsp. brown sugar

FILLING

2 - 8 oz. pkg. cream cheese
1 cup white sugar
1 cup Rich's Topping
4 eggs, well beaten
1 tsp. vanilla

Mix crust and press into bottom of 9" x 13" pan. Mix remaining ingredients and pour over graham cracker crust and freeze.

Remove from freezer 15–20 minutes before serving. Serve with any fruit glaze. Fresh strawberries, raspberries, or peaches are delicious!

FROZEN FLUFF
··· Mervin and Rhoda Hilty

2 eggs
1/2 cup sugar
2/3 cup milk
1 Tbsp. gelatin
1/2 cup cold water
1 tsp. vanilla
1 cup cream or whip topping, whipped
12 graham crackers, crushed
3 Tbsp. sugar
3 Tbsp. butter

Beat egg yolks, sugar, and milk and cook till thick. Soak gelatin in water and add. Chill. Fold in beaten egg whites, vanilla, and whipped topping. Make a crust with graham crackers, sugar, and butter. Press into pan and pour pudding on top. Sprinkle a few crumbs on top and freeze, or eat as it is. A 13" x 9" pan = 2 recipes of pudding and 1 recipe of crust.

RASPBERRY SWIRL
··· Mrs. Marion (Rachel) Mullet

Extract seeds from 1 cup raspberries and thicken fruit juice with clear jel, a little thinner than jelly. Cool.

Mix together:

3/4 cup graham cracker crumbs   3 Tbsp. butter, melted

2 Tbsp. brown sugar

Press into 7" x 11 1/2" pan. Bake 8 minutes at 375°.

Beat 3 egg yolks until thick. Add:

8 oz. cream cheese   1/8 tsp. salt

1 cup sugar

Beat until smooth. Beat 3 egg whites until stiff. Fold egg whites and 1 pt. Cool Whip into cheese mixture. Gently swirl thickened fruit through the cheese mixture. Pour onto cooled crust. Sprinkle a few graham cracker crumbs on top. Freeze at least 2 days before serving.

FROZEN DESSERT
··· Mrs. Firman (Deborah) Miller

1 box vanilla wafers   3 egg yolks, beaten

1/2 cup butter   1/2 cup chopped nuts

2 cups powdered sugar   3 egg whites, beaten

6 squares Baker's chocolate,   1 tsp. vanilla

    melted   1/2 gal. vanilla ice cream

Crush cookies and spread over bottom of oblong Tupperware. Cream butter and sugar; add egg yolks, chocolate, and nuts and beat until fluffy. Stir in egg whites and vanilla. Spread over crumbs. Spread ice cream evenly over chocolate layer. Sprinkle some cookie crumbs over top. Place in freezer.

BUSTER BAR DESSERT
··· Mrs. Roy (Freda) Miller

1 lb. Oreo cookies, crushed   2 cups powdered sugar

1/2 cup butter, melted   1 1/2 cups evaporated milk

1/2 gal. vanilla ice cream, softened   1 cup chocolate chips

1 1/2 cups Spanish peanuts   1/2 cup oleo or butter

Mix cookies and melted butter; press in bottom of 9" x 13" pan. Spread softened ice cream over crust and sprinkle with peanuts. Freeze.

Mix powdered sugar, evaporated milk, chocolate chips, and butter in saucepan. Bring to a boil and boil 8 minutes, stirring constantly. Cool. Pour chocolate over top and freeze.

FROZEN PUMPKIN DESSERT ··· Mrs. Linda Mae Troyer

1 cup canned pumpkin
$^1/_2$ cup brown sugar
$^1/_2$ tsp. salt

$^1/_2$ tsp. cinnamon
$^1/_2$ tsp. pumpkin spice
2 qt. vanilla ice cream

CRUST

2 cups graham crackers
$^1/_4$ cup butter

$^1/_4$ cup brown sugar
$^1/_2$ cup chopped pecans (optional)

Melt butter; add crumbs, sugar, and nuts. Press into a 9" x 13" pan. Mix together ice cream, pumpkin, sugar, and spices. Put on top of cooled crust and freeze. Remove from freezer 5–10 minutes before serving. Cut in squares. Garnish with whipped topping. Can also be frozen with whipped topping.

CHOCOLATE MALT SHOPPE PIE ··· Mrs. Linda Mae Troyer

1$^1/_2$ cups chocolate cookie crumbs
$^1/_4$ cup butter, melted
1 pt. vanilla ice cream, softened
$^1/_2$ cup crushed malted milk balls
2 Tbsp. milk, divided

3 Tbsp. instant chocolate malted milk powder
3 Tbsp. marshmallow creme
1 cup whipped cream

Combine crumbs and butter. Press into 9" pie pan. Freeze while preparing filling. In bowl, blend ice cream, crushed malted milk balls, and 1 Tbsp. milk. Spoon onto crust. Freeze for 1 hour. Blend malted milk powder, marshmallow creme, and 1 Tbsp. milk. Stir in whipping cream; whip until soft peaks form. Spread over ice cream layer. Freeze several hours or overnight. Garnish with whipped cream and milk balls.

CHART HOUSE MUD PIE ··· Mrs. Steve (Ruth) Schlabach

4$^1/_2$ oz. chocolate wafers
$^1/_4$ cup butter, melted
$^1/_2$ gal. coffee ice cream, soft

1$^1/_2$ cups fudge sauce
diced almonds

Crush wafers and add butter. Mix well. Press into a 9" pie plate. Cover with soft coffee ice cream. Top with cold fudge sauce. (It helps to put the fudge sauce in the freezer for a while to make spreading easier.) Store the Mud Pie in the freezer approximately 10 hours before serving. Slice into eight pieces and serve with whipped topping and diced almonds.

CHOCOLATE PEANUT LOAF   ··· *Mrs. Mary Esta Yoder*

1 1/2 cups Town House crackers,   3 Tbsp. powdered sugar
  crushed   3 Tbsp. melted oleo
1/2 cup chopped salted peanuts

Combine above ingredients and press half of mixture in 9" x 13" pan. Reserve other half. Place crust in freezer for 15 minutes.

First layer: Soften 1/2 gal. Fudge Ripple or Chocolate Swirl ice cream; put half on crust. Return to freezer.

Second layer:

1 - 3 oz. pkg. cream cheese,   1/3 cup milk
  softened   1/3 cup peanut butter
3/4 cup powdered sugar   1/2 cup Cool Whip

Beat cream cheese, peanut butter, and sugar until fluffy. Add milk gradually and fold in Cool Whip. Spread over frozen ice cream layer and freeze till filling is firm.

Third layer: Place remaining ice cream on filling. Sprinkle crumbs on top. Drizzle chocolate syrup over crumbs. Freeze.

RICE KRISPIE ICE CREAM DESSERT

··· *favorite of Kari Miller, age 8*

8 cups Rice Krispies   1/2 gal. ice cream
1 cup peanut butter   chocolate syrup
1 cup white Karo

Mix Rice Krispies, peanut butter, and Karo. Put half of mixture in the bottom of a 9" x 13" pan. Whip ice cream and spread on top of other mixture. Put remaining mixture on top and freeze. Chocolate syrup can be drizzled on when ready to serve (optional).

RICE KRISPIE PIE (FROZEN)   ··· *Mrs. Mary Esta Yoder*

2 cups Rice Krispies   1/2 cup marshmallow creme
1 Tbsp. melted butter or oleo   ice cream

Melt the butter in double boiler and blend in marshmallow creme. Stir till smooth; add cereal and mix well. While still warm, press in a greased pie plate to form a crust. Freeze for 20 minutes; fill crust with vanilla ice cream. Return to freezer. Serve with hot fudge sauce and nuts or fresh fruit filling. Simple and delicious!

FRIED ICE CREAM   ⋯ *Mrs. Linda Mae Troyer*

1 pt. ice cream	$^1/_2$ tsp. cinnamon
2 eggs, beaten	cooking oil for frying
$^1/_2$ tsp. vanilla	whipped cream
$2^1/_2$ cups sweetened corn flakes, crushed	cherries

Place 4 scoops (about $^1/_2$ cup each) of ice cream in a small pan. Freeze for 1 hour or until firm. Stir together eggs and vanilla. In another bowl, stir together cereal and cinnamon. Dip each frozen ice cream ball in the egg mixture, then roll it in cereal mixture. Return coated ice cream balls to pan and freeze for 1 hour or until firm. Remove coated ice cream balls from freezer. Repeat with egg mixture and cereal mixture. Return to pan. Cover and freeze until firm. Heat oil to 375° and fry frozen, coated ice cream balls 1 or 2 at a time for 15 seconds or till golden brown. Drain on paper towel. Return to freezer while frying remaining balls. Serve with whipped cream and garnish with a cherry.

MEXICAN ICE CREAM SUNDAE

⋯ *favorite of Danita Renea Troyer, age 10*

1 Tbsp. white sugar	$^1/_2$ tsp. instant coffee
$^1/_2$ tsp. cinnamon	1 Tbsp. butter
2 - 8" flour tortillas	$^1/_3$ tsp. vanilla
vegetable oil for frying	2 cups vanilla ice cream
1 oz. unsweetened chocolate	2 cups chocolate ice cream
$^1/_4$ cup sugar	whipped cream

Combine sugar and cinnamon; set aside. Using sharp knife, cut each tortilla into 8 wedges. Heat 1" oil in saucepan to 375°. Fry tortillas, a few at a time, 2–3 minutes, until golden and crisp. Remove and drain on paper towel. Sprinkle hot tortillas with cinnamon and sugar. Cool. In saucepan, heat chocolate with 3 Tbsp. water over low heat until chocolate is melted. Add sugar and coffee. Cook, stirring, until sugar dissolves and mixture is smooth and slightly thickened. Remove from heat. Stir in butter and vanilla. Cover and keep warm. To serve, place a scoop of ice cream on each tortilla wedge. Top with 2 Tbsp. sauce and whipped cream. Strawberry topping is also good.

DAIRY QUEEN ICE CREAM ··· *Mrs. Ammon (Esta) Brenneman*

2 Tbsp. gelatin   2 tsp. vanilla
$1/2$ cup water   1 tsp. salt
5 cups milk   2 cups cream
2 cups sugar

Soak gelatin in water. Heat milk, hot but not boiling. *HINT: If you pour sugar in the milk but do not stir, it will not burn.)* Remove from heat. Add gelatin, sugar, vanilla, and salt. Cool; add cream. Put in refrigerator to chill 5 or 6 hours before freezing. Makes 1 gallon. Freeze in ice cream freezer.

VARIATION: CHOCOLATE DAIRY QUEEN ICE CREAM

Mix together 3 Tbsp. cocoa and $1/2$ cup extra sugar. Heat with milk. Proceed same as vanilla flavor. This gets very fluffy.

HOMEMADE ICE CREAM   ··· *Mrs. Paul (Wilma) Schlabach*

Soak 2 pkg. gelatin in 1 cup milk. Thicken 1 qt. milk, 1 cup white sugar, and 2 Tbsp. cornstarch. Stir in gelatin while hot. Add 6 egg yolks (add a little milk to yolks) and 2 cups brown sugar. Now screen. When cooled, add vanilla, stiffly beaten whites, and a pint of cream or 1 can sweetened condensed milk. This recipe comes from Paul's mom, Mrs. Mose (Freda) Schlabach.

HOMEMADE ICE CREAM   ··· *Mrs. Jr. (Ruth) Miller*

2 pkg. unflavored gelatin $3/4$ cup cold water

Soak gelatin in cold water and set aside.

1 pint milk   2 Tbsp. cornstarch

Cook together milk and cornstarch. While still hot, add 1 cup white sugar, 6 egg yolks, and gelatin mixture. Later, when cooled, put in 1 tsp. vanilla, 1 tsp. salt, 2 cups brown sugar, and 1 qt. cream or 1 can Eagle Brand milk. Add beaten egg whites. Strain before putting into $1^1/2$ gal. can. Fill can with milk. I got this recipe from Mom soon after we married, and have always liked it.

*A hint is something we often drop
but rarely pick up.*

HOMEMADE "CUSTARD" ICE CREAM
··· *Naomi and Willard Schlabach; Zak and Jordan*

2 small boxes instant vanilla
  pudding
8 eggs, well beaten and heated
1 can Milnot milk

1 cup white sugar
1 cup brown sugar
milk

Make vanilla instant pudding as directed on box. Add warm, well-beaten eggs. Stir in sugar and Milnot milk. Pour into ice cream freezer, adding regular milk until freezer is $3/4$ full.

BUTTER PECAN ICE CREAM   ··· *Mrs. Wayne (Emma) Yoder*

Soften 3 pkg. Knox gelatin in some cold milk. Scald 2 cups milk. Add gelatin mixture and stir until dissolved. Add 2 cups white sugar, 1 cup brown sugar, and $1/4$ tsp. salt to milk. Beat 9 eggs. Add 3 cans Milnot evaporated milk, 1 box vanilla instant pudding, and 1 box butterscotch instant pudding. Then add milk and gelatin mixture. Add 4 tsp. vanilla and 1 tsp. butter flavor. Add $1/2$ cup toasted pecans and enough milk for 6 qt. freezer.

CHOCOLATE CHIP ICE CREAM ··· *Mrs. Lloyd (Bena) Miller*

Put $1^1/2$ squares Baker's unsweetened chocolate in a saucepan. Add 2 Tbsp. butter. Melt over low heat. Add a little sugar. (Do not use sweet milk chocolate.) After it is melted, pour into vanilla ice cream when it is almost frozen. Close lid and turn again till it is thoroughly mixed. For 1 or $1^1/2$ gal. freezer.

BUTTERSCOTCH ICE CREAM TOPPING
··· *Jeremiah Schlabach*

$3/4$ cup white sugar
$1/2$ cup corn syrup
a few grains salt

$1/4$ cup butter
1 cup cream
$1/2$ tsp. vanilla

Reserve half the cream. Mix together the other ingredients, except vanilla. Cook in saucepan over low heat, stirring constantly, to soft ball stage. Then stir in remaining cream. Cook until thick and smooth. Remove from heat; add vanilla. Yield: 2 cups.

HOT CHOCOLATE SAUCE   ⋯ *Mrs. Henry (Emma) Troyer*

1 cup white sugar   1 cup water
3 Tbsp. cocoa or carob   2$^1/_2$ level Tbsp. flour
$^1/_2$ tsp. salt
   Cook 3 minutes. Add 1 tsp. vanilla.

CHOCOLATE SYRUP   ⋯ *Mrs. Henry (Emma) Troyer*

3 cups honey $^1/_2$ tsp. salt
3 Tbsp. carob or cocoa   1 tsp. vanilla
$^1/_2$ cup water
   Heat to combine, then store in refrigerator. To keep on hand for chocolate milk or to drizzle over ice cream or frozen bananas.

ANGEL SAUCE   ⋯ *favorite of Willard Schlabach, age 9*

2 egg yolks $^1/_2$ cup sugar
$^1/_3$ cup pineapple juice, undiluted $^1/_3$ cup soft butter
$^1/_3$ cup milk
   Mix until smooth in blender. Cook over low heat till slightly thick. May be served over angel food cake or as ice cream topping. Yield: 1$^1/_2$ cups.

IMPATIENT DINER: "Look here, waiter, I ordered chicken pie,
but there isn't a bit of chicken in it!"

WAITER: "That's all right, sir. We also have cottage cheese,
but as far as I know, there's no cottage in it."

Pies

God's love is such a quiet thing,
And yet it's everywhere.
You feel it in a gentle rain
Or in an answered prayer.

Four People

"Everybody," "Somebody," "Anybody," and "Nobody"

There was an important job to be done and Everybody was sure Somebody would do it. Anybody could have done it, but Nobody did it. Somebody got angry about that because it was Everybody's job. Everybody thought Anybody could do it, but Nobody realized that Everybody wouldn't do it. It ended up that Everybody blamed Somebody when Nobody did what Anybody could have done.

A Hug

It's wondrous what a hug can do—
A hug can cheer you when you're blue.
A hug can say, "I love you so,"
Or, "My, I hate to see you go."
A hug is, "Welcome back again."

A hug can soothe a child's pain
And bring a rainbow after rain.
The Hug! There's just no doubt about it,
We scarcely could survive without it.
A hug delights and warms and charms;
It must be why God gave us arms!

CRISCO PIE CRUST   ··· *Mrs. Andy (Elsie) Schlabach*

4 cups flour

1 tsp. salt

1 Tbsp. sugar

1²/₃ cups Crisco

1 egg, beaten

¹/₂ cup water

1 Tbsp. vinegar

Blend together flour, salt, and sugar. Cut in Crisco. Mix together egg, water, and vinegar. Add to flour and mix well. Chill dough before rolling. Makes 4 - 9" pie shells.

NOTE: This will keep soft in refrigerator for several days.

A FLAKY CRUST   ··· *Mrs. Emanuel (Mary) Nisley*
··· *Joyce (Schlabach) Albritton*

2 cups flour (scant)

¹/₄ cup milk or water

1 tsp. white sugar (can be omitted)

¹/₂ cup oil

1 tsp. salt

Mix flour, salt, and sugar. Mix oil and milk together; add to flour. Stir until ball is formed. Roll dough between waxed paper. Makes 2 crusts. Very flaky. Joyce mixes all ingredients in pie pan and presses crust into shape. Prick with fork and bake.

PIE CRUST MIX ··· *Mrs. Kris Miller* ··· *Mrs. Wayne (Emma) Yoder*

5 lb. Gold Medal flour

3 lb. Crisco

6 tsp. salt

¹/₂ cup sugar

Combine all ingredients, mixing well. Store in tight container. When you want a crust, mix 1 cup mix with 2 to 3 Tbsp. water for one pie crust. Makes a very flaky crust.

BUTTER CRUNCH PIE CRUST ··· *Mrs. Reuben (Betty) Yoder*

¹/₂ cup butter

¹/₄ cup brown sugar, packed

1 cup flour

1 cup nuts

Heat oven to 400°. Mix all ingredients together. Spread in oblong pan. Bake 15 minutes. Remove from oven and press mixture on bottom and sides of a 9" pie pan.

NEVER FAIL PIE CRUST   ··· Mrs. Marion (Rachel) Mullet
··· favorite of Rita Renae Schlabach, age 8

Make crumbs of:

3 cups Softex flour   pinch of salt

1 cup Crisco shortening

Put in measuring cup and beat well:

1 egg $^1/_3$ cup cold water

1 Tbsp. vinegar

Pour egg and water mixture over flour and shortening crumbs; mix lightly. Roll out between 2 sheets of Saran Wrap. Makes 3 crusts. This is always flaky and never fails.

"DUTCH" CRUMBS FOR PIE   ··· Mrs. Mary Esta Yoder

1 cup flour $^1/_2$ tsp. soda

$^1/_4$ cup brown sugar $^1/_2$ tsp. cream of tartar

$^1/_4$ cup margarine

Mix with pastry blender to form crumbs. Enough for 1 pie.

FRY PIES   ··· Mrs. Marion (Rachel) Mullet ··· Lori Ann Schlabach

9 cups Hilite cake flour   3 cups Creamtex

1 Tbsp. salt   2 cups water

1 Tbsp. sugar   any desired flavor of thick pie filling

GLAZE

8 lb. powdered sugar   1 tsp. vanilla

$^1/_2$ cup cornstarch $2^1/_2$ cups water

$^1/_3$ cup Carnation milk

Cut Creamtex into dry ingredients. Add water. Roll out and cut into circles. Fill with pie filling, then seal dough with a fork. Deep-fry in Creamtex (380°–400°). Heat glaze ingredients a bit. Glaze Fry Pies immediately after frying. Yield: 35 pies. Lori uses only 4 lb. powdered sugar in glaze.

Count your age by friends, not years;
Count your life by smiles, not tears.

BASIC CREAM PIE   *··· favorite of Stephen Schlabach, age 9*

$^1/_2$ cup butter   5 egg yolks

8 cups milk   salt

2 cups sugar   vanilla

1 cup clear jel

Melt butter; add 7 cups milk and 1 cup sugar. Bring to a boil. Combine clear jel, 1 cup sugar, and 1 cup milk. Add egg yolks, salt, and vanilla. Add to hot milk. Bring to boil again. Cool!

FOR COCONUT CREAM PIE:

Use above filling. Add $^3/_4$ cup coconut for 1 pie. Spoon into pie crust and top with whipped cream.

FOR RAISIN CREAM PIE:

Cook 2 cups raisins in a little water for 10 minutes. Add $^1/_2$ cup brown sugar. Cool, then add to basic cream filling. Spoon in pie shells. Top with whipped cream.

FOR PEANUT BUTTER PIE:

CRUMBS

$^2/_3$ cup peanut butter   1$^1/_3$ cups powdered sugar

Mix well. Put half of crumbs in bottom of pie shell. Fill with Basic Cream Filling. Top with whip and add rest of crumbs on top.

CREAM PIES   *··· Mrs. Mike (Ruby) Sommers*
(PEANUT BUTTER, COCONUT, BANANA, ETC.)

5 cups milk   1$^1/_2$ cups sugar

THICKENING

3 egg yolks, beaten well   1 cup cornstarch

$^3/_4$ tsp. salt $^1/_2$ tsp. vanilla

1 cup milk

Pour sugar in saucepan. Add milk. Do not stir; sugar keeps it from scorching on the bottom. Heat till just before it boils. Meanwhile, mix thickening. Pour slowly into hot milk and stir. Bring to boil and remove from heat immediately. Add vanilla last. For chocolate pie, add $^1/_2$ cup cocoa to thickening. Use this pudding for Peanut Butter, Coconut, and Banana Cream Pie, etc.

RAISIN CREAM PIE

··· *Mrs. Albert (Verna) Yoder*

6 cups milk

6 Tbsp. flour

1 1/2 tsp. salt

6 egg yolks

3 Tbsp. butter

3 cups raisins

2 1/4 cups brown sugar

Cook raisins soft in water, enough to cover. Add milk and butter to this; heat to about boiling. Mix other ingredients with enough milk to stir. Add to milk and bring to a boil. Cool; stir in 1 tub of "ready whipped" whipped topping. Pour into 4 baked pie shells; put topping on top.

OLD-FASHIONED CREAM PIE

··· *Mrs. Marvin (Martha) Mast*

3 rounded Tbsp. flour

1 cup sugar

Mix together well.

1/2 pt. whipping cream

1/2 pt. milk

pinch of salt

1/3 tsp. vanilla

1 unbaked pie shell

Add whipping cream to first mixture and beat; add milk and beat well. Pour into crust. Bake at 375° till it bubbles in center.

COFFEE CREAM PIE FILLING ··· *Mrs. Paul (Linda) Schlabach*

Combine in saucepan:

1 cup sugar

3 Tbsp. flour

1 Tbsp. cornstarch

Blend in:

1 1/2 cups milk

1/2 cup evaporated milk

(or light cream)

1 Tbsp. instant coffee

1/4 tsp. salt

3 beaten egg yolks

1 tsp. vanilla

Cook over medium heat, stirring constantly, until thick. Stir in:

1/2 cup chopped pecans

Cool. Turn into baked pie shell. Spread with meringue. Bake at 350° for 10–12 minutes.

MERINGUE

Beat 3 egg whites, 1/4 tsp. cream of tartar, and 1/4 tsp. salt until soft mounds form. Gradually add 6 Tbsp. sugar. Beat well until stiff, glossy peaks form.

MILK FREE BUTTERSCOTCH PIES (2)

··· Mrs. Ammon (Esta) Brenneman

1 cup brown sugar	$^1/_4$ tsp. vanilla
$^1/_2$ cup boiling water	$^1/_4$ tsp. soda
2 Tbsp. butter	pinch of salt

Boil till taffy. Add:

2 cups hot water

Mix together:

1 cup cold water	1$^1/_2$ cups white sugar
1 cup flour	2 egg yolks

Add to hot mixture and bring to a boil.

BUTTERSCOTCH PIE   ··· Mrs. Ammon (Esta) Brenneman

$^1/_2$ cup butter or oleo	2 cups flour
2 cups white sugar	4 egg yolks
1$^1/_2$ qt. milk	4 baked pie shells
$^1/_2$ qt. milk	

Melt butter; add sugar. Brown while stirring constantly. When browned enough, add 1$^1/_2$ qt. milk very slowly. It can really sputter at first. Heat. Meanwhile, put $^1/_2$ qt. milk, flour, and egg yolks in blender. Blend, then add to heated mixture. Cook till thickened. Cool. When ready to serve, put in baked pie shells. Top with whip if desired.

PEANUT BUTTER CUP PIE   ··· Mrs. Albert (Verna) Yoder
BOTTOM PART

1$^1/_2$ cups white sugar	$^3/_4$ cup milk
3 Tbsp. flour	3 beaten eggs
3 Tbsp. cocoa	1$^1/_2$ tsp. vanilla

TOP PART

8 oz. cream cheese	8 oz. whipped topping, whipped
$^1/_2$ cup peanut butter	1 tsp. vanilla
1 cup powdered sugar	

Combine Bottom Part ingredients and pour into 2 unbaked pie crusts. Bake until set. Chill and add Top Part which has been mixed together. Put whipped topping on top and sprinkle with grated chocolate.

FROZEN PEANUT BUTTER PIE   *··· Mrs. Kris Miller*

8 oz. cream cheese
2 cups powdered sugar
$^2/_3$ cup peanut butter
1 cup milk

9 oz. Cool Whip
1$^3/_4$ stick of butter, melted
1$^1/_2$ Tbsp. sugar
2 pkg. graham crackers

Combine last 3 ingredients and press into pie pans. Cream cream cheese and powdered sugar until smooth. Add peanut butter and milk; mix well. Fold in Cool Whip. Pour into pans and refrigerate or freeze.

CHOCOLATE MOCHA PIE   *··· Jonas and Katie Raber*

Soak 1 Tbsp. gelatin in $^1/_4$ cup water. Heat:

2 Tbsp. cocoa
$^1/_8$ tsp. salt
$^3/_4$ cup sugar

1$^1/_4$ cups milk
1 tsp. instant coffee

Bring to a boil; remove from heat and add gelatin. Cool. When starting to thicken, add 1 cup whipped cream, 1 tsp. vanilla, and some nuts over top, if desired. Pour into baked pie crust.

HEAVENLY CHOCOLATE CREAM PIE

··· Mrs. Linda Mae Troyer

1 pkg. chocolate cake mix
$^3/_4$ cup butter
1 - 8 oz. cream cheese
1 cup powdered sugar

1 cup whipped topping
2 pkg. chocolate instant pudding
3 cups milk
2 cups whipped topping, divided

Grease 2 - 9" pie pans. Preheat oven to 350°. For crust, combine cake mix and $^3/_4$ cup butter. Put the crumbs in each pan. Press up sides and on bottom of each pan. Bake for 15 minutes. Cool.

First layer: Combine cream cheese and powdered sugar; fold in 1 cup whipped topping. Spread half the mixture evenly over each crust. Refrigerate.

Second layer: Prepare pudding mix by directions on package, using 3 cups milk. Spoon half the pudding over cream cheese mixture in each pan.

Third layer: Spread 1 cup whipped topping on each pie. Refrigerate until ready to serve. Lemon is also good.

CARAMEL PIE
··· Mrs. Mary Esta Yoder

1 cup brown sugar
2 cups milk
$^1/_2$ tsp. maple flavoring
1 Tbsp. flour

2 eggs, separated
pinch of salt
chopped nuts

Beat egg yolks; add sugar, flour, flavoring, salt, and a little of the milk. Scald milk and add to other ingredients. Beat egg whites and fold in last. Pour into unbaked 9" pie shell. Sprinkle nuts on top. Bake at 450° for 5 minutes, then at 325° for 40 minutes or till done.

CHOCOLATE MARBLE CREAM CHEESE PIE
··· Mrs. Linda Mae Troyer

1 - 8 oz. pkg. cream cheese, softened
$^1/_2$ cup white sugar
1 tsp. vanilla
2 egg yolks
1 tsp. unflavored gelatin

$^1/_4$ cup water
1 cup whipping cream
4 oz. semisweet chocolate, melted
Cookie Crust (recipe follows)
strawberries
pecan halves

Beat cream cheese, sugar, and vanilla until smooth. Beat in yolks one at a time until well blended. Combine gelatin and water in a saucepan over low heat. Stir until gelatin is dissolved. Cool slightly. Beat gelatin mixture into batter. Combine $^3/_4$ cup batter and melted chocolate. Whip cream until soft peaks form. Fold half of whipped cream into chocolate batter and remaining half into vanilla batter. Alternately place spoonfuls of chocolate and vanilla batter into crust until all batter is used. With knife, swirl batter to form marble pattern. Chill at least 3 hours. Garnish with strawberries and pecans (optional).

COOKIE CRUST
Combine $1^1/_2$ cups chocolate cookie crumbs, 2 Tbsp. white sugar, and 6 Tbsp. melted butter. Press mixture onto bottom and sides of 9" pie pan. Bake at 350° for 8 minutes. Cool.

CUSTARD PIE
··· Mrs. Jason (Fern) Schlabach

4 eggs
$^1/_2$ cup white sugar
$^1/_2$ cup brown sugar

dash of salt
2 Tbsp. flour
3 cups warm milk

Whip eggs and sugars till foamy. Add remaining ingredients and mix. Bake at 425° for about 15 minutes. Turn back to 375° until done.

CUSTARD PIE

··· Mrs. Paul (Wilma) Schlabach
··· Mervin and Rhoda Hilty

³/₄ cup brown sugar
1 heaping tsp. flour
¹/₄ tsp. salt
1 tsp. vanilla
¹/₄ tsp. maple flavoring

3 eggs, separated
2 cups milk
1 Tbsp. butter, melted
3 egg whites, beaten

Mix in order given. Pour into 9" unbaked pie shell. Bake at 425° for 10 minutes. Turn oven back to 350° and bake 30 more minutes or until done.

PEACH CUSTARD PIE

··· Mrs. Lloyd (Bena) Miller

Mix together:

3 Tbsp. sugar   2 Tbsp. flour

Spread about half this mixture over bottom of 9" unbaked pastry shell. Slice 3 or 4 fresh peaches over this; sprinkle remaining sugar and flour over peaches. Beat:

3 eggs

Combine with:

¹/₂ cup sugar   ¹/₂ tsp. vanilla
¹/₄ tsp. salt   ¹/₄ tsp. nutmeg

Slowly add 2 cups scalded milk. Pour over peaches in pie shell. Sprinkle with cinnamon. Bake at 450° for 10 minutes, then at 350° for 25 minutes.

PUMPKIN PIE

··· Mrs. Albert (Verna) Yoder

¹/₂ cup cooked pumpkin
¹/₂ cup sugar
2 eggs
2 Tbsp. flour
¹/₂ tsp. cinnamon
¹/₂ tsp. allspice

¹/₄ tsp. nutmeg
2 Tbsp. light Karo syrup
2 Tbsp. melted butter
1¹/₄ cups milk
vanilla

Mix pumpkin, sugar, spices, flour, and Karo. Beat egg yolks and add; also add butter and milk. Beat egg whites and add last. Pour into unbaked pastry shell and bake at 425° for 10 minutes or until golden over top. Quickly reduce heat to 300° or 325° and bake until set.

MOM'S A+ PUMPKIN PIE   ⋯ *Mrs. Marvin (Martha) Mast*

2 unbaked pie shells
1 cup pumpkin
1 tsp. cinnamon
1 tsp. pumpkin pie spice
6 eggs (use 2 whites to beat stiff
     and add last)

1 cup white sugar
$1/2$ cup brown sugar
2 Tbsp. flour
4 cups milk (I use 1 can evaporated
     milk and the rest reg. milk)

Bake at 450° for 12 minutes, then at 350° about 25–30 minutes.

PUMPKIN PIE   ⋯ *Mrs. Mary Kaufman*

Beat 4 egg yolks and add 2 cups fine pumpkin. Sift:

2 cups white sugar
2 Tbsp. flour
1 tsp. salt
1 tsp. cinnamon

$1/2$ tsp. ginger
$1/4$ tsp. cloves
$1/4$ tsp. nutmeg

Add this to pumpkin mixture and mix well. Add:

2 Tbsp. light Karo   4 cups rich milk

Fold in:

4 stiffly beaten egg whites

Pour into two 9" unbaked pie shells and bake at 375° until almost set.

PUMPKIN PIE   ⋯ *Mrs. Reuben (Betty) Yoder*

5 eggs, separated, whites beaten
$2^1/2$ cups brown sugar
$1/4$ cup flour
$2^1/2$ tsp. pumpkin pie spice

1 tsp. salt
$3/4$ cup pumpkin
3 cups milk
$2^1/2$ cups evaporated milk

Mix all together except the beaten egg whites. Beat well. Last, add egg whites. Pour into unbaked pie shells. Bake at 375° for 10 minutes, then at 325° for 20–25 minutes, until done. Makes 3 - 9" pies.

PUMPKIN PIE   ⋯ *Mrs. David (Susan) Nisley*

2 cups white sugar
2 cups brown sugar
4 Tbsp. flour
2 tsp. cinnamon
6 eggs

2 qt. milk
3 or 4 cups pumpkin
4 Tbsp. brown butter
2 tsp. pumpkin pie spice
4 egg whites, beaten

This makes 4 pies. Bake at 425° for 10 minutes, then at 350° for 30 minutes or till done.

PARADISE PUMPKIN PIE

··· Mrs. Mary Esta Yoder
··· Mrs. Linda Mae Troyer

1 - 8 oz. pkg. cream cheese
1/4 cup white sugar
1/2 tsp. vanilla
1 egg
1 - 9" unbaked pastry shell
1 1/4 cups canned pumpkin

1 can evaporated milk
1/2 cup sugar
2 eggs, beaten
1 tsp. cinnamon
1/2 tsp. pumpkin pie spice
dash of salt

Combine softened cream cheese, sugar, and vanilla, mixing until well blended. Add egg; mix well. Spread evenly in bottom of pastry shell.

Combine remaining ingredients; mix well. Carefully pour over cream cheese layer. Bake at 350° for 1 hour and 5 minutes.

LEMON MERINGUE PIE

··· Mrs. Ammon (Esta) Brenneman

1 - 9" baked pie shell
1 1/2 cups sugar
1/3 cup plus 1 Tbsp. cornstarch
1 1/2 cups water

3 egg yolks
3 Tbsp. butter
2 tsp. grated lemon peel
1/2 cup lemon juice

Heat oven to 400°. Mix sugar and cornstarch in medium saucepan. Gradually stir in water. Cook over medium heat, stirring constantly, until mixture thickens and boils. Boil and stir 1 minute. Gradually stir at least half the hot mixture into egg yolks. Blend into hot mixture. Boil and stir 1 minute. Remove from heat; stir in butter, lemon peel, and juice. Pour into baked pie shell. Heap meringue (recipe below) onto hot pie filling; spread over filling, carefully sealing meringue to edge of crust to prevent shrinking or weeping. Bake about 10 minutes or till a delicate brown. Cool away from draft.

MERINGUE

3 egg whites
1/4 tsp. cream of tartar

6 Tbsp. sugar
1/2 tsp. vanilla

Beat egg whites and cream of tartar until foamy. Beat in sugar. Add 1 Tbsp. at a time; continue beating until stiff and glossy. Do not underbeat. Beat in vanilla.

Jesus is the bridge over troubled waters.

LEMON SPONGE PIE ··· *Mrs. Emanuel (Mary) Nisley*

1 cup sugar (scant)
1 Tbsp. flour
2 egg yolks

1 cup milk
grated rind and juice of 1 lemon

Beat whites of 2 eggs stiffly and fold in last.

ORANGE PIE ··· *Mrs. Emanuel (Mary) Nisley*

1 egg yolk
3 Tbsp. melted butter
1 cup sugar
3 level Tbsp. flour

1 cup milk
rind and juice of 1 orange
pinch of salt

Beat egg white and add last. Bake in slow oven.

STRAWBERRY DANISH DESSERT

··· *Mrs. Mary Esta Yoder*

1 1/4 cups clear jel
2 cups sugar

2 pkg. strawberry Kool-Aid

Combine and mix well. Store dry mix until ready to use. To each 3/4 cup mix, add 2 cups water. Cook until thickened. Add fresh sliced strawberries when cool. Use as pie filling or dessert topping.

Variation: 3 oz. strawberry jello may be added to dry mixture for more flavor.

MILE HIGH STRAWBERRY PIE

··· *favorite of Martha Jean Schlabach, age 6*

2 egg whites
3/4 cup sugar
1/2 tsp. salt
1 Tbsp. lemon juice
1 cup fresh strawberries

1 tsp. vanilla
1 cup whipped cream or
    2 cups Cool Whip
1 graham cracker pie crust

Mix egg whites and sugar 15 minutes. Mix remaining ingredients except cream. Whip cream and fold in. Pour into crust. Pile high. Freeze. Do not take out till ready to serve. (Frozen strawberries may be used; just use a little less sugar.) If you don't like too much filling, put in 2 small crusts. A very refreshing pie!

STRAWBERRY PIE FILLING   ··· *Mrs. Reuben (Betty) Yoder*

3 oz. strawberry jello $^1/_4$ tsp. salt
$^1/_4$ cup clear jel   1 cup water
$^3/_4$ cup white sugar   1 cup 7-Up

Bring this to a boil. Cool, then add 1 qt. fresh sliced strawberries. You can make whatever flavor you wish by adding your favorite jello to whatever fresh fruit you will use.

STRAWBERRY PIE   ··· *Joyce (Schlabach) Albritton*

$1^1/_2$ cups sugar   1 box strawberry jello
$^1/_4$ cup cornstarch   1 qt. strawberries
$1^1/_2$ cups water

Cook sugar, cornstarch, and water until thick and clear (approximately 5 minutes). Let cool slightly and add jello. Put strawberries in pie crust; pour glaze over. Firmer if it sets up 2 to 4 hours or overnight.

FROSTY STRAWBERRY CREME PIE

··· *Ruth Ann Schlabach*

1 cup strawberries, mashed   3 tsp. lemon juice
1 unbeaten egg white   1 baked pie shell
$^1/_2$ cup sugar $^1/_2$ cup cream

Beat first 4 ingredients at high speed until thick and creamy. Whip $^1/_2$ cup cream till thick and fold gently into strawberry mixture. Spoon into pie shell and freeze 4 to 6 hours or overnight.

For variations, use peaches or raspberries. Also good on graham cracker crumbs for pudding (frozen).

PINEAPPLE COCONUT PIE   ··· *Mrs. Emanuel (Mary) Nisley*

3 eggs $^1/_2$ cup light corn syrup
1 cup sugar $^1/_4$ cup coconut
1 level Tbsp. cornstarch $^1/_4$ cup melted butter
$^1/_2$ cup drained pineapple, crushed

Beat eggs lightly; add remaining ingredients. Pour into 9" unbaked pie shell. Bake at 350° for 45–50 minutes or until slightly set.

SWISS COCONUT CUSTARD PIE

··· Mrs. Andy (Elsie) Schlabach

4 eggs, beaten	$3/4$ cup white sugar
2 cups milk	6 Tbsp. butter or oleo
$1/2$ cup flour	1 cup coconut
1 tsp. vanilla	$1/2$ tsp. baking powder
$1/4$ cup brown sugar	

Beat eggs, then add all the other ingredients together in a bowl. Pour into greased 10" pie pan. Bake at 350° for 50 minutes. When baked, crust will be on bottom, custard in the middle, and coconut on the top. Andy brought this recipe back from Switzerland.

CREAM CHEESE VANILLA CRUMB PIE

··· Mrs. Lloyd (Bena) Miller

2 - 9" unbaked pie crusts	1 beaten egg
8 oz. cream cheese	$1/2$ tsp. salt
$1/2$ cup sugar	1 tsp. vanilla

FILLING

2 cups water	1 cup dark corn syrup
1 cup sugar	1 beaten egg
1 Tbsp. flour	1 tsp. vanilla

CRUMB TOPPING

2 cups flour	1 tsp. baking soda
$1/2$ cup brown sugar	$1/2$ tsp. cream of tartar
$1/2$ cup softened butter or margarine	$1/2$ tsp. cinnamon

Beat together cream cheese, sugar, egg, salt, and vanilla. Spread in pie crusts. In a medium saucepan, bring 2 cups water to a boil. Combine sugar, flour, corn syrup, and egg. Stir into hot water. Bring to a boil, then set aside to cool. Add vanilla. When cooled, pour this over cream cheese layer. Mix the topping ingredients until crumbly. Spread over top of pie. Bake at 375° for 30–40 minutes. Yield: 2 pies.

*A selfish man is not a grateful man,
for he never thinks he gets as much as he deserves.*

MOUNDS PIE
··· Mrs. Reuben (Betty) Yoder

3 eggs
1 cup light corn syrup
2 Tbsp. butter
$1/4$ tsp. salt
1 tsp. vanilla
$1/2$ cup macaroon coconut
$1/2$ cup oatmeal
$1/2$ cup chocolate chips

Beat eggs; add corn syrup, butter, vanilla, and salt. Mix well. Add the remaining ingredients. Pour into unbaked pie crust. Bake at 350° for 45 minutes or until it is set. Very good! Makes 1 pie.

OATMEAL PIE
··· favorite of Emanuel Andrew Brenneman

2 eggs
$3/4$ cup sugar
$3/4$ cup dark corn syrup
2 Tbsp. flour
$1/4$ cup butter or margarine
1 tsp. vanilla
$3/4$ cup oatmeal
$1/3$ cup coconut (optional)

Preheat oven to 350°. Beat eggs till foamy. Gradually add sugar; beat until thick. Stir in remaining ingredients. Blend well. Pour into pie shell. Bake about 45 minutes, or until center of pie is firm.

PECAN PIE
··· Mrs. Alton (Nora) Nisley

7 eggs
2 cups light corn syrup
$1^1/2$ cups white sugar
$1/2$ cup butter, melted
1 tsp. salt
pecans

This makes 2 large pies. Bake at 350° for 45 minutes.

PECAN PIE
··· Mrs. Steven (Bena) Yoder

6 eggs
2 cups white Karo
1 cup brown sugar
$3/4$ cup white sugar
2 cups pecans
$1/2$ cup butter, melted
2 tsp. vanilla
1 Tbsp. flour

Beat eggs; add all the ingredients but the pecans. Put pecans in 2 unbaked pie shells. Pour the liquid ingredients on top of the pecans. Bake in a hot (450°) oven for 10 minutes, then reduce heat to 300° and bake till set. In all, bake 1 hour.

CREAM CHEESE PECAN PIE   ··· *Mrs. Mary Esta Yoder*

8 oz. cream cheese
1 egg, beaten
1 tsp. vanilla
$^1/_2$ cup sugar

$^1/_2$ tsp. salt
1$^1/_4$ cups chopped pecans
1 - 10" unbaked pie shell

TOPPING

3 eggs
$^1/_2$ tsp. vanilla

1 cup light Karo

Cream together softened cream cheese, sugar, egg, salt, and vanilla. Spread over bottom of pie shell. Sprinkle pecans over cream cheese layer. Combine topping ingredients and beat until smooth. Pour over pecan layer. Bake at 375° for 35–45 minutes, until pecan layer is golden brown.

SOUTHERN PECAN PIE   ··· *Mrs. Freeman (Marie) Schlabach*

2 eggs
$^1/_2$ cup corn or pancake syrup
$^1/_2$ cup oleo, melted
2 Tbsp. flour
1 cup sugar

$^1/_2$ tsp. salt
1 tsp. vanilla
1 tsp. maple flavoring
2 Tbsp. milk
$^1/_2$ cup pecans, chopped

Beat eggs; add sugar, flour, and oleo. Beat, then add the remaining ingredients except pecans and beat again. Pour pecans in pie shell and the rest on top. Bake at 350° till set. Serve with ice cream and coffee.

DUTCH APPLE PIE··· *Mrs. Kris Miller* ··· *Mrs. Paul (Rebecca) Nisley*

7 apples, shredded
$^1/_2$ cup brown sugar
3 Tbsp. flour

1 tsp. cinnamon
2 Tbsp. butter

TOPPING

4 Tbsp. butter, melted
$^3/_4$ cup flour

$^1/_2$ cup brown sugar

Mix sugar, flour, and cinnamon with apples. Put in pie shell and dab with butter. Mix butter, flour, and sugar and put on top of apples. Bake at 375° for 45 minutes.

Variation: Rebecca adds 4 Tbsp. cream over top of crumbs.

MOST UNUSUAL APPLE PIE   ··· Mrs. Owen (Elsie) Nisley

1 cup unsifted flour	$^3/_4$ cup sugar
1 tsp. baking powder	pinch of salt

Mix together. Add:

$^1/_2$ cup butter	1 egg, beaten

Mix all this with a fork. Will be thick like paste. In the meantime, put 4 or 5 apples, sliced, into a square Pyrex dish. Put above mixture over the apples in big spoonfuls. Sprinkle with cinnamon and sugar. Bake at 325° for 30–40 minutes, until done. Serve warm with ice cream or whipped cream.

YELLOW DELICIOUS APPLE PIE

··· Mrs. Andy (Elsie) Schlabach

3 cups shredded apples	$^1/_2$ tsp. cinnamon or apple pie spice
1 cup sugar	2 Tbsp. margarine or butter
3 Tbsp. flour	3 Tbsp. rich milk

Mix apples, flour, sugar, and spice together. Blend well. Place mixture in 9" unbaked pie shell. Add dots of butter and milk. Put lattice or crust on top. Bake at 375° for 40–45 minutes.

TIP: For a nice brown crust, brush top with milk and sprinkle with sugar.

CREAM CHEESE RHUBARB PIE

··· Mrs. Marion (Rachel) Mullet

1 unbaked pie shell	8 oz. cream cheese
$^1/_4$ cup cornstarch	2 eggs
$^1/_2$ cup water	whipped cream
pinch of salt	slivered almonds for garnish

1$^1/_2$ cups white sugar, divided

3 cups fresh or frozen rhubarb, cut into $^1/_2$" cubes

Combine cornstarch, 1 cup sugar, and salt in saucepan. Add $^1/_2$ cup water; stir until thoroughly combined. Add rhubarb. Cook, stirring often, until mixture boils and thickens. Pour into pie shell. Bake at 425° for 10 minutes.

Meanwhile, for topping, beat cream cheese, eggs, and remaining $^1/_2$ cup sugar till smooth. Pour over rhubarb layer. Return to oven and reduce heat to 325°. Bake until set, about 25 minutes. Cool; chill several hours or overnight. Garnish with whipped cream and almonds.

RHUBARB PIE
··· Mrs. Henry (Emma) Troyer

2 eggs, beaten
1 1/2 cups granulated sugar
2 Tbsp. flour
5 Tbsp. water
2 cups rhubarb, cut fine

Put in unbaked pie crust and sprinkle butter and cinnamon on top. Bake at 350° till done.

GROUND CHERRY PIE
··· Mrs. Lloyd (Bena) Miller

1 1/4 cups ground cherries
1 cup water
1 cup (or less) sugar
2 Tbsp. clear jel
1/4 tsp. salt
1 Tbsp. butter
1 Tbsp. lemon juice

Put cherries in saucepan; add water, salt, and 3/4 cup sugar. Bring to a boil; thicken with clear jel. Reduce heat; boil for 2 minutes. Take off stove; add butter, rest of sugar, and lemon juice. Pour into pie shell and put crust on top. Bake at 450° until golden brown. Our family favorite.

DOUBLE CRUST RAISIN PIE
··· Mrs. Ralph (Sarah) Schlabach

2 cups raisins
1 qt. water
1 cup white sugar
1 cup brown sugar
1/2 tsp. salt

Soak the 2 cups raisins in 1 qt. water overnight. Next morning, add the remaining ingredients and cook about 30 minutes, then add another 2 cups water and thicken with clear jel.

JAPANESE FRUIT PIE
··· Mrs. Freeman (Marie) Schlabach

1 cup sugar
1 Tbsp. vinegar
1 stick oleo, melted
dash of salt
1 Tbsp. flour
1 tsp. vanilla
2 eggs
1/2 cup raisins
1 cup coconut
1/2 cup nuts, chopped

Beat eggs and add sugar, oleo, vinegar, flour, salt, and vanilla. Stir in raisins, coconut, and nuts. Pour into unbaked pie shell. Bake 30 minutes at 350° or till set.

MOCK MINCE PIE
··· *Mrs. Freeman (Marie) Schlabach*

2 eggs	1 1/2 cups bread crumbs
3 cups sugar	1 tsp. cinnamon
2 cups water	1 tsp. cloves
1 cup raisins	1 tsp. nutmeg
1/2 cup vinegar	1/2 cup butter (scant)

Beat eggs and add all remaining ingredients except butter. Melt butter and add. Pour in pie shell and bake at 350° till set.

A smile takes but a moment, but the memory of it sometimes lasts forever.

Candy,
Snacks &
Children's
Corner

Roses can mean, "I love you,"
Daisies can enthrall ...
But a weed bouquet in a chubby fist—
Oh my, that says it all!

Children

A child is a lovable patch of skin
To poke rock candy and pudding in;
Torture somehow in the tub,
For giggling and splashing as they scrub;
To powder and put fresh play clothes on...
Two minutes later the pressing is gone.
To scatter the toys and rough the rug;
They melt your annoyance with a hug.
To amaze you with all the things they know—
They're sharper than you were years ago!
They keep your ego at reasonable levels,
And change your frowns to blessed revels;
They make you important, even sublime,
Two jumps ahead of you all the time.

History of the Pretzel

Way back in the early days of the Christian church, an old German monk discovered the idea of little cakes to be given to the children who learned their prayers well and he fittingly called them "Pretiolas," meaning "little rewards." So ingenious was he that he made these cakes in a shape that would signify their very purpose. He rolled the dough into a long strip, formed it into a circle, then crossed the ends in an attitude of prayer. His plan was so effective that other monks adopted it, and soon "Pretiolas" were being made in the small quaint ovens of many monasteries. Little did these monks know that these cakes would be handed down from generation to generation and would be called pretzels someday. The next time you enjoy these little snacks, remember their beginning and always remember to have an attitude of prayer.

BUTTER CREAMS
··· *Leona Sue Miller*

2 cups white sugar

$^1/_4$ tsp. cream of tartar

1 cup cream

$^1/_2$ cup butter

Boil sugar, cream, and butter for 5 minutes. Add cream of tartar and continue to boil to soft ball stage. Do not stir while cooking. Remove from heat and let cool completely. When cold, beat until creamy.

Mold in small balls and coat with melted chocolate. This is a Miller family tradition at Christmastime.

CHOCOLATE DROPS
··· *Mrs. Steve (Bena) Yoder*

2 cups brown sugar

1 cup cream

$^1/_4$ tsp. cream of tartar

chocolate

Combine all ingredients. Use a candy thermometer and cook over low heat to soft ball stage. Do not stir while cooking. Cool until the bottom of the pan feels warm or a little cool. Then stir and stir till it doesn't look shiny anymore, about 15–30 minutes. Then let set for 5–10 minutes. Shape in balls and dip in chocolate.

CARAMELS
··· *favorite of Wendall David Miller, age 4*

$^1/_2$ lb. butter

2 cups white sugar

Bring to a boil. Add:

1 can Eagle Brand milk

1 cup corn syrup

$^1/_2$ cup walnuts

Bring to soft boil (240°). Cool. Cut into small pieces and wrap in waxed paper.

SUGARLESS DATE AND NUT CANDY
··· *Mrs. Emanuel (Mary) Nisley*

2 cups chopped dates

$^1/_2$ cup oleo or butter

2 well beaten eggs

Cook slowly about 15 minutes or until thick. Add:

1 cup pecans

1 tsp. vanilla

$2^1/_2$ cups Rice Krispies

Mix well and while still warm, shape into balls and roll in coconut, or pat in pan and put coconut on top.

EASTER EGGS
··· *Leona Sue Miller*

$3/4$ lb. butter or margarine
2 pkg. regular pudding mix
$1/2$ cup milk

1 lb. powdered sugar
1 tsp. vanilla
dipping chocolate for eggs

Melt butter; add pudding and stir until blended. Add milk and blend well. Cook over low heat, stirring constantly. Let boil for 2 minutes. Remove from heat; add powdered sugar and vanilla. Mix until smooth. When cool enough to handle, shape into eggs. Chill thoroughly, and when cold, melt chocolate and coat eggs.

VARIATIONS

Chocolate Eggs: Use chocolate pudding, 1 tsp. vanilla, and chopped nuts.

Cherry Eggs: Use vanilla pudding, 1 tsp. almond flavoring, a few drops of red food coloring, and $1/2$ cup very well drained, cut-up maraschino cherries.

Maple Nut Eggs: Use butterscotch pudding, 1 tsp. maple flavoring, and $1/2$ cup (or more) chopped nuts.

HEAVENLY HASH CANDY
··· *Hannah Yoder*

2 lb. white chocolate
5 cups Cheerios
5 cups Cap'n Crunch cereal
(peanut butter flavor)

3 cups mini marshmallows
(funmallows)
3 cups Spanish peanuts

Mix cereals, peanuts, and marshmallows in a large bowl. Melt chocolate over low heat and pour over mixture; stir well. Spread on waxed paper. Let cool; break into pieces and enjoy!

HOPSCOTCH CANDY
··· *Mrs. Mary Esta Yoder*

Melt in double boiler:
$1/2$ cup peanut butter
Pour over:
1 - 3 oz. can La Choy chow mein
noodles

1 - 6 oz. pkg. butterscotch chips

2 cups mini marshmallows

Stir until blended. Drop by tsp. onto waxed paper. Chill.

CLARK BARS
··· *Julia Yoder*

1 cup margarine
1 lb. crunchy peanut butter
2^1/$_2$ cups powdered sugar

3 tsp. vanilla
1 lb. graham crackers, crushed
chocolate

Mix first 5 ingredients. Roll in bonbon size balls. Dip in melted chocolate.

WHITE TRASH
··· *favorite of Lavern Yoder, age 6*

6 cups Crispix
4 cups small pretzels
2 cups dry roasted peanuts

1 lb. M&Ms
1^1/$_4$ lb. white chocolate

Melt chocolate over medium heat in double boiler. Pour over snack mixture and mix to coat. Spread on waxed paper or trays to cool.

PUPPY CHOW
··· *favorite of Rachel Kay Schlabach, age 8*
··· *Erica Kaufman* ··· *Iva D. Nisley* ··· *Sarah Schlabach*

1 cup chocolate chips
1 stick butter
^{1}/$_2$ cup peanut butter

9 cups Chex cereal
2 cups powdered sugar

Melt chocolate chips, butter, and peanut butter in saucepan, then pour over cereal, stirring until well coated. Pour cereal into a paper bag containing powdered sugar and shake vigorously. Place mixture on a cookie sheet to dry a few hours or overnight.

CHURCH WINDOW COOKIES
··· *Hannah Yoder*

^{1}/$_2$ cup butter or oleo
1 - 12 oz. pkg. chocolate chips
1 cup chopped nuts

1 - 10 oz. pkg. funmallows
1 - 14 oz. pkg. flake coconut

Melt butter and chocolate chips over low heat. Allow to cool slightly. Stir in funmallows and nuts. Shape into 2 rolls. Spread coconut on waxed paper. Roll in coconut and wrap in waxed paper. Refrigerate for 24 hours. Cut in ^{1}/$_2$" slices.

Variation: Can also be made without coconut.

ROCKY ROAD SQUARES   ··· *favorite of Larisa Yoder, age 9*

graham crackers   1 cup powdered sugar
2 cups mini marshmallows   1 egg, beaten
6 oz. butterscotch chips $^1/_2$ cup oleo

Line 9" x 12" pan with whole graham crackers. Arrange marshmallows over cracker layer. Melt oleo and chips in double boiler; add beaten egg and powdered sugar. Heat to boiling point. Cool slightly. Pour over cracker–marshmallow layer. Cool in refrigerator. Break into squares to serve.

S'MORES   ··· *Mrs. Linda Mae Troyer*

graham crackers   chocolate chips
small marshmallows   peanut butter

Place a layer of graham crackers on a cookie sheet; top with marshmallows. Put in a 350° oven until marshmallows are melted. Remove; put milk chocolate chips on top. Add another layer of graham crackers which have been spread with peanut butter. Return to oven until melted. Derrick's favorite snack.

MARSHMALLOW HATS   ··· *Hannah Yoder*

12 Ritz crackers   peanut butter
12 large marshmallows

Spread each cracker with peanut butter. Put one marshmallow on each cracker. Put in oven till nicely browned. Enjoy with friends!

CARAMEL CRACKERS   ··· *Mrs. Mary Esta Yoder*

2 - 9 oz. boxes Ritz Bits $^1/_2$ cup Karo
1 cup dry roasted peanuts   1 tsp. vanilla
$^1/_2$ cup margarine   1 tsp. soda
1 cup white sugar

Combine crackers and nuts in a large shallow pan. In a saucepan, bring margarine, sugar, and Karo to a boil. Boil for 5 minutes. Remove from heat and add vanilla and soda. Stir; pour over cracker mixture and mix well. Spread on baking sheet and bake 1 hour at 250°, stirring every 15 minutes. Pour onto waxed paper and break apart before completely cool. Store in airtight container.

QUICK CRACKER SNACKS
··· favorite of Kristine Joy Yoder, age 6

Spread a Ritz cracker with:
— peanut butter with M&M candies
— softened cream cheese topped with a fresh strawberry
— salsa, a drop of sour cream, and mozzarella cheese
— ham and a slice of cheese

SEASONED CRACKERS   *··· Mrs. Wayne (Emma) Yoder*

1 cup vegetable oil
3 Tbsp. cheddar powder

3 Tbsp. sour cream and onion
powder

Pour over 1 lb. white crackers or oyster crackers. Bake 20 minutes at 250°.

ZESTY PRETZELS   *··· Julia Yoder*

24 oz. pretzel sticks
1 cup vegetable oil
1 pkg. Hidden Valley Ranch mix (dry)

1 Tbsp. dill weed
$^3/_4$ tsp. garlic powder

Mix together ingredients and pour over pretzel sticks. Mix thoroughly. Store in a covered bowl. They get better as they set! It takes 2–4 hours to fully absorb the flavors.

HONEY CRACKLE *··· Mrs. Henry (Emma) Troyer ··· Rosanna Nisley*

3 qt. fresh popped corn
1 cup almonds or peanuts
$^1/_2$ cup butter

1 cup brown sugar
$^1/_4$ cup honey
1 tsp. vanilla

Put corn in shallow roasting pan. In qt. saucepan over low heat, melt butter; stir in brown sugar and honey. Over medium heat, bring to boil. Boil gently, without stirring, for 5 minutes. Remove from heat; stir in vanilla. Pour mixture over popped corn and nuts. Stir until well mixed. Bake in 250° oven, stirring every 15 minutes, for 1 hour. Cool and break apart. This recipe comes from Grandma Schlabach's *Women's Household Magazine*.

CARAMEL POPCORN   *··· Mrs. Linda Beachy*

1 cup brown sugar   2^1/$_2$ sticks of butter
^{3}/$_4$ cup white Karo   7^1/$_2$ qt. popcorn
pinch of salt

Melt butter, then add sugar, Karo, and salt. Boil 5 minutes. Pour over popcorn. Put on cookie sheet and bake for 1^1/$_4$ hours at 200°. Stir every half hour.

CRISPY CINNAMON POPCORN *··· Mrs. Mary Esta Yoder*

7 qt. popped popcorn   1 tsp. salt
1 cup white sugar   1 cup oleo
1 cup cinnamon Imperial candies   1 tsp. vanilla
^{1}/$_2$ cup white Karo ^{1}/$_2$ tsp. soda

In heavy saucepan, boil sugar, Karo, salt, candies, and oleo. Stir till candies are dissolved. Boil 5 minutes. Add vanilla and soda. Stir well. Pour over popcorn and mix well. Place on cookie sheets and bake 1 hour at 250°, stirring every 10–15 minutes. When cold, store in airtight container.

PARTY MIX   *··· Mose A. Schlabach*

1 box Rice Chex   2 sticks oleo or butter
1 box Corn Chex   2 tsp. celery salt
1 box Cheerios   1 tsp. Lawry's seasoning salt
1 pack thin pretzel sticks   2 tsp. garlic powder
nuts to taste   2 tsp. onion powder
2 Tbsp. Worcestershire sauce

Melt oleo; add salts and sauce. Pour over cereal mixture; mix well. Put in pans and heat in 250° oven for 1^1/$_2$ hours, stirring every 15 minutes. From my experience, this mixture is a prizewinner.

PEANUT BUTTER PLAY DOUGH (IT'S EDIBLE)

··· Marnita Yoder, age 2

18 oz. peanut butter   nonfat dry milk and flour to make
6 Tbsp. honey   right consistency of play dough

Shape and decorate with raisins. Enjoy with friends!

PLAY DOUGH
··· favorite of Rachel Schlabach

1 cup salt
2 cups flour
2 cups water

4 tsp. cream of tartar
2 Tbsp. cooking oil

Add food coloring. Mix all together. Cook 3 minutes or until dough sticks together. Knead. Store in airtight container.

PLAY DOUGH
··· Mrs. Steven (Bena) Yoder
··· Mrs. Wayne (Emma) Yoder

1 cup flour
$^1/_2$ cup salt
$1^1/_2$ Tbsp. oil

2 tsp. cream of tartar
1 cup water
food coloring to suit color

Combine all ingredients. Cook over low heat for about 3 minutes, stirring constantly. When cooked to dough, it will pull away from pan; place on waxed paper. Knead when cool and place in airtight container. My children love to watch me make play dough.

SILLY PUTTY OR GAK
··· Marita Mast ··· Sarah Schlabch

FIRST BOWL
Mix well:

2 cups Elmer's glue

$1^1/_2$ cups water

SECOND BOWL
Dissolve 2 level tsp. of 20 Mule Team borax in 1 cup warm water; add any food coloring desired. Slowly combine the 2 mixtures and mix together. You may have to use hands to mix thoroughly. Store in an airtight container.

PUMPKIN SEEDS
··· favorite of Rachel Schlabach

1 pumpkin
1 Tbsp. butter

1 tsp. Worcestershire sauce

Separate seeds from pumpkin flesh. Boil 10 minutes in water. Drain. For each cup of drained seeds, add 1 Tbsp. butter and 1 tsp. Worcestershire sauce. Mix well. Spread on cookie sheets and sprinkle with seasoning salt. Bake 30 minutes at 350°, stirring occasionally, until dry.

CINNAMON ORNAMENTS

··· *Mrs. Philip (Denise) Schlabach*

$^3/_4$ cup ground cinnamon
1 Tbsp. ground allspice
2 Tbsp. ground cloves
1 Tbsp. ground nutmeg
1 cup applesauce

Combine all the spices, blending well. Stir in applesauce. Mix well. Roll out to $^1/_4$" thickness. Cut out shapes with cookie cutters. Put on ungreased cookie sheet and let dry 4–5 days. You may then store in plastic bag and seal. Don't forget to put a hole in each for ribbon ties.

POTPOURRI – SCENT OF CHRISTMAS   ··· *Julia Yoder*

3 Tbsp. ground cinnamon
2 Tbsp. ground cloves
1 tsp. ground nutmeg
1 tsp. ground ginger
1 Tbsp. anise seed (optional)

Mix all ingredients; add 1 qt. water. Simmer on low or simmer in a potpourri pot.

BIRD FEED   ··· *Leona Sue Miller*

Melt 1 lb. lard. Add:
1 lb. peanut butter
1 lb. oatmeal
1 lb. yellow cornmeal

Mix together and pour into pans. When set, cut into chunks for bird feeder. For a special treat, I like to add some unsalted raw sunflower seeds.

PRESERVED CHILDREN   ··· *copied by Mrs. Owen Schlabach*

Take one large grassy field, half a dozen children, 2 or 3 small dogs, a pinch of brook, and some pebbles. Mix the children and dogs together well and put on field, stirring constantly. Pour the brook over the pebbles. Sprinkle the field with flowers, spread over all a deep blue sky, and bake in the sun. When children are brown, set away to cool in the bathtub.

Kindness is the oil that takes the friction out of life.

KINDERGARTEN COOKIES

1 small child	4 drops of safety rules
5 to 6 years of tender loving care	$1/2$ tsp. humor
1 lb. of patience	generous pinch of reading time
2 heaping measures of good manners	10 sticky fingers

If dough is wiggly, add a few extra hugs until desired consistency is obtained. Allow to stand 5–10 minutes for proper discipline. Place in desired world with interest and pride. Set goals at a degree that will give a child a feeling of accomplishment. Will produce a creative, enthusiastic, capable child. CAUTION: Will crumble easily; must be reassured often.

BIRTHDAY GIFT IDEAS

On a large piece of cardboard, print this birthday message, using candy bars to complete the message.

Mr./Mrs. **WHATCHAMACALLIT,**

We were going to give you **100 GRAND**, but the money slipped through our **BUTTERFINGERS** and we couldn't wait till **PAYDAY**, so we looked on **FIFTH AVENUE** and found a trip to **MARS** and the **MILKY WAY**, but neither seemed appropriate.

We wish you **MOUNDS** of **ALMOND JOY** as you **CRUNCH** through another year.

Sincerely,
MR. GOODBAR
THE 3 MUSKETEERS
BABY RUTH

P.S. We promise not to **SNICKERS** at your age!

Favorite Recipes

_____

_____

_____

_____

_____

_____

_____

_____

_____

_____

_____

_____

_____

_____

_____

_____

_____

_____

_____

_____

_____

_____

_____

_____

Large

Quantity

Recipes

If a task is once begun,
Never leave it till it's done.
Be the labor great or small,
Do it well or not at all.

CHICKEN AND DRESSING FOR 250 PEOPLE

··· Mrs. Freeman (Marie) Schlabach

12 gal. dry bread crumbs
1 gal. minced celery
2 qt. minced onion
2 qt. minced parsley
4^1/$_2$ gal. cut-up chicken or turkey
    meat

5^1/$_2$ gal. broth
5 lb. melted butter
5 doz. eggs, beaten
salt and pepper to taste
8 cubes bouillon or chicken base
poultry seasoning to taste

Pour butter over crumbs; mix well. Add all other ingredients. Put in large roasters. For a wedding, put in oven at 7:00 at 225°. When browned, turn back temperature. Do not stir.

CHICKEN DRESSING

··· Mrs. Mary Esta Yoder

2 loaves white bread, cubed
1 loaf wheat bread, cubed
2 qt. deboned chicken
2 cups celery, diced
2 cups carrots, diced
4 cups potatoes, diced
12 to 14 eggs
1 qt. chicken broth

^{1}/$_4$ cup parsley
1 Tbsp. Lawry's seasoning salt
1 tsp. pepper
2 Tbsp. salt
^{1}/$_4$ tsp. onion salt
2 Tbsp. chicken base
3 qt. milk

Cook vegetables until tender. Toast cubed bread in butter. Put bread in a large mixing bowl; add vegetables and chicken. Beat eggs and milk; add broth and seasonings. Pour over all and mix well. Fry in skillet. May also be frozen.

HAM POTATO CASSEROLE

··· Mrs. Freeman (Marie) Schlabach

20 lb. cooked diced potatoes
10 lb. smoked ham, diced
1 gal. milk
1^1/$_2$ cups flour

4 Tbsp. salt
1 tsp. pepper
1^1/$_2$ cups butter
1 lb. Velveeta cheese

Heat milk and flour after mixing till there are no lumps. Add butter, salt, and pepper. Mix and add ham and potatoes. Add cheese last. Bake till heated through. Serves 60–75 people.

SCALLOPED POTATOES   ··· *Mrs. Lloyd (Bena) Miller*

10 lb. potatoes
2 qt. milk
1$^1/_3$ cups flour
3 Tbsp. salt
$^1/_2$ tsp. pepper

1$^1/_4$ cups butter
1 lb. Velveeta cheese
1 medium onion, chopped
2 tsp. Worcestershire sauce
5 lb. ham, cubed or sliced

Cook potatoes in jackets. Cool; peel and slice. Put potatoes into a large baking dish. Melt butter in saucepan. Add flour; stir well. Add milk, cheese, salt, pepper, and Worcestershire sauce. Heat until cheese is melted. Mix ham and onions with potatoes. Pour cheese mixture over potatoes and bake at 350° for 1 hour. Serves 30.

EL PASO CASSEROLE   ··· *Mrs. Lloyd (Bena) Miller*

1$^3/_4$ lb. Velveeta cheese
2 lb. ham

1$^1/_2$ lb. noodles

WHITE SAUCE

$^1/_2$ lb. butter
1 cup flour

$^1/_2$ gal. milk

Cook noodles in water. Blend cheese and ham into white sauce. Pour over noodles in greased casserole dish. Sprinkle with toasted bread cubes. Bake at 350° for 25 minutes. Serves 30.

TRASH CAN MEAL   ··· *Mrs. Linda Beachy*

Place 6" of corn husks in the bottom of a clean, new metal trash can.

$^3/_4$ gal. water
10 lb. potatoes
4 lb. carrots
3 heads of cabbage

2$^1/_2$ doz. ears of corn
7 lb. ham
4 lb. sausage
4 lb. smoked sausage

Place ingredients on top of corn husks in order given. Cover with tinfoil and cook over an outside fire (placed on blocks or stone) for 1$^1/_2$ hours. Don't uncover. Have fire very hot. Serves about 25 people.

NOODLE RECIPE
··· *Mrs. Lloyd (Bena) Miller*

Brown $^1/_2$ lb. butter in large cooker. Add:

5 large cans College Inn chicken   6 - 8 oz. pkg. Inn Maid noodles
   broth   3 cans cream of chicken soup
2 heaping Tbsp. chicken base

Bring broth to a boil; add noodles and chicken base. Cook 5 minutes. Add soup which has been heated. Cover and let set till done. Do not add water. Serves 70.

BAR-B-Q SAUCE FOR 55 TO 60 CHICKEN HALVES
··· *Mrs. Jr. (Ruth) Miller*

1 gal. and 1 qt. water   2 lb. oleo
1 gal. and 1 qt. vinegar $2^1/_2$ cups salt
2 lb. butter $1^1/_2$ bottles Worcestershire sauce

Heat until butter and oleo are melted. Do not use sparingly on chicken. It works best to put sauce in a small sprayer.

POTATO AND HAM SOUP
··· *Mrs. David (Susan) Nisley*

1 large onion, diced   enough flour to make a paste
3 sticks butter

Mix and make a paste, then brown. Add:

5 qt. shredded potatoes that have   5 qt. milk
   been heated to boiling

Add milk and potatoes, water and all. Add enough water to cover; boil.

5 to 6 lb. turkey ham, cut in small cubes

Add this after other ingredients are hot. Salt to taste. Add:

1 - 2 lb. box Velveeta cheese

Makes 5 gal.

LIME FLUFF
··· *Mrs. Freeman (Marie) Schlabach*

32 oz. whipped topping   3 - 15 oz. cans mandarin oranges,
6 oz. lime jello, dry   drained
32 oz. small curd cottage cheese

Combine topping, jello, and cottage cheese. Fold in oranges. This recipe taken 4 times serves 100 people.

LETTUCE DRESSING   *... Jonas and Katie Raber*

1 qt. Miracle Whip   3 cans Milnot milk
$^1/_2$ bottle Catalina or Country   2 Tbsp. mustard
   Kitchen French dressing   3 tsp. salt
$^1/_2$ bottle Sweet 'n' Sour dressing   vinegar, if necessary, to suit your taste
4 cups sugar
   Beat with egg beater. Makes 1 gallon.

CHOCOLATE CHIP COOKIES (BIG BATCH)

10 cups shortening   vanilla
10 cups brown sugar   10 tsp. soda
10 cups white sugar   8 tsp. salt
20 eggs   32 cups flour
2$^1/_2$ cups hot water   8 cups chocolate chips
   Mix all together and bake at 350°.

BUTTERMILK COOKIES (BIG BATCH)

   Cream:
8 cups shortening   16 cups brown sugar
   Add:
16 eggs   16 tsp. soda
8 cups buttermilk   16 tsp. baking powder
vanilla   3 tsp. salt
32 cups flour
   Drop onto baking sheet. Bake at 350°. Frost with caramel icing while still
warm for a glossy appearance. Yield: Approximately 40 doz.

PEANUT BUTTER SPREAD   *... Mrs. Alton (Nora) Nisley*

4 cups brown sugar $^1/_4$ cup light Karo
2 cups boiling water   2 tsp. maple flavoring
   Bring to a boil. Remove from heat. Cool and add 2$^1/_2$ lbs. peanut butter
and 1 qt. marshmallow topping. Double batch is enough for church.

ELEPHANT STEW

1 medium sized elephant   salt and pepper to taste
2 rabbits (optional)

Cut elephant into small, bite sized pieces. This should take about 2 months. Add enough brown gravy to cover. Cook for about 4 weeks at 465°. Will serve about 3,800 people. If more people are expected, the two rabbits may be added, but do this only if necessary, as most people do not like hare in their stew.

CALCULATING FOOD

Figuring approximate amounts for groups is not as difficult as many people think. Amounts needed, of course, will also vary with the number of items on the menu. The more items guests have to choose from, the less they usually take of each.

One-half ($1/2$) cup does make a nice serving of many foods. All you need to do is multiply the number of guests and you have a good idea of the total amount needed.

The following amounts are approximate because of variations in menus and in eating habits.

Bread — 10 servings per loaf (homemade)
Meat Loaf — 4 servings per 1 lb. of meat
Noodles — 10 servings per 8 oz. pkg.
Corn — 10 servings per qt.
Tossed Salad — 25–30 servings per Fix 'n' Mix bowl
Mixed Fruit — 40 servings per Fix 'n' bowl
Jello Prepared with Fruit — 2 - 6 oz. pkg. serves 20–25
Cake — 9" x 13" cake is 20 servings
Potatoes — 1 lb. is 4 servings
Lettuce — 1 head is 6–8 servings
Soup (1 cup serving) — 1 gal. is 16 servings
Cheese for Cheese Plate — 8 servings per 1 lb. sliced
Ice Cream — 1 gal. is 25 servings

Canning &

Freezing

Success comes in cans—
"I can"
"You can"
"We can"

Home canning is a very rewarding experience! It is very satisfying to see the many jars of fruits and vegetables lined up on a shelf, ready at your fingertips to feed your family and friends.

When canning, it is important to process your filled jars at 212°F for the right amount of time to destroy the bacteria, molds, and yeast which exist everywhere, or they will grow in your canned food and cause it to spoil.

Following is an approximate timetable of processing times in boiling water. Time for fruit varies in families.

Meats — 3 hours   Peaches — 5 minutes
Vegetables — 3 hours   Pears — 5 minutes
Bologna — 1 hour   Applesauce — 5 minutes
Pizza and Spaghetti Sauce — 10–20 minutes
Green Beans — $1^1/_2$–2 hours (add 1 Tbsp. lemon juice to each qt.,
    then only process 1 hour)
To Freeze Peas — Bring water to boiling; turn to low. Do not boil. Add peas.
    After 10 minutes, remove and cool; drain on paper towel to dry. Freeze.
To Freeze Peaches: Add orange juice and pineapple juice.

APPROXIMATE YIELDS

Legal weight of a bushel of fruits or vegetables varies in different states. These are average weights.

FOOD	FRESH	CANNED
Apples	1 bushel (48 lb.)	16–20 qt.
Berries, except Strawberries	24 qt. crate	12–18 qt.
Strawberries	1 qt.	$1^1/_2$ pt. crushed, frozen
Peaches	1 bushel (48 lb.)	18–24 qt.
Pears	1 bushel (50 lb.)	20–26 qt.
Tomatoes	1 bushel (53 lb.)	15–20 qt.
Lima Beans in Pods	1 bushel (32 lb.)	6–8 qt.
Snap Beans	1 bushel (30 lb.)	15–20 qt.
Beets, without Tops	1 bushel (52 lb.)	17–20 qt.
Sweet Corn, in Husks	1 bushel (36 lb.)	8–9 qt.
Sweet Corn	1 doz. ears	1 qt. frozen
Green Peas, in Pods	1 bushel (30 lb.)	12–15 qt.

CANNING STRAWBERRIES   ··· *Mrs. Lloyd (Bena) Miller*

1 qt. berries
1 cup sugar

$^1/_2$ cup water

Bring water and sugar to boil before adding strawberries. Add berries and cook for 7 minutes. Put in jars and seal.

CANNING STRAWBERRIES   ··· *Mrs. Albert (Verna) Yoder*

3 pt. strawberries, mashed or
  chopped
1$^1/_2$ cups water

1 cup white sugar
1 Tbsp. minute tapioca

Mix all together; boil about 20 minutes. Skim off foam. Pack in hot jars. Can put more than 1 batch in a large kettle. Very good and quickly done!

RHUBARB JUICE   ··· *Mrs. Mary Esta Yoder*

Cook together in an 8 qt. saucepan:

4 qt. water   4 lb. rhubarb, chopped

Boil 10 minutes. Strain, then add:

2 cups sugar   1 cup orange juice
1 cup pineapple juice

Bring to a boil; pour in clean jars. Seal; cold pack 10 minutes. To serve, add 7-Up or Sprite to taste.

APPLE PIE FILLING   ··· *Mrs. Mary Esta Yoder*

28 cups apples, shoestring,
  Golden Delicious
7 cups water
3 cups fresh cider
4$^1/_2$ cups white sugar

1 tsp. salt
2 tsp. cinnamon
1 cup clear jel
3 Tbsp. lemon juice

Bring water, cider, and sugar to a boil. Dissolve clear jel in 1 cup of the water (cold). Mix cinnamon and salt; add to boiling syrup. Stir till clear and thickened; add lemon juice and apples. Remove from heat; cover for 10 minutes. Put in jars and cold pack 20 minutes. Yield: 7 qt.

MINCEMEAT FOR PIE

··· *Mrs. Emanuel (Mary) Nisley (from Mother's cookbook)*

1 gal. (or more) chopped apples
1/2 gal. cooked ground beef
1/2 lb. raisins, cooked a few
    minutes

1 tsp. each cinnamon, allspice, and
    nutmeg
sugar and salt to taste
some vinegar

Grind apples with food chopper (not too big). Add some water. Cold pack 1–2 hours.

CANNED PEACH PIE FILLING

··· *Mrs. Freeman (Naomi) Miller* ··· *Mrs. Reuben (Betty) Yoder*
··· *Mrs. Marion (Rachel) Mullet* ··· *Mrs. Mary Esta Yoder*

6 qt. peaches
3 cups pineapple juice
3 cups water

7 cups sugar
1³/₄ cups Perma-Flo or Clo-Flo
1³/₄ cups water

Peel and slice peaches into a large mixing bowl. In a 6 qt. saucepan, combine, 3 cups water, pineapple juice, and sugar. Bring to a boil. In another bowl, mix Perma-Flo with 1³/₄ cups water. Slowly stir into hot juice mixture. Bring to boil and stir until thick. (It will be very thick!) Add to sliced peaches and mix well. Put in jars and cold pack 20 minutes. Very simple and delicious topping for Delights, for pie with crumbs, or even for Peach Cobbler. A double batch takes half a bushel of peaches and yields 14 qt.

CHERRY PIE FILLING
··· *Mrs. Mary Esta Yoder*

3 qt. pitted sour cherries
4 cups white sugar
6 cups water

1¹/₂ cups clear jel
red food coloring (optional)
1 pkg. cherry Kool-Aid

Place water, sugar, cherries, food coloring, and Kool-Aid in a large saucepan. Bring to a boil. Mix clear jel and 1¹/₂ cups cold water and dissolve well. Add to cherry mixture and cook till clear and thickened. Spoon into jars. Process for 20–25 minutes. Yield: 6–7 qt.

STRAWBERRY PRESERVES
··· *Mrs. Mary Esta Yoder*

4 cups crushed strawberries
7 cups white sugar

Cook together 10–12 minutes. Add 1 tsp. Epsom salt. Skim; ladle into jars and seal. Yield: 4 pt.

PEACH–PINEAPPLE JAM ··· *Mrs. Paul (Linda) Schlabach*

5 cups chopped peaches   7 cups sugar
1 - 16 oz. can crushed pineapple   1 - 6 oz. box orange jello

Boil peaches, pineapple, and sugar for 15 minutes. Remove and add jello. Stir until dissolved. Put in jars and seal.

GRAPE BUTTER ··· *Mrs. Henry (Emma) Troyer*

1 qt. whole grapes   2 Tbsp. water
1 qt. sugar

Cook 20 minutes, then put through colander. Bring to boiling point again and pour in jars and seal.

ORANGE ZUCCHINI JAM ··· *Mrs. Reuben (Betty) Yoder*
··· *Mrs. Marion (Rachel) Mullet*

6 cups zucchini, shredded fine   1 - 20 oz. can crushed pineapple,
6 cups sugar   drained
2 Tbsp. lemon juice   1 - 6 oz. box apricot jello

Boil sugar and zucchini for 10 minutes. It will make its own syrup. Stir in jello before removing from heat. Remove from heat; add pineapple and lemon juice. Stir until well blended. Pour into jars and seal. Process for 10–15 minutes in hot water bath. I like to blend my pineapple in the blender for a smoother jam.

SOUTHERN MIXED FRUIT ··· *Rosanna Nisley*

8 qt. bowl full of each:
watermelon   peaches
muskmelon

Cut up in small chunks. Add 1 gal. pineapple tidbits and sugar to suit your taste. Put in jars and cold pack for 15 minutes. Very good!

PEACH SLUSH (TO FREEZE) ··· *Mrs. Mary Esta Yoder*

1 peck (14 lb.) peaches, sliced   8$^1/_2$ lb. bananas
6 - 20 oz. cans pineapple   9 cups sugar
3 - 12 oz. cans frozen orange juice   10 cups water
    concentrate   1 liter 7-Up

Dissolve sugar in hot water; add orange juice concentrate and prepared fruits. Add 7-Up last. Mix in 21 qt. canner.

FREEZER PICKLES

··· Mrs. Firman (Deborah) Miller
··· Mrs. Owen (Elsie) Nisley

2 qt. pickles, sliced

onion, sliced fine

2 Tbsp. salt

Pour salt over onion and pickles. Refrigerate 24 hours. Drain. Mix together:

1³/₄ cups sugar   ¹/₂ cup vinegar

Stir mixture and pour over pickles. Refrigerate 24 hours, then freeze. If freezing for church, take pickles out of freezer the evening before.

ILLINOIS LIME PICKLES

··· Mrs. Emanuel (Mary) Nisley

1¹/₂ pt. canning lime and
    enough water to cover

9 lb. pickles, sliced crosswise

Let stand 24 hours and stir often. Take out and put in clear water for 3 hours. Wash off lime and drain. Bring 2 qt. vinegar, 4 lb. sugar, 4 Tbsp. mixed pickle spice, 2 Tbsp. salt, and 1 tsp. celery seed to a boil. Pour over pickles. Let stand overnight. Put on to boil next day and can. Instead of boiling 3 minutes, just heat, put in jars, and cold pack 10 minutes. Put spices together in bag and take out before putting into jars.

HINT: Heating before putting in jars makes pickles greener.

CINNAMON STICK PICKLES

··· Mrs. Wayne (Emma) Yoder
··· Mrs. Mary Esta Yoder

Peel big cucumbers; seed and slice into sticks (about 2 gal.). Put in crock or enamel canner with 2 cups pickling lime and enough water to cover. Soak 24 hours. Drain and wash several times. Soak again in plain water for 4 hours. Drain and cover with the following: 1 cup vinegar, 1 Tbsp. alum, red food coloring, and water to cover. Simmer for 2 hours. Drain and throw away liquid. Make syrup of the following: 1 Tbsp. salt, 2 cups water, 2 cups vinegar, 12 oz. pkg. red cinnamon candy, and 10 cups sugar. Bring to a boil and pour over cooked pickles. Let stand for 24 hours. Drain and bring syrup to a boil again. Pour over pickles. Do this 4 days. Drain and pack in jars. Heat syrup to a boil; pour in jars and cold pack 10 minutes. It takes about a week to make these and they are a lot of work, but we all enjoy them in the winter months.

MILLION DOLLAR PICKLES ··· *Mrs. Paul (Wilma) Schlabach*

Salt 3 gal. crock of pickles in salt brine strong enough to carry an egg. Stir every day for a week.

Eighth day: Drain and cover with boiling water.

Ninth day: Drain off water. Cut in slices or chunks. Put pickles back in crock and add 1 - 6 oz. jar horseradish and 2 Tbsp. alum. Cover with boiling water.

Tenth day: Drain and cover with boiling water.

Eleventh day: Drain. Mix 2 qt. vinegar and 10 lb. white sugar. Tie 1 Tbsp. cloves, 1 tsp. celery seed, and several sticks cinnamon in bag. Boil vinegar, sugar, and spices; pour over well drained pickles.

Twelfth day: Drain off syrup. Heat syrup to boiling; pour over pickles.

Thirteenth day: Repeat.

Fourteenth day: Repeat.

Fifteenth day: Take out spice bag. Pack pickles in jars. Pour boiling syrup over pickles and seal. This batch makes 10 qt. Very crisp!

ARISTOCRAT PICKLES ··· *Mrs. Lloyd (Bena) Miller*

1 gal. cucumbers, sliced   1 cup salt to 1 gal. water

Soak cucumbers in salt brine. Let stand 5 or 6 days, stirring each day. Drain. Boil in water to cover with alum the size of an egg for 10 minutes. Drain. Cover with water which has 2 Tbsp. ginger added. Boil 10 minutes. Drain. Add the following, tied in a bag: 1 Tbsp. celery seed, 1 Tbsp. allspice (whole), 1 Tbsp. cloves (whole), and 1 stick cinnamon. Add 3 cups water, 3 lb. sugar, and 3 cups vinegar. Boil until transparent (30 minutes). Pack in jars. Put vinegar over pickles and seal.

SWEET DILLS ··· *Mrs. Jr. (Ruth) Miller*

Fill pt. jars with lengthwise cut cucumbers, adding 1 bunch dill (home-grown is best) and 1 or 2 garlic cloves. Pour the following over cucumbers: 1 qt. weakened vinegar ($^1/_2$ water may be added), 1 pt. water, $^1/_4$ cup salt, and 4 cups sugar. Bring syrup to a boil, then pour in jars. Cold pack just long enough to seal. These are my husband's favorite.

LIME PICKLES   *... favorite of Christina Sue Miller, age 9*

7 lb. sliced pickles   2 cups lime

SYRUP

2 qt. vinegar   1 tsp. salt
1 Tbsp. whole cloves   1 tsp. celery seed
4 1/2 lb. white sugar   1 tsp. mixed pickle spices

Mix lime to 2 gal. water. Soak pickle slices in lime water 24 hours, then rinse in 3 different cold waters. Soak 3 hours in ice water, then drain. Make syrup. Pour over pickles and let stand overnight. Next morning, bring to a boil and boil for 35 minutes. Put in jars and seal. I usually put my spices in a small cloth bag, then take them out when done boiling. These usually turn out very crisp and crunchy. A favorite.

RED BEETS, TO CAN   *... Mrs. Albert (Verna) Yoder*

4 cups vinegar mixed with   7 tsp. salt
  2 cups water   14 cups white sugar
6 cups water

Bring to a boil; pour over a large (13 qt.) stainless steel bowl full of beets which have been cooked and sliced. Let stand overnight. Put in jars and cold pack 10–15 minutes.

CANNING RED BEETS   *... Mrs. Lloyd (Bena) Miller*

10 cups beet water   2 Tbsp. pickling spice tied in bag
3 cups vinegar   salt to taste
5 cups sugar

Cook beets; slip off skins and cut in chunks. Heat the above to boiling; add beets and bring to a boil. Pack in jars and seal. I have used this recipe for years and they are very good in wintertime.

RED BEETS   *... Mrs. Jr. (Ruth) Miller*
... Mrs. Reuben (Sara Etta) Schlabach

5 qt. cooked and skinned beets   5 cups white sugar
3 cups vinegar   3 Tbsp. salt
1 cup juice from beets

Cold pack just long enough to seal. Mom always had the best beets, and they were made exactly like this.

HEINZ CATSUP
··· *Mrs. Mary Esta Yoder*

1 peck tomatoes

3 large onions

green and hot peppers (optional)

Boil till soft, then put through Victorio strainer. Drain in bag for 2 hours. To the pulp, add:

1 - 12 oz. can tomato paste

4 cups white sugar

3 tsp. salt

1 pt. vinegar

$^1/_2$ tsp. cloves

$^1/_2$ tsp. cinnamon

$^1/_2$ tsp. dry mustard

Boil 10 minutes. Pour into jars and cold pack 10 minutes. Double recipe = 9 pt.

KETCHUP
··· *Mrs. Wayne (Emma) Yoder*

4 qt. tomatoes

2 Tbsp. salt

1 Tbsp. cinnamon

1 tsp. ground mustard

3 cups sugar

1 Tbsp. mixed pickle spice

$^1/_2$ tsp. red pepper

2 cups vinegar

3 small onions

Cook together tomatoes, onions, and pickle spice for 1 hour. Run through sieve. Mix all other ingredients together and cook. Thicken with 2 Tbsp. cornstarch. More cornstarch can be used if you prefer thicker catsup. Cook 10 minutes more and put in bottles. Instead of adding cornstarch, I prefer to boil the tomatoes down for a few hours, then add the remaining ingredients.

MARIE'S PIZZA SAUCE
··· *Mrs. Freeman (Marie) Schlabach*

$^1/_2$ bushel tomatoes

6 to 8 qt. tomato juice

3 lb. onion

1 pt. oil

11 - 7 oz. cans tomato paste

15 - 4 oz. cans mushrooms

$1^1/_2$ cups white sugar

$^1/_4$ cup salt

2 Tbsp. Italian seasoning

Cook onions in oil till tender and blend till liquefied. Add to juice and other ingredients. The mushrooms and Italian seasoning are very important. Simmer 20 minutes. Cold pack 10–20 minutes. Yield: 10–12 qt. I use this for pizza, lasagna, spaghetti, etc.

ITALIAN SAUCE
··· *Mrs. Marvin (Martha) Mast*

$^1/_2$ bushel plum tomatoes
48 oz. Ragu spaghetti sauce
   with meat
3 to 4 cups sugar
2 tsp. oregano

2 tsp. onion salt
24 oz. tomato paste
8 tsp. salt
2 tsp. garlic salt
2 pkg. spaghetti mix with mushrooms

Cook tomatoes in sauce. Add the remaining ingredients. Stir well and bring to boiling point. Pour in jars and seal. We use this for spaghetti and lasagna.

PIZZA SAUCE TO CAN
··· *Mrs. Reuben (Sara Etta) Schlabach*

1 bushel tomatoes
10 onions

8 large peppers
2 garlic bulbs

Cook together and put through strainer. Add:

1 tsp. red pepper
2 tsp. black pepper
1 Tbsp. Lawry's seasoning salt
1 Tbsp. chili powder
1 Tbsp. paprika
1 Tbsp. taco seasoning
4 Tbsp. oregano

1 Tbsp. garlic salt
1 cup salt
3 cups sugar
3 cups clear jel mixed with juice, or
   add some tomato paste, then not
   as much clear jel

Cook everything except clear jel together for 3 hours before adding thickener. I sometimes just use canned tomato juice. Fill the canner (stainless steel) $^3/_4$ full of juice, add spices, and thicken. We love this sauce!

PIZZA SAUCE
··· *Mrs. Jr. (Ruth) Miller*

$^1/_2$ bushel tomatoes
8 onions
$1^1/_2$ tsp. red pepper
1 cup vegetable oil
2 Tbsp. basil leaves

6 Tbsp. flaky oregano
$2^1/_2$ cups white sugar
$^1/_3$ cup salt
4 - 12 oz. cans tomato paste

Cook tomatoes and onions $2^1/_2$–3 hours. Put through Victorio strainer. Add oil, sugar, and seasonings. Boil 1 hour more. Add tomato paste. Put hot sauce in hot jars and seal or cold pack 10 minutes. Makes 20 pt. This recipe takes some time, but I have always liked it.

SPAGHETTI SAUCE   *··· Mrs. Mary Esta Yoder*

Brown in 6 Tbsp. butter:

8 lb. hamburger	3 Tbsp. garlic salt
6 Tbsp. parsley flakes	$1^1/_2$ Tbsp. black pepper

Combine with:

3 - 12 oz. cans tomato paste	3 onions, chopped
3 cans water	3 peppers, diced
6 qt. tomato juice	3 small cans mushrooms, chopped
3 Tbsp. salt	$1/_2$ cup cooking oil
2 cups sugar	2 large jars Ragu spaghetti sauce

Cook 1 hour. Put in jars and cold pack 2 hours. Yield: 13 qt.

SALSA SAUCE   *··· Mrs. Marion (Rachel) Mullet*

14 lb. or 7 qt. tomatoes, cooked and juiced	$1/_4$ cup sugar
	$1/_4$ cup salt
6 hot peppers, chopped	$1^1/_2$ Tbsp. cumin (optional)
6 to 8 green peppers, scalded and skinned	3 cloves garlic or 1 tsp. garlic powder
	2 Tbsp. chili powder
4 onions, chopped	$1/_2$ to 1 cup clear jel
1 cup vinegar	1 cup water

Cook peppers and onions in tomato juice; put through blender (unless you prefer chunky salsa). Add remaining ingredients, except clear jel and water. Bring to a boil and cook for 15 minutes. Mix clear jel and water; add to juice. Cook another 5–10 minutes. Put in jars and seal. Cold pack 10 minutes.

THREE-GALLON CHILI SOUP   *··· Mrs. Jr. (Ruth) Miller*

$4^1/_2$ lbs. hamburger	$2^1/_2$ cups brown sugar
2 large onions, browned with meat	4 tsp. chili powder
9 Tbsp. flour added to hamburger	5 tsp. salt
1 large can kidney beans	1 tsp. red pepper
3 large cans tomato juice	$3/_4$ tsp. black pepper

Simmer for 30 minutes. Pressure cook 1 hour for quarts.

CHICKEN NOODLE SOUP ··· Mrs. Mary Esta Yoder

1/2 lb. butter
3 qt. deboned chicken broth
1/4 cup soup base
1 qt. shoestring potatoes, precooked
2 pt. shoestring carrots, precooked

1 cup diced celery, precooked
1 cup minute rice, uncooked
2 lb. fine noodles (4 - 8 oz. pkg. Inn Maid)
2 cans cream of chicken soup
2 cans cream of celery soup

In a 20 qt. canner, brown butter; add cut-up chicken and enough broth to fill canner half full. Add chicken base and bring to a boil. Add vegetables, rice, and noodles. Cream soups with 2 cans water and add last. Bring to a boil, then cover and let set until noodles are tender. Add hot water to fill canner 2 1/2" from top. Cold pack 2 1/2 hours. Yield: 18–20 qt.

VEGETABLE SOUP ··· Mrs. Freeman (Naomi) Miller

5 qt. tomato juice
2 qt. beef broth
1 pkg. sloppy joe seasoning
1 pkg. meat loaf seasoning
2 pkg. beef stew seasoning
2 to 3 lb. hamburger, fried
1 qt. each of potatoes, carrots, and celery

1 qt. each of corn, peas, and green beans
2 cups onions, chopped
1 large can pork and beans
1 box ABC macaroni
1 cup sugar

Combine tomato juice, beef broth, seasonings, and sugar. Cook potatoes, celery, carrots, and macaroni till soft. Fry hamburger. Combine all ingredients; add salt and pepper to taste. Put in jars and cold pack 3 hours. Makes 16–17 qt.

HOT PEPPER BUTTER ··· Mrs. Linda Mae Troyer

40–45 hot peppers, ground, with seeds
1 qt. prepared mustard
1 qt. white vinegar

1 Tbsp. salt
5 cups white sugar
1 1/2 cups flour
2 cups water

Bring to a boil and add 1 1/2 cups flour mixed with 2 cups water. Cook until thickened. Put into jars. Yield: 8–9 pt.

SIMPLE VEGETABLE SOUP   ⋯ *Mrs. Mary Esta Yoder*

1 1/2 gal. potatoes (shoestring) cooked in 1 1/2 gal. chicken broth
   Add:
1 - 1 lb. box spaghetti, cooked
   Fry:
6 lb. ground beef   3 medium onions, chopped
   Drain, then add:
3 qt. tomato juice   1/2 cup brown sugar
   Cook:
4 pkg. mixed vegetables, frozen   1 pkg. peas, frozen
   Mix all together. Put in jars and cold pack 2 hours. Yield: 19 qt.

CANNED MINIATURE STUFFED PEPPERS

⋯ *Mrs. Mary Esta Yoder*

red and yellow mini peppers   1 1/2 tsp. mustard seed
   (sweet)   4 2/3 cups sugar
3 qt. cabbage, shredded fine   4 2/3 cups cider vinegar
2 1/2 cups canning salt   2 cups water
1 1/2 tsp. celery seed

   Remove seeds from peppers and rinse well; drain. Combine cabbage with canning salt. Let stand 20 minutes, then squeeze cabbage and discard liquid. Add celery seed, mustard seed, 2/3 cup sugar, and 2/3 cup vinegar. Mix well and stuff into peppers. Place into pint jars, approximately 15 to a jar.
   Combine 4 cups sugar with the remaining 4 cups vinegar and 2 cups water, and bring to a boil to make a syrup to pour over peppers. Fill jars to 1/2" from top. Seal; process in hot water bath for 15 minutes.

CANNING MEATBALLS   ⋯ *Mrs. Mary Esta Yoder*

   Mix 1 tsp. salt and 1/4 tsp. black pepper to each 2 lb. meat. Form into balls (about walnut size) and place in a 6 or 8 qt. kettle. Cover with cold water and bring to a boil over medium heat. Boil 10 minutes. Skim off foam; strain broth. Fill qt. jars with meatballs and cover with broth. Seal and cold pack for 2 1/2 hours. Very handy to use for noodles or beef stew with fresh garden vegetables.

CANNING SWEET POTATOES   ··· *Mrs. Mary Esta Yoder*

Peel and slice sweet potatoes. Pack in jars. Cover with syrup of 1 cup white sugar and 2 cups water. Do not add salt. Cold pack for 1 hour.

GERMAN BRATWURST ··· *Mrs. Reuben (Sara Etta) Schlabach*

25 lb. ground pork
$1/2$ cup paprika
3 Tbsp. garlic salt

4 oz. salt (regular table salt)
$1/4$ cup black pepper
3 Tbsp. onion salt

A very delicious sausage mix.

SEASONINGS FOR SAUSAGE
(TO FREEZE OR CAN)   ··· *Mrs. Paul (Linda) Schlabach*

100 lb. sausage meat
$1^3/4$ cups salt
5 Tbsp. red pepper (less if you
    want milder sausage)

5 Tbsp. black pepper
8 Tbsp. sage (optional)
2 cups brown sugar
2 tsp. dry mustard

Mix all together and sprinkle over meat before you grind it. Mix in well, then grind. Stuff with sausage stuffer in 3" muslin bags instead of casings. Tie firmly and smoke for several hours. Remove bags; cut tubes of meat in desired lengths. Wrap and freeze. Or, can unsmoked meat.

Tips & Hints

A Christian Mother

I have a special job in life—I am a mother and a wife.
I am not paid a salary; all the work I do is free.

I rise each morning and I pray that God will use my life today
To touch the lives He's given me with words and deeds of charity.

I cook and wash; I sew and clean. It never ends, it seems to me.
I hug and kiss; I teach and guide. I read and play; I laugh and cry.

I love my life...the bad and good. I would not change it if I could.
I find great joy, peace, and pleasure in being one of life's priceless
    treasures.

Yes, I'm a mother and a wife...there is no greater job in life.

EQUIVALENTS
BAKING ITEMS
Bread Crumbs, dry . . . . 1 cup = 3 to 4 dried bread slices
Bread Crumbs, soft . . . . 1 cup = 1^1/$_2$ fresh bread slices
Flour, all-purpose. . . . . 1 lb. = 4 cups
Gelatin, unflavored . . . . 1 envelope = 1 Tbsp.
Graham Cracker Crumbs. . . . . . 1 cup = 13 squares, finely crushed
Margarine, solid regular . . . . . 1 stick = 8 Tbsp. = ^{1}/$_2$ cup = ^{1}/$_4$ lb.
Margarine, soft. . . . . 1 container = 1 cup
Marshmallows, miniatures . . . . 100 to 110 = 1 cup
Nuts, chopped (peanuts, pecans, walnuts) . . . . . . 4^1/$_2$ oz. = 1 cup
Sugar, brown . . . . 1 lb. = 2^1/$_4$ cups packed
Sugar, confectioner's . . . . 1 lb. = 4^1/$_2$ cups sifted
Sugar, granulated . . . . 1 lb. = 2^1/$_4$ cups

CHEESES
Natural Chunk or Process. . . . . . . 4 oz. = 1 cup shredded or cubed
Cottage . . . . 1 lb. = 2 cups
Cream . . . . 8 oz. = 1 cup

FRUITS & VEGETABLES
Apples . . . . 3 medium (1 lb.) = 3 cups sliced
Coconut, shredded . . . . 3^1/$_2$ oz. can = 1^1/$_3$ cups
Lemon or Lime . . . . 1 medium = 2 to 3 Tbsp. juice
= 1 Tbsp. grated rind
Onion . . . . 1 medium = ^{1}/$_2$ cup chopped
Orange . . . 1 medium = ^{1}/$_2$ cup chopped = 1 to 2 Tbsp. grated rind
Potatoes. . . . . 3 medium (1 lb.) = 2^1/$_4$ cups mashed

RICE & PASTAS
Macaroni, uncooked. . . . . 4 oz. (1 cup) = 2 cups cooked
Noodles, uncooked. . . . . . . 4 oz. (1^1/$_2$ to 2 cups) = 2 cups cooked
Rice, precooked . . . . 1 cup = 2 cups cooked
Rice, uncooked. 1 cup = 3 cups cooked
Spaghetti, uncooked . . . . 1 lb. = 6^1/$_2$ cups cooked

PAN AND BAKING DISH SIZES

Cooking need never become a crisis if you know what to substitute when you don't have the size the recipe calls for.

4 CUP BAKING DISH

  9" pie plate

  8" x 1^1/$_4$" round layer cake pan

  7^3/$_8$" x 3^5/$_8$" x 2^1/$_4$" loaf pan

6 CUP BAKING DISH

  8" or 9" x 1^1/$_2$" round layer cake pan

  10" pie plate

  8^1/$_2$" x 3^5/$_8$" x 2^5/$_8$" loaf pan

8 CUP BAKING DISH

  8" x 8" x 2" square pan

  11" x 7" x 1^1/$_2$" baking pan

  9" x 5" x 3" loaf pan

10 CUP BAKING DISH

  9" x 9" x 2" square pan

  11^3/$_4$" x 7^1/$_2$" x 1^3/$_4$" baking pan

  15" x 10" x 1" jelly roll pan

12 CUP AND OVER BAKING DISH

  13^1/$_2$" x 8^1/$_2$" x 2" glass baking pan = 12 cups

  13" x 9" x 2" metal baking pan = 15 cups

  14" x 10^1/$_2$" x 2^1/$_2$" roasting pan = 19 cups

TOTAL VOLUME OF VARIOUS SPECIAL PANS AND DISHES

  10" bundt pan = 12 cups

  10" angel food cake pan = 18 cups

  8" x 3" springform pan = 12 cups

  9" x 3" springform pan = 16 cups

  8^1/$_2$" x 2^1/$_4$" ring mold = 4^1/$_2$ cups

  9^1/$_4$" x 2^3/$_4$" ring mold = 8 cups

  small Tupperware mold = 5 cups

  large Tupperware ring mold = 6 cups

CONTENTS OF CANS

SIZE	AVERAGE CONTENT
8 oz.	1 cup
No. 300	$1^3/_4$ cups
No. 1 tall	2 cups
No. 303	2 cups
No. 2	$2^1/_2$ cups
No. $2^1/_2$	$3^1/_2$ cups
No. 3	4 cups
No. 10	12–13 cups

EQUIVALENT MEASURES

Dash or speck= less than $^1/_8$ tsp.	16 Tbsp. . . . . = 1 cup
3 tsp.. . . . . = 1 Tbsp.	2 cups . . . . = 1 pint
4 Tbsp. . . . . = $^1/_4$ cup	4 cups . . . . = 1 quart
$5^1/_3$ Tbsp. . . . . = $^1/_3$ cup	4 quarts. . . . . = 1 gallon
8 Tbsp. . . . . = $^1/_2$ cup	8 oz.. . . . . = 1 cup
$10^2/_3$ Tbsp. . . . . = $^2/_3$ cup	4 oz.. . . . . = $^1/_4$ lb.
12 Tbsp. . . . . = $^3/_4$ cup	16 oz.. . . . . = 1 lb.

BABY WIPES:

1 roll Bounty paper towels   2 Tbsp. baby bath or baby shampoo
$2^1/_4$ cups water   1 Tbsp. baby oil

Cut roll of paper towels in half and remove cardboard. Mix water, shampoo, and oil in plastic container. Place half a roll in container; put on lid and turn upside down to let towels soak thoroughly. When ready to use, pull towels through center of roll.

If your child is hesitant about starting school, pack some unique encouragement in his lunchbox. For example...on the skin of a banana, draw a smiling face and a short message.

This homemade cleaner can be used on windows, chrome, and painted surfaces in bathroom in kitchen.

Combine:

1 pt. rubbing alcohol	1 Tbsp. dishwashing liquid
1 Tbsp. household ammonia	1 gal. water

Store in a gallon jug. Be sure to add label.

The backs of spelling tests, book reports, and other papers brought home by your children are usually blank. Youngsters can use them as writing paper for letters to grandparents or friends, and show off their schoolwork at the same time.

Attach two clothespins to either end of a length of ribbon or thick yarn. When you are eating out with your child, clip the napkin to the clothespins to create a bib. You don't have to wash this one because you leave the napkin at the restaurant—just take home the clothespins.

Be sure to set a simple but tasteful table. Set placemats and utensils straight. Use napkins and place flowers on the table. Use your best dishes sometimes.

If in doubt about how much seasoning to use, remember Grandmother's rule and "season to taste."

Before following a recipe from a cookbook, slip the open book into a clear plastic bag. It will protect the pages from splatters and spills.

Write notes or changes in your cookbook margins. Then you know how you made the recipe before. After all, the book is *yours*.

When bread is baking, a small dish of water in the oven will help to keep the crust from getting hard.

A pie crust will be more easily made and better if all the ingredients are cool.

Use whole wheat flour to roll out pie dough for better flavor.

Brush cream, then sprinkle sugar on top of two-crust pies. Browns beautifully.

Brush the inside of your bottom crust with egg whites when making fruit pies. This prevents juice from soaking through.

To prevent stringy tapioca, do not stir while it is cooling.

In a hurry to fry hamburger? Shape the burgers with a hole in the center. They will cook faster and the holes will disappear when done.

When icing a layer cake, slide 3 dry sticks of spaghetti through the layers to prevent them from sliding before the icing sets.

$1/2$ cup clear jel thickens 1 qt. liquid. 1 Tbsp. or 1 pkt. unflavored gelatin will jell 2 cups liquid. Substitute: 2 Tbsp. flour = 1 Tbsp. cornstarch.

To measure honey or other sticky syrups, oil the measuring cup with cooking oil and rinse under hot water before using.

Add a bit of white sugar (without stirring) to milk being scalded to prevent scorching.

Use a strawberry huller to peel potatoes which have been boiled in their "jackets."

It is easy to remove the white membrane from oranges, for desserts and salads, by soaking them in boiling water for 5 minutes before you peel them.

When cooking cabbage, place $1/2$ cup vinegar on the stove near the cabbage, and it will absorb all odor from it.

A leaf of lettuce dropped into the pot absorbs the grease from the top of soup. Remove lettuce as soon as it has served its purpose.

To add variation to mashed potatoes, add $1/2$ to $3/4$ tsp. dill weed and $1/4$ cup sour cream.

If a lemon is put in hot water a few minutes before juicing, it will yield more juice.

Have eggs or egg whites at room temperature and they will beat up easier.

Before scalding milk in saucepan, rinse the pan in cold water and it will not scorch so easily.

Most vegetable soups are tastier after being marinated for a day or two. Just set in refrigerator.

Honey substituted for sugar in rolls and bread dough makes the crust brown better and it stays softer.

For fluffy meat loaf, add 1 tsp. baking powder.

Instead of buying toothpaste, mix equal amounts of baking soda and salt. Leaves mouth with a clean, refreshing feeling.

When making Rice Krispie candy, try using corn flakes instead of Rice Krispies.

For easy slicing of lasagna dishes, put first layer in lengthwise, for second layer cut noodles to fit diagonally, and finish last layer lengthwise.

If your cream pudding is too thin, add dry instant vanilla pudding and mix slowly while stirring.

For an attractive melon basket, draw a zigzag pattern on melon with a non-toxic marker. Cut along pattern and separate halves. Seed, then fill with melon balls and fruit.

Add powdered sugar to whipped cream or fruit to prevent it from being too thin and juicy.

Roll raisins in flour before adding to cake and cookie batter to prevent them from going to the bottom.

To prevent lettuce from rusting, line the bottom of the container with paper towels. The towels absorb the excess moisture, keeping fruits and vegetables fresh longer.

Baking cupcakes or muffins, and don't have enough muffin tins? Place canning jar rings on cookie sheet to hold cupcake liners while baking.

When baking cookies, save the crumbs you scrape from the cookie sheets and add to your graham cracker crumbs.

To dry tea, preheat oven to 200°. Put the tea on cookie sheets in the oven. Turn off heat. The tea is usually dry by the time the oven is cooled off. If not, turn to 200° again for a short time. I also use this method to dry parsley. It stays nice and green.

A small new paintbrush works well as a pastry brush.

Keep a toothbrush handy at the kitchen sink—you will find it useful in cleaning rotary egg beaters, graters, choppers, and similar utensils.

Rub vinegar or rubbing alcohol on hands just before hanging out wash in cold weather. Dry hands thoroughly before going out. This keeps them from getting so cold.

To keep wash from freezing on the line in wintertime, wipe line with vinegar.

Add vinegar to your water when cold packing meats to keep jars free from grease.

Use a damp paper towel to pick up small slivers of broken glass.

Spray your vegetable plants with a solution of 3 tsp. Epsom salt to a gallon of water, just when they start to bud and have their first blooms, to make them bloom heartily for a heavy yield of vegetables!

Never put manure on the area where potatoes are to be planted if you want smooth potatoes instead of scabby ones!

When planting carrot seeds, add 1 tsp. radish seeds. The radishes will grow faster, thus marking your row. When the radishes are pulled to use, it thins the carrot row.

To eliminate potato bugs, plant cabbage plants beside the potatoes.

Hair spray removes ink from clothes.

Shampoo is an excellent grass stain remover. I also dilute it (1:1) and use on collars and cuffs before washing.

Baking soda takes black marks off linoleum.

Use Murphy's Oil Soap on grass stains on laundry. Also good on other stains.

To remove paint from clothes, mix equal parts of ammonia and turpentine and saturate spots thoroughly. This mixture should even remove paint spots that have hardened.

Soak mildew for several hours in a weak solution of chloride of lime. Rinse in cold water.

To get rid of flies at an upstairs or attic window, set a small tin can of kerosene on the windowsill. For some reason, the flies tumble in.

Make a paste of cream of tartar and vinegar to put around your water faucets that lime up. Let set 1 hour or longer. Your lime will clean off.

Use vinegar and soda to clean your oven and stove top. It does an amazing job!

To remove contact paper, brush paint or varnish remover on the contact. When paper starts blistering, pull off.

To take off water spots or anything that gathers lime with water sitting in it, put 1 tsp. cream of tartar in hot water, fill it up, let set overnight, and wash it. It comes out sparkling!

If your window screen develops a small hole that's large enough for mosquitoes or other insects to get through, fix it with clear household cement. Holding the tube directly over the hole, squeeze on a dab of cement.

For a child with a nervous stomach who has a hard time relaxing and falling asleep: Fill water bottle with very warm water and lay against abdomen. This usually helps.

Index

Meats & Main Dishes

Cakes & Icings

Desserts

Candy, Snacks, & Children's Corner